THE INSTA
COMPANY SECRETARY

An A-Z Guide to
Duties and Responsibilities

David Martin

THOROGOOD

Published by Thorogood Publishing
2017, reprinted 2021
10-12 Rivington Street
London EC2A 3DU

Telephone: 020 7749 4748
Email: info@thorogoodpublishing.co.uk
Web: www.thorogoodpublishing.co.uk

A CIP catalogue record for this book is
available from the British Library.

Paperback ISBN: 978185418 900 4
eBook ISBN: 978185418 901 1

Designed and typeset by Driftdesign:
www.getyourdrift.com

Contents

Preface

The average UK company has to comply with around 25,000 legal enactments – with more added every year. The person to whom the Board of Directors has a right to look to advise them to keep their company legal is their Company Secretary. Yet the Companies Act 2006 allows LTDs the option of doing without that appointment! This option would remove:

- the focal point for legal matters and interpretation

- the person to whom the board have every right to look for guidance on matters legal

- the logical point of contact for third parties with the legal persona (or 'unnatural person') that is a company

- the custodian of the board's confidential data or *secrets* (from which the job title is derived) and

- the logical person to construct the minutes – the legally required written record of board and general meetings.

Whilst the position can be abandoned, legal compliance remains and, in view of its seriousness, a senior manager or board member must take responsibility. This title seeks to provide an instant and basic guide to the legal obligations particularly for that person who usually will have many other duties. As well as updated guidance on legal obligations, examples of wordings, forms, policies, checklists etc. are included which, with a little customizing, may be able to be used immediately. Case studies demonstrate where others have gone wrong – highlighting actions and procedures etc., to be avoided.

Of the UK's 3.5 million companies, over 3.4 million are private LTDs. This book is primarily for them, although in the interests of completeness (and since more than a few LTDs become PLCs) some PLC obligations are referred to. During the new Act's consultation period, it was mooted that there should be a separate Act for LTDs but this did not materialise – so the smallest family LTD is subject to the same Act as the largest international PLC. In both the legal minefield and the following matters there may be more than a suggestion that their complexities outweigh their value. Corporate Governance (CG) obligations on listed PLCs are not included; indeed it is arguable that if a company complies properly with CA06, CG requirements should be unnecessary. 300 years ago, satirist Jonathan Swift said that laws are 'like spiders webs – they catch the small flies but hornets blast through'. Swift's words ring true today, as the CG code totally failed to stop breaches by some of our largest companies – alleged fraud/bribery (Barclays), tax avoidance issues at various internet companies (Google, Amazon and Facebook) and others (Starbucks, Apple), cheating customers (Royal Bank of Scotland), convicted fraud (HBOS) employee benefit exploitation (BHS), money laundering (HSBC), illegal employment practices (JD Sports, Uber) and so on, whilst the instances of household name organisations illegally hounding legitimate whistleblowers abound. These examples of the unacceptable face of capitalism not only defraud those cheated and oppressed but also taint the legitimate and law-abiding majority of companies and their boards. Morality in some businesses seems the exception rather than the rule as cupidity fosters stupidity.

As a plain guide to an LTD's requirements the content should suffice in over 90% of the cases where guidance is sought. In the remaining areas legal advice may be necessary – in which case the book should help the reader to ask the right questions, without which there may be little hope of ever obtaining the right answers!

David M Martin
Buddenbrook Consultancy

Note: As this book went to press it was announced that the Financial Reporting Council has been asked to compile a Corporate Governance Code for 'large' LTDs (i.e. those with 1000 or more employees). Compliance is to be voluntary.

Using this book

1. The *'expanded index'* format allows each subject to be dealt with comprehensively under its own title, but leads to some duplication as well as cross-referencing to other sections – whose titles are set in upper case within the text.

2. Abbreviations:
   - CA followed by the last two digits of the year of the Act is used for Companies Acts with (where appropriate) the relevant section following (Section 257 of Companies Act 2006 = CA06s257)

   - CH: Registrar of Companies and/or Companies House

   - CDDA86: Company Directors Disqualification Act 1986

   - CMA: Competition and Markets Authority

   - DBEIS: Dept of Business, Energy & Industrial Strategy (formerly DBIS, formerly the DTI)

   - EAT: Employment Appeal Tribunal

   - ET: Employment Tribunal

   - FCA: Financial Conduct Authority

   - FRC: Financial Reporting Council

   - HSE: Health & Safety Executive

   - LTD: private limited company (limited by shares or guarantee)

   - PLC: public limited company

   - SAIL: Single Alternative Inspection Location

   - SBEEA: Small Business, Enterprise and Employment Act 2015

   - *Traded companies*: PLCs whose shares are listed on the main Stock Exchange

   - *Non-traded companies*: LTDs, PLCs quoted on the Alternative Investment Market, and unlisted/unquoted PLCs.

3. CA06 grants LTDs options (LTDs are not obliged to appoint a Secretary, do not need to hold an AGM, only need give 14 days notice of their AGM and special resolutions). Options do not overrule a company's Articles and can only be used providing the Articles are silent or do not prohibit them. If the Articles require the board to appoint a Secretary, or to hold an AGM each year, etc. then that company must comply – unless it changes its Articles.

4. Traditionally, companies had a Memorandum (setting out its 'objects clauses') and Articles. A CA06 company's Memorandum consists only of details of its country of registration, number, address, and details of the promoters. Any objects clause must be in its Articles. The objects clauses of preCA06 companies are now deemed to form part of their Articles.

5. CA06 applies to all companies now being formed which may pose a challenge to those also administering companies formed under a previous CA unless they bring the Articles of pre-existing companies into a similar format and content.

6. Traditionally any meeting other than a company's AGM has been called an Extraordinary General Meeting (EGM). CA06 specifies that meetings other than the AGM are General Meetings. However most companies registered prior to CA06 have Articles based on drafts in those Acts (e.g. Table A of CA85) which refer to EGMs. CA06 does not override the Articles and thus unless (and until) the Articles of all those companies are changed, requirements regarding holding an EGM continue to apply.

7. Each CA has been accompanied by or incorporates pro forma sets of Articles which apply if a company does not adopt its own. A majority of the companies in existence prior to CA06 used Table A of CA85 either in whole or in part as their Articles. Company Articles need to be checked to ensure whether the Table A regulation referred to has been incorporated.

8. The current (subject to periodic revision) definitions of companies' 'sizes' are:
Micro-entities: does not exceed two of:
- turnover: £632,000;
- balance sheet aggregate: £316,000;
- 10 employees.

Small: Does not exceed two of:
- turnover: £10.2 million;
- balance sheet aggregate: £5.1 million;
- 50 employees.

Medium-sized: a company that exceeds the parameters for a small company but does not exceed two of:
- turnover £25.9 million;
- balance sheet aggregate £12.9 million;
- 250 employees.

Large: a company that exceeds at least two of the last set of parameters.

9. All references to companies (other than in case studies) are for example only and not representative of any real company.

10. Use of the masculine includes the feminine.

Readers seeking more details could refer to Roger Mason's *The Company Secretary's Desktop Guide* and the author's *The Company Director's Desktop Guide* – both published by Thorogood.

Opinions expressed are those of the author.

Table of Cases

- HMRC v O'Rourke (2013 UKUT 0499 All ER(D) 150)

- HMRC Commissioners v McEntaggart (2006 1 BCLC 476)

- Holland v The Commissioners for HMRC and anor (2011 All ER 430)

- IBM v Web-Sphere Ltd (04 EWHC 529)

- Item Software (UK) Ltd v Fassihi & ors (High Court 2003 IRLR 769)

- Lexi Holdings Plc (in administration) v Luqman & ors [2009 EWCA Civ 117]

- Muncipal Mutual Insurance v Harrap (1998)

- Neufeld v A & N Communication in Print Ltd (2008 All ER (D) 156)

- Nesbitt & Nesbitt v Secretary of State for Trade and Industry (2007 All ER (D) 23/9)

- Pemberton v Claimstart t/a Parkin Westbury & Co (15.5.98 EAT 1093/97)

- Pharmed Medicare Private Ltd v Univar Ltd (2002 EWCA Civ 1569)

- PNC Telecom plc v Thomas (2002 EWHC 2848)

- R v Owide (A v U) (EAT IRLB 6.1.04)

- R v Sale (2013 EWCA Crim 1306 All ER (D) 367)

- Ranson v Customer Systems plc (2012 EWCA Civ 841 All ER(D) 186)

- Regal Hastings Ltd v Gulliver (1967 2 AC 134 HL)

- Re Mea Corporation, Secretary of State for Trade and Industry v Aviss (2006 All ER (D) 291)

- Re UKLI; DBIS V Chohan & ors (2013 All ER 253 Mar)

- Re Westmid Packing Services Ltd (No 2) [1998 2 ALL ER 124 CA]

- Secretary of State for DBIS v Aaron & ors (2009 EWHC 3263 Ch)

- Secretary of State for Trade and Industry v Holler (2006 All ER 232)

- SMC Electronic Ltd v Akhter Computers Ltd (20011 BCLC 433)

- Smith & Fawcett Ltd (1942 Ch 304 CA)

- Smith v Henniker-Major (High Court 17 October 2001)

- Stack v Ajar-Tec Ltd (CA 2015 EWCA Civ46)

- Tesco Stores Ltd v Pook (2004 IRLB 618 EAT)

Agenda and notice

KEY POINTS

- The foundation of an efficient productive meeting is a well thought out Agenda.

- If a meeting is a maze, the agenda is its map.

- Members must have time to consider matters requiring their decisions so papers should be issued (say) 5 working days prior to a meeting.

A meeting has been called a maze. Galbraith called them 'a great trap' and commented 'They are indispensable when you don't want to do anything.' Proper planning and attention will help ensure our meetings do not meet his description. That starts with an Agenda.

Board meetings

A detailed agenda can provide:

- guidance through the *maze;*

- assistance to the chairman in achieving the meeting's aims;

- guidance to what is required to be achieved; and

- (a benefit for the Secretary!) a foundation for the first draft of the legally required record of the meeting – the MINUTES.

EXAMPLE: Detailed board agenda

ANY COMPANY LTD
For a meeting of the Board to be held on Thursday 30th March 2XXX,
Boardroom at 10.00 a.m.

Apologies for absence

1. MINUTES of Board Meeting held on 29th February (attached).

2. DIRECTORS INTERESTS – review new entries in Register.

3. RISK – consider reassessment of risks identified which could impact
    the company (review attached).

4. SHARES
    a) Resolution to approve share transfer in favour of Mr PQR.
    b) Recommendation that share registration work of the company be
        placed with Share Registrars Ltd. (Report and contract attached.)

5. FINANCE
    i)   Management accounts to 28th February 2XXX. (Set to be distrib-
         uted by Finance Dept by 25th March.)
    ii) Recommended change to calculation of depreciation charge.
         (Report on effect from Finance Dept attached.)
    iii) Capital expenditure
         a) Proposed purchase of (units).
         b) Capex project 13/2XXX.
    iv) Cash flow. (Projection for remainder of 2XXX attached.)
    v)   Bank Mandate – new format (attached).
    vi) Borrowings. (The Secretary to report concerning latest negotia-
         tions with the company's bankers regarding additional borrowing.)

    Draft resolution required: THAT the chairman and Mr UVW be and
    they hereby are empowered to sign such documents and take such
    actions to provide the company's bankers with the documentation to
    facilitate the additional borrowing requirement.

6. CURRENT TRADING – managing director's report (enclosed).

7. PERSONNEL
    a) Wage negotiations for review 1st July 2XXX (see report from
        divisional director (personnel) attached).

b) Impact of recent employment legislation. (Secretary to table report with recommendations.)

8. PROPERTY

    i) Board approval required for items X, XX, XXX in attached report.

    ii) Progress on sale (facility).

9. SAFETY MATTERS

    i) General report (attached).

    ii) Report re [new project] implementation.

10. SEALING – Approval required for items 345 to 361 in sealing register.

11. BOARD MEETINGS IN 2XXX

Suggested additional dates as follows 28th April, 30th May, 30th June, 28th July, 31st August, 29th September, 25th October, 23rd November, and 21st December.

Note: Draft MINUTES reflecting this agenda appear in that section.

This agenda seeks to aid the efficiency of the meeting. Advance drafting of a formal resolution such as is shown in item 5 (vi) may avoid drafting on the day and save valuable time. If the agenda and the reports tabled are kept with the minutes these can show what information was before the board at the time of the decision-making process.

Annual General Meeting (AGM)

Although PLCs must hold an AGM each year within 6 months of the company's FINANCIAL YEAR END, LTDs are no longer required to hold an AGM, unless their Articles, the members, or the directors require it. An LTD's AGM must be held within 10 months of the company's year-end. Everyone entitled to attend must be given adequate notice. Thus:

- to convene the AGM of a PLC, which can only be waived in whole or part if all the members agree (see GENERAL MEETINGS) 21 days notice is required (20 *working* days for a traded company);

- to convene the AGM of an LTD CA06 requires 14 days notice although the Articles must be checked in case any longer period is required. Notice for an LTD's AGM can be waived if 90% (which the Articles can increase to 95%) of the total voting strength of the members agree.

Whilst accidental failure to give notice to one or more members will not usually invalidate the meeting, every effort should be made to ensure that members' addresses are kept updated. With the authority of their members, companies can now serve such notices by electronic means – email or fax.

Case study: Faxed notices of AGM

In *PNC Telecom plc v Thomas* the Court held that serving notice of a meeting by fax was valid.

Although standard business is required to be conducted at an AGM, this does not prevent other business being considered, the Articles being checked for requirements. If business other than that covered in the agenda below is to be considered then full details must be given – special RESOLUTIONS and special notice of an ordinary resolution require specific periods and types of notice.

Example: Draft notice/agenda for an AGM

ANY COMPANY LTD
NOTICE

Is hereby given that the XXTH ANNUAL GENERAL MEETING of the members of the Company will be held at 9.30 a.m. at the [registered office] on Friday, 14th March 2XXX, to consider the following business:

1. Notice of Meeting.

2. Apologies for absence.

3. Directors/strategic report for the year ended 30th September 2XXX.

4. Profit and Loss a/c for the year ended 30th September 2XXX and Balance Sheet as at that date.

5. To consider and if thought fit authorise payment of a final dividend of X% (Y pence per share) to ordinary shareholders on the register as at [date].

6. Retirement and proposed re-appointment as directors of:

   a) Ms C Smith

   b) Mr B Jones

   who retire by rotation and, being eligible, offer themselves for re-appointment.

7. Retirement and proposed re-appointment as a director of Mr A Robinson who was appointed a director on 1st January 2XXX and retires and offers himself for re-election.

8. Appointment and remuneration of auditors.

By order of the board

[Name]

Company Secretary   15th February 2XXX

A member entitled to attend and unable to do so may appoint one or more proxies to attend, vote and speak in his place. Such proxies should be sent to the Registered Office of the company to arrive not later than 48 hours before the commencement of the meeting. Proxies do not have to be members of the company.

Notes:

1. A Secretary who is also a director would sign 'On behalf of the board'.

2. The ARTICLES of some companies require a proportion of the board to retire ('*by rotation*') at each AGM and to offer themselves (if they wish and are eligible) for re-election. However, under Articles incorporating regulation 84 of Table A of CA85, only non-executive directors are required to retire by rotation. Directors of FTSE350 companies are required to retire/seek re-election each year.

3. Any director(s) who has/have been appointed since the previous AGM must retire at the following AGM and may (if they wish and are eligible) offer themselves for re-election.

4. Special rules apply regarding the appointment at a general meeting of anyone other than the retiring AUDITORS.

5. Only members and auditors have a right of attendance at a general meeting, although directors have a right of attendance (and to address the meeting) should their REMOVAL be proposed.

6. The Agenda for an LTD limited by guarantee would be slightly different since there are no shares and thus there can be no dividend.

7. The Articles of some older companies may stipulate that a proxy 'must be a member of the company' but CA06s324 negates this restriction.

General Meetings

CA06 specifies (only for companies formed under that Act or those that change their Articles to conform with it) that meetings of members other than the AGM are called general meetings (GMs), although the requirements are identical to the previous requirements for ExtraOrdinary General Meetings (EGMs). Most of the nearly 3 million companies registered under legislation that preceeded CA06, used as a base for their Articles pro forma drafts accompanying previous CAs – e.g. Table A of CA85 and such drafts (and often the Articles of those companies adopting them) refer to EGMs.

[E]GMs are usually convened for specific purposes, although there is nothing to stop such business being conducted at the AGM if the timing is appropriate and providing any special rules regarding the business to be considered are adhered to.

Example: Draft notice/agenda for a(n) [E]GM

ANY COMPANY LTD
NOTICE

Is hereby given that a(n) [EXTRAORDINARY] GENERAL MEETING of the members of the Company will be held at 9.30 a.m. at the [registered office] of the company on Wednesday 18th June 2XXX to consider the following business:

1. Notice.

2. Apologies for absence.

3. SPECIAL RESOLUTION: that the share capital of the company be and it hereby is increased from £10,000 to £2,000,000 by the creation of:

   a) 990,000 new ordinary shares of £1 each ranking in all respects *pari passu* with the 10,000 existing ordinary shares of £1 of the company,

   b) the creation of 1,000,000 [X]% net p.a. Cumulative Redeemable Convertible Preference Shares of £1.

4. SPECIAL RESOLUTION: that the name of the company be changed to ANY OTHER COMPANY LTD.

By order of the board

[Name]

Company Secretary   20th May 2XXX

A member entitled to attend and unable to do so may appoint one or more proxies to attend, vote and speak in his place. Such proxies should be sent to the Registered Office of the company to arrive no later than 48 hours before the commencement of the meeting. Proxies do not have to be members of the company.

Notes:

1. An (E)GM normally requires 14 days' notice, but longer notice may have to be given if a special resolution is to be considered. CA06 specifies 14 days' notice (formerly 21) is required of special resolutions, but a pre CA06 company's Articles may stipulate a longer period.

2. Unless specified in its Articles, a company formed under CA06 does not need an authorised share capital – the company has whatever share capital the directors decide it needs and such a resolution would be unnecessary.

3. At a meeting a special resolution requires a minimum support of 75% of the votes *cast* (whether present or by proxy) and must be filed with CH within 15 days of being passed. For a special resolution to be passed by written resolution it requires support of 75% of *all* the votes – i.e. not just of the votes cast.

4. The notice period of an (E)GM of a traded company is usually 21 days but this can be reduced to 14 if the shareholders have agreed and the company offers its shareholders the 'facility for shareholders to vote by electronic means'.

5. *Pari passu* means the shares have exactly the same rights etc.

6. Although Articles of older companies may stipulate that a proxy 'must be a member of the company' this is overridden by CA06s324.

Allotment and transfer of shares

KEY POINTS

- Details of all shares issued must be recorded in the Register of Members and advised to CH.

- Directors may need authority from existing shareholders before issuing additional shares.

- Articles and any Shareholders Agreement should be checked for any issue restrictions.

- LTDs must not issue shares publicly.

- Share transfers may attract stamp duty.

Authority

The maximum value of, as well as any denominations of, the share capital of pre-CA06 LTDs is stated in the Memorandum. Shares in the defined CLASSES can be issued up to maximum, but before any are issued in excess, shareholders' authority is required (i.e. to increase the authorised share capital). For CA06 companies, *authorised share capital* as a limitation no longer exists unless there are restrictions set out in the Articles – a company with only one class of share can have whatever share capital its directors (with required authority) determine by board resolution.

Shareholders will often have a right of pre-emption (i.e. a requirement that when new shares are issued, they have *first refusal* on taking them, in the proportion that their shares bear to the total). This means that the board is precluded, without first gaining shareholder approval, from issuing more shares to others. Further restrictions could include a prohibition on issuing additional shares that would result in any one holder owning more than (say) 50% of the total and thus having voting control of ordinary business. Exceptions to a pre-emption rule (i.e. those that do not need the members to waive their pre-emptive rights) are as follows:

- shares issued for employee share schemes;
- issue of non-participating preference shares and similar securities, or of any other non-equity securities;
- allotment of shares for a non-cash consideration;
- allotment of shares under a renounceable letter of allotment.

Administration

Shares that are not fully paid (that is the full issue price has not yet been paid for them) must be numbered and such numbers must be used in all transactions, so that their partly paid status is made clear to anyone involved. Once all shares are fully paid they no longer need numbers. Before new shares are allotted, the authority of the board is required and a record of this resolution, with the effective date, must be recorded in the board minutes. Entries (i.e. full details of the new shareholders or the addition of new shares to an existing shareholding) must be made in the Register of Members and under CA06s555 a return of allotments (form SH01) must be filed at CH within one month of the resolution. The following board minute might be appropriate

Example: Allotment board minute

Board Meeting: 1st December 2XXX

It was resolved that – the following shares be and they hereby are allotted as follows, amounts in respect of the subscription monies referred to having been received from each person – and that the Secretary should issue share certificates, make the necessary entries in the share register and notify the Registrar.

New shareholder	Number of shares	Cash rec'd
A Bloggs	1000 Ordinary shares of £1	£1000
B Jones	2000 Ordinary shares of £1	£2000
J Smith	10000 Ordinary shares of £1	£10000

Payment – and non-payment

The nominal amount (either in whole, or if the shares are issued part paid, in part) is due from the subscribing shareholder. The issue of shares partly paid means only an initial amount is originally due, with the balance subject to *call* in due course (sometimes on stated dates). Where the directors issue a *call* notice for the amount due, and that amount is not paid, the shares may be subject to forfeiture. A forfeiture notice is issued to the shareholder stating a date (not less than 14 days later) by which the amount due (plus interest) is required. If the amount due is not paid then the directors could resolve that the shares be forfeited and the shareholder's name be removed from the Register.

Controlling who holds the shares

Many of the Articles of LTDs limited by shares grant the right to their directors to prevent (by refusing to accept a transfer form) someone unacceptable to the board becoming a shareholder (hence such companies being referred to as *private companies*). Under CA06s771, any board wishing to block a transfer of a share must be prepared to give reasons for the refusal within two months of receipt of the share transfer. If an LTD RE-REGISTERS as a PLC, this right of the directors must be abandoned.

Payment, premiums and part payment

The original subscribers of a PLC must pay for their shares in cash. Shares in an LTD (and subsequent share issues by PLCs) can be issued in exchange for the rights to property, patent(s), intellectual property or a new process, etc. Where a PLCs shares are issued other than for cash, the asset(s) must be passed to the company within five years of the date of the share issue. If transfer of the asset(s) does not take place within that time, the allottee is liable to pay cash (and any premium) plus interest instead. If shares are to be issued in exchange for an asset, the value of the asset must be assessed by an expert (a person capable of acting as an auditor) and stamp duty may be payable.

A PLC must have an issued share capital of at least £50,000 and cannot allot any shares unless at least 25% of the nominal value of such shares (together with any premium) has been paid in cash. Where shares have a nominal value (e.g. £1, 50p, 25p etc.) the prospective shareholder normally pays the full amount for each share. However, a company could issue shares at more than the nominal value: e.g. they could issue new £1 shares at (say) £1.50 each. If so, in respect of each share issued, £1 will be credited to the company's Share Capital account and 50p to its Share Premium account. The balance in a Share Premium account is subject to restrictions- it cannot, for example, be used to pay a dividend.

If a company has authority under its Articles, shares may be able to be issued *partly paid*. However an LTD using the CA06 model Articles is not permitted to do so (unless it removes that restriction). If the ordinary shares have a nominal value of £1, they (or further shares of that class) could be issued on the basis that the subscribers will pay initially (say) 50p per share. The new £1 shares are then described as *partly paid* and the remaining 50p per share which has not so far been paid is *uncalled capital*. There may be contractual obligations (e.g. timing) regarding the payment of the uncalled capital but, subject to those, the board can *call* the remaining amount in whole or part and the shareholders must pay up (or sell their shares *partly paid* – but obviously at a lower price than a fully paid share).

Should the company become insolvent, an insolvency practitioner will demand that shareholders owning partly paid shares immediately pay the *uncalled* amount in respect of each share.

Share transfer

Shareholders can transfer their shares by completing a signed (and, if the value exceeds £1,000, an Inland Revenue stamped) stock transfer form (STF) and giving it and their share certificate(s) to the company for action. However if a shareholder dies, is sectioned under the Mental Health Act, or is declared bankrupt, and thus cannot sign an STF, the shares can be vested in another person under share *transmission* arrangements. The authority to deal with the shares is vested in the shareholder's personal representative(s) (executor, administrator or deputy), committee or receiver, or trustee in bankruptcy. For CA06 companies, on the death of a shareholder, subject to production of Probate or Letters of Administration, the shares can be put into the name of a *transmittee* (i.e. a person entitled to the shares) and the directors cannot object to that person holding the shares. However a *transmittee* is not a full member of the company and has no right to attend or vote at GMs. LTD directors have the right to refuse to accept a subsequent transfer from the *transmittee* to a third party who is unacceptable to them.

Stamp duty

Until March 2008 stamp duty had to be paid on all share transfers (other than exempted transactions) in proportion to the value of the shares (*ad valorem* duty). The shares had to be valued – a relatively easy requirement for companies with shares listed on a stock exchange but more difficult for non-listed companies, where usually an auditor's valuation would be needed. If a company receives an unstamped STF in respect of a transaction where the value exceeds £1000, the form should be returned to the shareholder with a request that it be sent to HMRC for duty stamping. If an STF is submitted to HMRC more than a month after it is dated, excess charges may be required. A non-duty paid STF which is acted upon when duty was due, fails to give a good title to the transferee, and those responsible can be fined £300.

The following transfers are also exempt from stamp duty subject to confirmation (by a certificate required to be completed on the reverse of the STF) that the transaction falls within one of the categories, i.e. it is:

- of property in the name of a trustee to a new trustee;
- by way of security for a loan;
- to a beneficiary under a will;
- to a beneficiary from an intestate's estate;
- to a residuary legatee;
- on, and in consideration of, marriage and/or a civil partnership;
- by the liquidator;

- not on sale and not arising from sale where no beneficial interest passes (e.g. from one nominee to another nominee);
- by way of gift.

Finally, stamp duty is not levied when securities listed on growth markets (e.g. the Alternative Investment Market) are transferred.

Record and title

The issue of a share certificate acts as both receipt for the money subscribed and evidence of title. However, some Articles stipulate that a share certificate is only valid as evidence of title if it bears the common SEAL of the company. If a company wishes to dispense with its seal, either its Articles should be changed to ensure share certificates can be issued validly without being sealed, or alternatively a *securities seal* could be retained purely for the purpose of authenticating share certificates.

Single member company (SMC)

If a share transfer results in the company having only one member i.e. creating an SMC, a note of this fact and the date must be entered in the register of members for the sole member. Should an SMC issue share(s) to (an) additional person(s) then the fact that the company is no longer an SMC and the date should be added to the entry in the share register. The Articles of a company that becomes an SMC should be examined for any implications – e.g. the quorum for general meetings may be *two*! After six months, the surviving shareholder of a company which becomes an SMC by default (e.g. shares are sold to one remaining shareholder) has unlimited personal liability for the acts of the company.

Reduction of share capital

Provided there is nothing in its Articles to prevent it, a company by special RESOLUTION can reduce its share capital. Since this could prejudice the interests of the creditors, in addition to passing the resolution, a PLC must gain Court authority to a scheme of arrangement. Under CA06ss.642/643, LTDs no longer need Court permission (although they can use that procedure); if not, then following the passing of the special resolution, the directors must sign a solvency statement confirming that each director has formed the opinion that

- there is no ground on which the company could be unable to pay its creditors or discharge its debts;
- during the year ahead the company will be able to pay its debts as they fall due;
- (if it is intended to wind the company up in the following year) the company will be able to pay its debts in full within a year of the commencement of the winding up process.

Copies of the special resolution or the solvency statement must be filed with CH within 15 days of the passing of the resolution.

Buying back shares

There are strict rules regarding share buybacks and audit/legal advice should be sought. Providing their Articles allow, and with agreement of their shareholders, under CA06s725 PLCs are permitted to buy back up to 10% (of the nominal value) of their shares. However CA06 (Amendment of Part 18 Regulations) 2013 now require only an ordinary resolution (unless the Articles stipulate otherwise) rather than the previous special resolution. The regulations also allow LTDs (with the authority of the Articles) each year to buy back shares worth the lower of £15,000 or 5% of the company's share capital. Normally the buy back is financed by distributable profits, but with a director's solvency certificate, a special resolution and notification to CH (form SH04) (i.e. requirements similar to a reduction of capital) they could be financed out of capital if the buyback is in connection with an employee share scheme.

If the shares are *bought back* out of distributable profits, they can be held by the company *in treasury;* their voting rights are suspended and they do not rank for dividends. They can be re-issued at any time (when CH must be informed – form SH05) and will then be treated in exactly the same way as other shares. Shares held *in treasury* could be cancelled which would result in a reduction in capital – and require the authority related thereto (see above) including notifying CH (form SH06).

Annual report

Whilst the annual report of a high-profile listed PLC requires considerable investment in both time and money, for most LTDs, although the required content is similar, a far more modest document will usually suffice.

a) The chairman's statement

Under Stock Exchange requirements listed PLCs must include a chairman's statement which is often the focal point of the whole document not least since it looks forward whereas much of the report is reflective. Such a statement is not required for LTDs but, if desired, the following would need to be addressed.

CHECKLIST: Preparation of chairman's statement

✓ Decide on theme and style

✓ Collate background data (previous statements, media comment and interviews, results of competitors)

✓ Collate data on external factors – political, economic, environmental etc. – which have impacted/could impact business

✓ Assess impact of results on current and future prospects

✓ Report on capability of personnel current and anticipated and steps being taken to ensure adequate skills supply

---

b) Report of the directors

This is a legally required statement and the advice from the company's AUDITORS (whose report covers its contents) should be sought to ensure compliance with the latest requirements. The main contents include statements regarding:

- trading results;

- transfers to and from reserves and any movements in assets in the period under review;

- dividends paid and proposed;

- acquisitions and disposals;

- details of DIRECTORS during the year under review and, for those seeking re-election at the AGM, of any service agreements;

- the AUDITORS and a note regarding their re-election or replacement;

- developments in employment, employee involvement, disabled employees and health and safety;

- donations made, separating political donations from others;

- major shareholdings (if any) in the company;

- the development of the business;

- any share option and/or share ownership scheme(s);

- activities of significance that have taken place since the date of the balance sheet;

- that the directors take responsibility for the financial statements and accounts;

- (for listed PLCs) greenhouse gas emissions.

In addition 'large' LTDs (and all PLCs) are now required to include 'non-financial' data such as:

- environmental matters (i.e. the impact of the companies activities on the environment)
- employment matters
- social matters
- respect for human rights
- anti-corruption and anti-bribery matters.

c) Annual Accounts

The accounts and statements must give a true and fair picture of the company's financial state, and, unless the company is exempt, or is under the audit threshold, be backed by an auditor's statement to that effect. The accounts package will normally comprise a profit and loss statement, funds flow statement, balance sheet, details of accounting policies and any change(s) thereto, plus explanatory notes.

d) Notice and agenda of the Annual General Meeting

It is customary to include the notice and AGENDA of the Annual GENERAL MEETING in the Report as the accounts and balance sheet, together with a note of any dividend proposed, must be given to the members.

e) Auditors statement

The accounts must include the AUDITORS statement indicating that the accounts give a true and fair view of the company's financial affairs as at the date of the balance sheet. Auditors can qualify their statement, stating the scope of the qualification. Companies whose annual turnover does not exceed £10.2 million (unless they are charities or involved in financial services) are not required to have their accounts audited.

f) Statement of compliance with requirements of the UK Corporate Governance Code (UKCGC)

Listed PLCs are required to include such a statement covering a range of topics which are constantly being added to. Advice should be taken. A company that does not comply with the detailed requirements of the code must provide an explanation for such non-compliance. In addition the following information is required to be disclosed either in the Annual Report or on the company's website:

- the terms of reference of the board's nomination, remuneration and audit

- committees, explaining their roles and authority;

- non-executive directors terms and conditions of appointment;

- a statement, if any remuneration consultants were appointed, of whether they had any other connections with the company.

Where there is a resolution regarding the re-election of directors / auditors, the company must also provide:

- biographical details that will enable shareholders to take an informed decision on such persons election or re-election;

- the reason(s) for someone being appointed a non-executive director;

- if the re-election of a non-executive director is to be considered, the chairman's confirmation that the person's performance has been evaluated and has been found to be effective; and

- if the re-election of an auditor is to be considered and the audit committee's recommendation is not accepted by the board, a statement showing both the recommendation and the reason(s) for the board opposing the recommendation.

The Strategic Report

The CA06 (Strategic Report and Directors Report) Regulations 2013 requires for all but small companies, the production of a Strategic Report to be signed by a director – plus an annual Directors Statement containing more detailed reporting and disclosure requirements.

The Strategic Report must contain information regarding:

- the strategy of the company and its business model to the extent necessary for an understanding of the development, performance or position of the company's business;

- human rights; and

- gender diversity giving details of the persons of each sex who were, directors, senior managers and employees. (A senior manager is defined as a person with responsibility for planning directing or controlling a strategically significant part of the company.)

Directors are personally liable for the content of the report and could be held liable to compensate anyone for any loss they suffer as a result of any untrue or misleading statement in, or any omission from, the report, if they knew (or were reckless as to whether) the statement was true – or knew the statement to be a dishonest concealment of a material fact.

Other possible inclusions

Recent developments in corporate reporting may require companies to address such matters within their reporting material – since failure to do so may generate enquiry.

a) Tax evasion

Legislation is pending which would require corporations to prevent anyone acting on their behalf from facilitating tax evasion. For there to be a criminal liability, prosecutors would need to show that the most senior members of an organisation (e.g. members of the board of directors) were involved in the matter: for example, '*a company X Ltd would* be guilty of an offence if a person associated with X Ltd commits a UK tax evasion facilitation offence when acting in the capacity of a person associated with X Ltd'. However, X Ltd would have a defence if it can show that it had 'such prevention procedures as it was reasonable in the circumstance to expect X Ltd to have'.

As is similarly and already required in legislation outlawing Bribery and Modern Slavery, for there to be at least the foundation of a defence, detailed guidance would need to be developed and publicised in a staff handbook or similar, for example:

'This company is committed to the principle that it should pay the appropriate amount of tax (as reduced by genuine and permitted allowances etc. only) on its activities as intended under legislation from time to time determined. The company is equally committed to outlawing any deviance from the above principle and regards

a) any employee operating or acting in the name of the organisation and being in breach of this commitment as being guilty of gross misconduct (and thus subject to dismissal), and

b) any other person (e.g. an agent or consultant etc.) acting in breach of these requirements of the organisation, rendering the relationship and any contract evidencing that relationship null and void.

Anyone involved in any way with the company and becoming aware of activities being carried on in breach of this rule, is expected to report such matters to [named person]. Providing it is made in good faith, the position of any person making such a report will be protected under the organisation's 'whistleblowing' commitment.'

b) Gender pay reporting

Employers with 250 or more UK–based employees are required to publish details of pay on a gender basis on a searchable website available to employees and the public. The information must be signed by a director; and evidence that the requirement has been complied with must be submitted to a Government sponsored website. The initial data must be published by April 2018 reflecting the information from April 2017 (hence a data base must be set so that data can be generated). Organisations need to publish:

- the mean gender pay gap (i.e. the difference between the average hourly earnings of the organisation's female and male employees, each taken as a single group).

- the median gender pay gap (i.e. the difference between the median hourly earnings of the organisation's female and male employees, each taken as a single group). The median is obtained by listing (by gross hourly rate) the number of people of each gender in a group and identifying the persons whose earnings are in the middle of the two lists. Gross pay must include basic pay, paid leave, maternity pay, sickness pay, area allowances, shift premiums, bonus pay etc.; but not overtime pay, expenses, redundancy pay, benefits in kind or tax credits.

- the gender bonus gap (i.e. the difference in average bonus pay paid to female and male employees during a 12 month period to the previous April each year as well as the proportion of female and male employees who received any bonus pay in that period).

An organisation's workforce must be divided into 4 quartiles; each stating the number of employees of each gender. An employer can determine its quartiles, but all its employees must be encompassed within the 4 groups.

At present there are no penalties for failure to comply – other than potential damage to reputation since presumably pressure groups will wish to 'name and shame' those where there is an unexplainable gender pay gap. As there may be sound reasons for such gaps, companies would be well advised to seek to explain these – and any steps being taken to eradicate them – with the published data.

Directors pay

Other than for small companies, details of rewards given to directors must be provided as follows:

- single total figure of remuneration for all directors (with separate figures for non-executive directors);
- payments to past directors;

- payments for any director's loss of office;

- statements of directors' shareholdings and share interests;

- the rewards for the chief executive officer; and

- the remuneration policy for the following financial year.

Preparation

The preparation of an annual report is a lengthy and complex operation. The main areas requiring attention are:

1. Appoint project leader.

2. Determine impression to be given (e.g. forward looking, high quality, retrenching, expansionist, etc.).

3. Decide on theme and, if reports are written by a number of executives, ensure this theme is used consistently.

4. Determine type of report required in relation to company and brief those invited to contribute.

5. Check space requirements with auditors (i.e. new or revised accounting requirements may mean a greater space being required).

6. Gain approval for budget.

7. Prepare draft layout and content.

8. Decide size, paper, typeface, and style.

9. Prepare detailed timetable, allowing flexibility.

10. Prepare proforma report and obtain quotation from typesetters and printers based on proforma and specification.

11. Agree timetables with all involved (including accounts staff, public relations advisers, auditors, designers, typesetters and printers, registrars and despatch).

12. Agree timetable with chairman/board.

13. Publish timetable and contact names/telephone numbers to all involved.

14. Agree proofing turnaround and discussion procedure with those involved. Advise printers numbers of proof copies required and destinations.

15. Communicate each step with all involved. Chase those writing items for the report as deadlines approach.

CHECKLIST: Timetable for the production of the annual report

Item D: Despatch Day

✓ Prepare budget and timetable (in liaison with interested parties)
D minus 100 days

✓ Prepare editor's brief, board specification and commitment to theme, style, design, concept, etc. Prepare mock-up.

✓ Prepare proforma and send to auditors to assess space requirements
D – 95

✓ Notify public relations advisors of publication and check possible clashes (i.e.. are major companies or competitors likely to report around the same time?) D – 90

✓ Photographer/illustrator specifications drafted

✓ Chairman's Statement lst draft

✓ Executives Reports lst draft

✓ Employee Report lst draft

✓ Proxy and other cards lst draft

✓ Chairman's Statement, etc. 2nd draft D – 80

✓ Photographer/illustrator commissioned *

✓ Analyse numbers of report required D – 70

✓ Chairman's Statement 3rd draft and copy to typesetter/printer D – 60

✓ Liaise with Registrars & provide checklist

✓ Liaise with corporate public relations (PR)

✓ Liaise with brokers

✓ First proof back, checked & returned to printers   D – 50

✓ Second proof to company/auditors

✓ Photographs reviewed and agreed   D – 40

✓ Third proof (colour) to company/auditors

✓ Preliminary announcement   D – 30

✓ Insert figures in third proof for printers (Hold period: D – 30 to D – 25)**

✓ Commission Dividend Warrants

✓ Final proof checked by company/auditors agreed

✓ Print order given. Printers liaise with registrars re mailing addresses
                                                            D – 20

✓ Report despatched externally   D – 1

✓ Report despatched internally   D day

* Some companies retain photographers to capture events during the year so that a choice of illustrations is available.

** A *hold* period allows time for an objective consideration of the production when no deadlines are pressing, although in practice, it tends to be used to catch up on previous time slippages!

Approval and filing

The board must approve the company's individual (and any consolidated) accounts and balance sheet as well as the directors' report and strategic review. A director must sign the balance sheet although the directors' report can be signed either by a director or the Secretary. The signatories' full names must be shown on the printed copies. The accounts and balance sheet are then presented to the members of the company in general meeting and a copy) filed with CH by the end of the ninth month after the ARD for LTDs (sixth month for PLCs).

CH has powers under CA06 to insist not only that all filing be carried out electronically but also that all company formations use this format. To file accounts electronically, the company must use software compatible with CH systems – contact www.companieshouse.gov.uk/accounts.

Failing to file accounts within the time limits renders the company liable to a fine from £150 to £15,000 depending on the type of company, the filing delay and any repetition and, for those responsible, potential prosecution and disqualification under CDDA86. If accounts are filed late repeatedly the amount of the fines can be doubled.

The accounts of a newly incorporated company must be filed not more than nine months (PLC – 6 months) after the first anniversary of its incorporation or not more than three months after its first ARD whichever is the later.

Despatch to owners

CA06 permits companies to communicate with their shareholders (e.g. sending reports etc.) by electronic means (email, fax, disk in post, etc.).Website communication is also allowed and unless a shareholder specifically opts out they will be regarded as having *received* the document if it is posted there. If they opt out then they must be sent the information in some other way. However companies using website posting must notify their shareholders of this – using hard copy, unless the shareholders have agreed they can be notified electronically.

Under the Companies Registrar, Languages and Trading Disclosures Regulations 2006, companies using a website must display their name and registered number and office, country of registration and VAT number (if appropriate). Similar information has been required to be displayed on external correspondence including emails under CA85s.349/351 – a requirement far more noted for its breach than its observance!

Wherever electronic communication is used a shareholder still has the right to a hard copy version (even if he has agreed to receive documents in electronic form) within 21 days of such a request.

Companies can:

- publish their annual reports and accounts on their website and simply advise shareholders that they are so available;

- allow shareholders to use fax and e-mail to appoint proxies and give their proxy(ies) voting instructions;

- publish other information on their website making it clear whether such information has been subject to audit or not.

CA06 requires PLCs to publish their annual reports on their websites as soon as they are available and immediately after they have been approved by the board and auditors. It is recommended that this should happen within 120 days (roughly four months) of the year-end. All the UK's FTSE100 companies publish financial information electronically. Companies adopting this option should liaise with their auditors since they may wish to ensure it is made clear what information is (and is not) subject to audit. Suitable security of the website is essential to prevent unauthorised changes.

Corporate social responsibility (CSR)

The previous Business Link service defined CSR as *'understanding your business impact on the wider world and considering how to use that impact in a positive way. It means taking a responsible attitude, going beyond the minimum legal requirements and following straightforward principles that apply whatever the size of your business',*

Listed PLCs are required to publish a CSR statement within their Annual Report that could address:

- The ethos of the company and employment matters;

- Its treatment of the environment;

- Whether the company deals in or with raw materials or products considered to be unethical.

This obligation is to be both extended in scope and required of other (non-listed) large companies under a draft EU directive. 'Large' in this respect includes companies:

- whose turnover is £34 million or more: and

- whose balance sheet total is £17 million or more: and

- who have 500 employees or more.

If a company has a turnover of £36 million or more it is subject to the Modern Slavery Act. Under that Act (see GIFTS) businesses must set out what steps they have taken in the year under review to ensure they:

a) (and/or their supply chains) do not exploit workers;

b) check the supply chain and business generally; and

c) have trained their employees about the risk of slavery and human trafficking.

Articles of Association

Adoption

All companies must have and file Articles and if a company does not adopt its own, it is deemed (CA06s20) to operate under the standard Articles related to the CA under which it was registered. New model Articles (for PLCs, and LTDs limited by shares or guarantee) are set out in the Companies (Model Articles) Regulations 2008 (as amended by the Mental Health (Discrimination) Act 2013). Any company feeling it can operate with standard rules, could simply adopt these, although they are intended to be used as a foundation. Thus most companies *cherry-pick*, taking the sections they want from the pro forma, and drafting their own Articles in substitution for those they discard, or in addition thereto. Alternatively a company can draft its own Articles – legal advice should be sought. Once adopted, such provisions become binding. The original Articles are adopted by being signed by each subscriber to the MEMO-RANDUM (each signature must be witnessed) and filed with CH as part of the company's INCORPORATION.

A new company can be formed electronically at CH virtually instantly but the standard Articles under CA06 must be used. Obviously, if time is of the essence, this service could be used to set the company up, then a General Meeting could be convened to approve customised Articles.

Notes:

1. If regulations from the pro forma are used, it is helpful to set out the wording in full plus any customised Articles in a complete version. Unfortunately the Articles of many companies simply cross-refer to the standard regulations of the relative Act, leaving the reader to source those before they can comprehend the full obligations. Then two detailed documents must be read as one. A 'cut and paste' procedure would be best used to gain one comprehensive document.

2. There are up to 2.8 million UK companies whose Articles are based on the pro formas either of CA85 or an earlier Act. The CA85 versions were drafted in the early 1980s, and it is unlikely that operating a company with such dated Articles is entirely appropriate now and these would be best updated.

Changing the Articles

Articles should support the directors – not constrain their legitimate actions. To update or change its Articles, the company must obtain the approval of its members by means of a special RESOLUTION (requiring the support of at least 75% of the votes *cast* in person or by proxy) at a GENERAL MEETING or by written RESOLUTION (needing the approval of 75% of the *total* voting strength). Such a resolution must be filed with CH within 15 days.

If the change(s) is/are minor (or only affects part of the Articles), the wording of the special resolution for consideration by the members could simply include details of the change(s) although pre-CA06 companies who wish to change their Articles must now incorporate any objects clauses (either transferred directly from their Memorandum or as revised with the authority of the shareholders) so these details would also have to be set out in the resolution. As a result of CA06, the availability of the new drafts, and the requirement to incorporate the objects clauses, it may be felt more appropriate to update the entire Articles. This may be particularly apposite for groups with subsidiaries registered under earlier Acts as any new subsidiary must now be formed under CA06, leading to the challenge of dealing with sets of Articles derived from different legislative enactments. The opportunity could be taken to, as far as possible, give subsidiaries similar Articles.

As well as the new wording, the reason for each change and its effect should be outlined in the notice to the members, with the advice that a copy of the proposed new Articles can be made available to those who wish to inspect it (alternatively the proposed version could be sent with the notice).

The proforma Articles for a CA06 LTD limited by shares are much shorter (only 53 clauses; 86 for a PLC) than CA85 Table A (118 regulations). Companies wishing to use the latest version may wish to retain some of those that have been omitted, included in the following checklist.

Checklist: CA85 Table A regulations (in brackets) for consideration for retention when using CA06 draft as basis

- Granting the right to the company to have a lien over shares where the shareholder has not paid in full for the amount due. (CA85, Table A reg. 8)

- Alternatively consideration could be given to reserving the right to disenfranchise shares where calls made have not been paid.

- The administration by which the board can make calls on shares issued partly paid (reg. 12).

- How shares are to be transferred (regs. 23 and 25-31).

- If an LTD wishes to continue to convene AGMs the provisions concerning such meetings need to be added (regs. 36- 63).

- If an LTD wishes to continue to operate with a Secretary it might be as well to make this clear (reg. 99).

Companies are not permitted to:

- make any Article unalterable;

- increase the size of the majority required to authorise a change in its Articles beyond that required for a special resolution (that is 75% of the votes cast when voting in person or by proxy at a meeting or, if by written resolution, 75% of the total voting strength). However if entrenched provisions have been inserted these may be subject to more restrictive procedures/conditions – e.g. unanimous consent;

- increase the financial liability of its members without their written authority, or require members to subscribe for additional shares. However where there are different classes of shares, a company may be able to incorporate Articles, the effect of which could be to restrict the rights of holders of those shares. Legal advice should be sought if this is required as the law gives protection where any such interests might be prejudiced.

The ultra vires rule

Directors who fail to act in accordance with the Articles are acting *ultra vires* (beyond their powers) and can be held personally liable for any losses thereby incurred. The Secretary should have a good working knowledge of the Articles' principal requirements – not least to avoid *ultra vires* action being taken.

Case study: Acting *ultra vires*

In *UK Safety Group Ltd v Hearne,* a managing director (one of six directors) seeking to delegate his responsibility for sales, met a young, ambitious, effective salesman who seemed an ideal sales director. Concerned that any appointee could in the future set up his own business in competition using the customer contacts made whilst working for his company, the MD's advisers devised a watertight contract including a *garden leave* clause to minimise this danger. After the appointee signed the contract, the MD *appointed* him a director and advised CH.

Within 18 months the sales director left to start his own business in competition. Relying on the *garden leave* clause, the MD went to Court to prevent its breach. The company lost the initial action since it was pointed out that the sales *director* had not been properly appointed. The Articles stipulated that directors could only be appointed at a 'properly convened and constituted Board meeting' – which had not taken place.

Further, since in making the false appointment, the MD had exceeded his authority, he was acting *ultra vires* and the company's shareholders could hold him liable for any loss(es) suffered by the company (see DERIVA-TIVE CLAIMS).

It is not only directors who could lose out because the requirements of the Articles are overlooked.

Case study: Restriction in Articles

In *T A King (Services) Ltd & Cottrell (C) v King (K)*, C held 75% of the shares and K the remaining 25%. When C died, his shares were transmitted to his widow (Mrs C). K objected because the Articles stipulated that on a member's death their shares had first to be offered to the remaining member at a price to be determined by the auditors. The High Court held that the transmission was void. Mrs C had to transfer C's shares back to C's estate, and the executor of the estate had then to offer the shares to K at valuation and the proceeds would fall into C's estate. Ironically, since he held 75% of the shares, C could have changed the Articles by a special resolution taking out the provision – unless, of course the obligations under a SHAREHOLDERS AGREEMENT precluded him from doing so.

Note: Since they must be filed at CH, a company's Articles are a public document and the law must be observed in framing them. However many LTDs shareholders enter into SHAREHOLDERS AGREEMENTS. CA06 stipulates that anything agreed between the parties in such an agreement which would have needed a Special Resolution must be filed at CH. Those in charge of a company where there is such an Agreement should ensure its contents are not in conflict with the Articles. Where a Shareholders Agreement contains rights to exercise control over the board etc., details of such rights will need to be disclosed in the company's register of PERSONS WITH SIGNIFICANT CONTROL.

Auditors

KEY POINTS

- Unless they are dormant, exempt or their turnover is under the audit threshold, companies' accounts must be audited by authorised accountants.

- Auditors have rights to look at all company records and to require answers to their questions from directors and employees.

- An auditor has a right to notify shareholders of any matter than gives them concern.

- Auditors can be held liable for errors and mistakes – even those carried out by the directors.

Qualification

An auditor must have a recognised accountancy qualification supervised by Recognised Qualifying Bodies (RQB) whose operation is regulated by Recognised Supervisory Bodies (RSB). Only registered auditors are eligible to audit company accounts. If accounts are audited by an unregistered auditor, CH can reject the accounts and require them to be properly audited – the directors being responsible for any additional costs.

By virtue of their appointment by the members, auditors are required to hold an independent view of the activities of the company and the board and to report to the members. Although they may need to work closely with the board and Secretary, their first duty is to the members and should there be irregularities, answers should be demanded. An auditor has a right to notice of, and to attend and to speak at the company's general meeting.

Appointment and term

The first auditors are appointed by the directors prior to the first ANNUAL GENERAL MEETING (AGM) (which must be held within 18 months of the company's incorporation date). At the first and subsequent AGMs auditors are appointed (or re-appointed) by the members and hold office from the conclusion of one AGM until the conclusion of the next – or, if the company does not hold AGMs, until their appointment is terminated. If an auditor resigns, the directors can appoint a replacement who holds office until the conclusion of the next following AGM. It can be adminis-tratively convenient for auditors to be replaced – for example, if a parent company acquires a new subsidiary, it might be logical for the parent's auditors to audit the accounts of the new subsidiary.

A resigning auditor is required to lodge at the company's registered office a statement if there are any matters that he feels should be brought to the attention of the members and creditors. If the auditor has lodged such a statement that the company wants suppressed, it has 21 days to take the matter to Court, and, if so, must notify the Auditor that it has taken such action. If, within 21 days of lodging the statement, the Auditor has been advised that an appeal has been made to the Court he must lodge his original statement with CH. The Court has the authority either to suppress the statement or to require that copies be distributed to the members.

A resigning auditor who feels that there are matters of which members should be made aware, can call upon the directors to convene a (extraordinary) General Meeting. Notice must be given within 21 days of the request and the meeting must be held within 28 days of the notice. The auditor also has the right to have a statement distributed to members and to be heard at the meeting, although no further action can be taken, unless (a) member(s) so wish(es).

If an auditor resigns prior to the end of his term there is no longer a requirement to advise CH although the relevant audit authority must be informed. There is, however, no need to make such a declaration if the auditor has ceased to be an auditor; or if the company:

- is no longer required to have its results audited (i.e. its turnover etc., is under the threshold; or
- is being wound up under an insolvency procedure; or
- is a subsidiary of a UK parent (and the new auditor is auditing the group accounts including those of the subject subsidiary).

Removal

An auditor can only be removed from office by ordinary RESOLUTION of the members in general meeting. Special Notice must be given of such a proposal:

- A member proposing that a current auditor not be re-appointed must give notice of this proposal (which can only be made once in each year) to the company's registered office.
- The Auditor has seven days to respond and make any representations why he should not be removed.
- The proposal (together with any representations from the Auditor) must be sent to the members with 21 days notice of the meeting. If the resolution is passed, then the auditor's office terminates at the end of the current financial year. If, however, such a notice is lodged within 14 days of the issue of the accounts for the previous financial year, the auditor's appointment may cease with effect from the end of the financial year being reported upon.

Rights

In addition to the right to attend and be heard at general meetings, auditors have rights of access to all records of the company including board minutes necessary for them to be able to complete their audit, and to require directors and staff of the company to provide information, and answer their questions. The auditors must also be sent a copy of every written resolution. Failure to comply can result in a £500 fine.

Payment

Fees paid to auditors must be determined by company in general meeting although it is customary for the members to delegate this duty to the board. Auditors' fees must be disclosed in the accounts, split between charges for audit and any other work, for example, taxation advice and calculations, consultancy, etc.

Exemption from or retention of audit

Under company law, the following companies are exempt from the requirement to have their accounts audited:

- a charity whose gross income does not exceed £500,000 (or £250,000 where gross assets are £3,260,000 or more) although such a company may still need an audit under charity law or its own constitution.

- a small company (i.e. one whose turnover does not exceed £10.2 million provided it is not a PLC, bank, insurance company or broker registered under the Financial Services and Markets Act 2000 or the Trade Union and Labour Relations (Consolidation) Act 1992.

Dispensing with an audit has been taken up by fewer than 10% of the companies entitled. There are several reasons. The role of the directors is to take risks and to drive the company forward in accordance with the law. Some may fail to conform (either accidentally or deliberately) to legal and accounting convention practices. Knowing that such practices could be challenged by the auditors can act as a brake on such activities. Without this 'audit brake' such practices can go unchecked – and potentially unnoticed – until the company fails. An independent view may not only highlight genuine mistakes but also provide suggestions and guidance. Further many involved may feel their interests could be prejudiced if there are no audited accounts. These could include: trade creditors and lending banks (which might preclude the company obtaining credit – or being required to have the accounts audited probably by the bank's own – and possibly more expensive – auditors); shareholders and non-executive directors (who would lack an independent view of the results); regulatory bodies and insurers; as well as the directors themselves as without an auditors advice they may find difficulty calculating the company's tax liability (and ensuring the company gains all the exemptions and allowances to which it is entitled – and complies with the latest disclosure requirements).

Liability

Although it is the officers who take responsibility for the accounts, increasingly auditors can be held to account where there are breaches which they should have queried and/or rectified. As a result of the investigation following the scandal of the failure of the MG Rover group, which was being run by the so-called 'Phoenix 4', although the four culpable directors plea-bargained an agreement not to be involved in the operation of a UK company for 6, 5, 5, and 3 years respectively, Deloittes, the auditors, were found guilty of 'significant misconduct' and fined £3 million (then [PwC just been fined £5.1M] the largest fine ever imposed on an audit firm), whilst the partner in charge of the company's audit was fined £175,000 and given a severe reprimand by the Financial Reporting Council.

Current developments

1. The EU has proposed exempting companies whose turnover is less than Euro 1,000,000 and who have fewer than 10 employees from the need to file accounts at all. This could put such companies at an even worse disadvantage than companies which at least have unaudited accounts available.

2. The abolition of audits for subsidiaries, other than for quoted subsidiaries or for companies in the financial services sector, providing their parent company guarantees their debts (implemented by CA06s479).

3. HMRC has recently adopted a policy of contacting companies to check how:

   a) the business is operated;

   b) business records are kept; and

   c) the business deals with cash receipts and payments.

   Gaining an input from the auditors before providing a response could be valuable.

4. The Companies (Disclosure of Auditor Remuneration and Liability Limitation Agreements) Regulations 2008 (SI 2008/49 as amended by SI 2011/2198) provide updated guidance regarding the disclosure of remuneration for accounts auditing and non-audit services.

5. Under the latest International Standard of Auditing requirements, auditors are required to issue a Basis of Opinion confirming:

   a) the audit was conducted in accordance with ISA and legal requirements,

   b) the part of the report that details the auditor's responsibilities,

   c) the auditor is independent of the entity being reported on, and

   d) they believe the evidence available is sufficient and appropriate to provide a basis for the opinion being given.

Authority, control and delegation

KEY POINTS

- Controls are essential when delegating authority to ensure that only authorised persons can commit the company contractually.

- Levels of delegated authority should be set out clearly on a chart (which should be periodically updated).

- Suppliers could be provided with such a chart to confirm authority levels.

Members

A properly approved resolution of its member is the highest authority in the company binding it, for example to approve/change the rules under which the company operates contained in its ARTICLES. Any changes need the approval of a majority of the votes *cast* at a general meeting (either a simple or a 75% majority depending on the resolutions' subject matter) or of the *total* votes if a written RESOLUTION is utilised.

Directors

Board authority is derived from the members via the Articles or their resolutions and operates on the basis of collective responsibility. Decisions are required to be taken by the board in meetings and evidenced by minutes of those meetings – the compiling and retention of which is a legal obligation. In dealing with third parties, it may be convenient to pass a resolution at a board meeting and, as evidence of such authority, provide the third party with a copy of the appropriate minute. Usually the extract from the minutes will need to be certified as a true copy by the chairman.

Example: Extract from board meeting minutes

Board meeting of Bloggs (Steel Fabricators) Ltd held on 29th November 2XXX at [address] Minute 157 – Brazilian contract RESOLVED that the company enter into a contract with San Paulo Constructiones for the supply of steel [amount / brief specification] for part of the Olympic park in Rio de Janeiro for a contract price of [sum], on terms to be agreed in discussion and that T Smith [a director] be and he hereby is authorised to agree such terms and sign the contract on behalf of the company.

Certified a true copy of Minute 157 _____

J Bloggs, Chairman _____ Date _____

Collective authority of the board is granted to the contract itself, whilst T Smith is granted individual authority to agree its terms and to sign it on behalf of the company. Although many commercial contracts require only a signature, possibly witnessed, some overseas organisations insist that the document bears the common SEAL and/or other additional attestation (e.g. by being sworn before a Notary Public) etc. Directors required to sign contracts not only need to ensure they have the requisite authority but also that it is clear they are signing on behalf of the company and not in their personal capacity

Case study: Check the paperwork

In *Hamid v Frances Bradshaw Partnership*, a director signed a contract bearing the trading name of a company (of which he was sole shareholder/director) but not the company name. Since there was no indication he was signing on behalf of the company itself he was found personally liable.

Notarial certification

Many overseas organisations insist on contracts being attested by a Notary Public.

Retaining a local Notary and arranging for him or her to meet the officers may assist as the Notary can then rely on personal knowledge of the signatories, otherwise it may be necessary to provide an *audit trail* to prove to the satisfaction of the Notary that the person signing a document is who they say they are, holds the position stated and is authorised to sign on behalf of the company.

Officers

Directors are company officers and as such have authority to bind it. However for their own protection it may be advisable to delineate the levels of authority attaching to each director and manager. Like the directors, the Secretary is an officer and is often referred to as the company's *chief administrator*. The Secretary has authority to bind the company in administrative duties (*'ostensible'* authority) but may not be able to enter into new commercial contracts except with board authority. If, however, it has been customary for the Secretary to sign particular contracts for some time, authority to continue to sign such contracts may actually be *derived* from what has gone before and been accepted previously. Under *actual* authority the board could grant the Secretary authority to sign (for example) a contract, the terms of which have been approved previously by the board.

Some companies prefer to enter brief details of each contract in a contracts register, entries in which, like the Register of Seals, are periodically approved at board meetings.

Other signatories

The value of an authority chart is that it not only sets out limits of authority for those lower down the chain of command (and can help reduce the likelihood of fraud or, at least, the exploitation of loopholes) but also it grants express authority to signatories; and, not least, demonstrates a degree of control.

Case studies:

Supplier correctly assumed authority

In *Pharmed Medicare Private Ltd v Univar Ltd* two employees described as managers of an organisation placed a number of small orders that were fulfilled by the supplier and paid for by their organisation. They then placed a much larger order under a pro forma invoice. There was then a dispute about paying for the goods, with the buying organisation stating the supplier should have known that the two managers who placed the order did not have authority. The supplier successfully claimed that the employees concerned had ostensible or derived authority since previous transactions entered into by them had been honoured by the buying organisation (i.e. it had paid for the goods they ordered).

Perceived authority

Allowing (even encouraging) a person to *hold themselves out* as having authority can mean the company being unable to avoid liability for their actions. In *SMC Electronic Ltd v Akhter Computers Ltd*, an employee, encouraged by his company to use the title Director of Power Supplier Unit Sales, signed a contract on behalf of the company. The Court held that the company could not repudiate the contract he signed since it was reasonable for the other party to assume they were dealing with someone with power to bind the company, given the job title his employers wished him to use.

Example: Authorities chart

BUSINESS NAME AUTHORITY LEVELS

Approval to contracts and/or the commitment or disposal of company resources is only permitted by suitably appointed personnel, in accordance with the following stated levels.

CONTRACTS

All contracts between the company and third parties, other than those covered by items set out below, must be channelled through the Company Secretary's office, to ensure correct status (i.e. whether they are to be regarded as a Deed or not) and approval.

The Secretary will arrange the passing of suitable board resolutions granting approval to specified person(s) to sign on behalf of the company. Sufficient time to obtain such a resolution should be allowed.

CASH COMMITMENT
Capital projects

- Authority for all projects (no low cut off) Board (All items must be supported by a Capital expenditure – Capex – form)

- Repairs and renewals, purchase of furniture and fittings (All items must be supported by a Capex form)

- Up to £1000   Manager – level...

- Over £1000 and up to £5000   Director

- Over £5000   Board

Vehicles

- (Supported by Capex form, for new allocations, or replacement form for write-offs and replacements)   Board

- All purchases to be in accordance with Policy

Expense items

- Up to £500   Manager – level...

- Over £500 and up to £1000   Senior Manager

- Over £1000 and up to £5000   Director

- Over £5000   Board

Committed expenditure

- Rent, rates, utility costs – where no change or increase is less than rate of inflation Manager – level... – where change has taken place

  Director

Bought ledger

- Raw materials, services etc., in accordance with budgeted level of production   Purchasing Manager

- Not in accordance with level of production   Director

Personnel matters

- Recruitment – as per plan   Director

  – additional to plan   Managing Director

- Wage adjustment

  - Annual Review   Board

  - Other than annual review, or for new staff, or replacement at other than at old rate

- Salary up to £18,000 p.a.   Manager – level...

- Salary over £18,000 p.a.   Board

- Warnings – written (grades...)   Director

  - written (grades...)   Managing Director

  - verbal   Manager

- Dismissal   Managing Director

In course of business

- Credits (cash or stock), samples, etc.

- In accordance with policy and less than £1000   Manager – level...

- Over £1000   Director

- Gifts, donations (cash or stock)

- In accordance with policy and budget   Personnel Manager

- Stock write-off and/or authority to dispose in stated area (e.g. to market trader, staff shop, by gift, etc.)

- Up to £1000   Sales Manager

- Over £1000   Sales Director in liaison with Finance Director

Personal expenses (inc. telephone bills etc.)

- Up to £500 by level above level submitting the expense claim (i.e. using the required company form). Over £500 by level two levels above person submitting expense claim.

Removal expenses

- In accordance with range of reimbursement agreed at time and may only be authorised by a Board Member. All invoices should be submitted in the name of the company to allow recovery of VAT.

Loans

- Loans to assist a new employee during the first weeks of his/ her employment (i.e. during the working of the 'week in hand' arrangements)   Personnel Manager

- All other loans   Board

Tips and inducements

- Other than normal business entertaining and acknowledging special service, the acceptance or provision of inducements and bribes etc. in the name of the organisation is expressly forbidden, being a criminal offence. Any instance where this is expected or required should be referred to [name]. All employees are expected to act to prevent bribery, breach of this obligation being a dismissible offence. Employees and agents are reminded of the following areas [specify] where it is possible that bribes etc. could be offered, expected or required.

- [Details of areas]

Price fixing

- It is illegal for any organisation to conspire with another to fix the price of any product or service – indeed even discussing prices might infringe the rules. Sanctions include imprisonment. On no account is any employee permitted to discuss prices with a competitor or to enter into any arrangement regarding prices no matter how informal. Any instance where this is expected or required should be referred to [name]. Breach of this rule is gross misconduct.

Issued by finance director on (date) To be updated 6 monthly (Next review due...)

(Figures are purely illustrative.)

Notes:

1. Whilst delineating and defining levels of authority is a sound control mechanism, it may also be necessary to advise third parties that a former employee no longer has authority to bind the company. If a dispute has resulted in summary dismissal for instance, those with whom the employee dealt (particularly if that person was involved in either buying or selling) should be advised immediately by e-mail or fax.

2. The reference to outlawing tips and inducements is included to try to ensure compliance with the Bribery Act. The Ministry of Justice has stated that, if facing an allegation of bribery, in order to success-fully use the defence that *reasonable steps were taken to prevent it* a company must be able to show that:

    a) it regularly assesses the nature of bribery risks to which it is exposed

    b) prevention of bribery is a top-level consideration and the commit-ment to operating without bribery is clearly communicated to everyone

    c) there are adequate policies and practices that cover all parties to a business relationship

    d) it has implemented its anti-bribery policies and procedures and these are set out in practical terms (i.e. examples are provided – see GIFTS) and

    e) that it monitors its requirements to ensure compliance.

    The guidance on the Act however states that normal business enter-taining is to be exempt from prosecution. However, it is an offence to provide *hospitality* if it can be proved that the intent was to persuade someone not to act *in good faith, impartially, or in accordance with a position of trust.*

3. The reference to price-fixing is included to draw the attention to those involved in buying or selling that there are criminal penalties for those that breach the Competition and Enterprise Acts. Any organisation that engages in anticompetitive practices (participating in a cartel, price-fixing, collusive tendering, bid-rigging, customer allocation, etc.) can be fined up to 30% of its turnover whilst individuals responsible (directors, Secretaries, senior managers etc.) can be jailed for up to five years. In addition anyone (which could be an individual) who has suffered loss because of such arrangements can sue the organisation(s) involved for losses sustained.

4. Whilst this is essentially a document aimed at enhancing internal controls mechanisms, it could be helpful to provide a copy (and regular updates) to suppliers so that they are advised *'who can bind the company and to what level'.*

5. It might also be advisable to insert reference to the organisation's commitment to ensuring it complies with the outlawing of Modern Slavery. The fact that the guide is re-issued every 6 months should assist keeping the attention of those in receipt of these requirements, negating for anyone in breach, the use of the 'I didn't know' defence.

Board meetings

KEY POINTS

- Company law requires owners to appoint directors to run their company – effected normally by regular directors meetings.

- Despite there being no legal obligation for directors to hold board meetings, failing to do so could make it difficult, if challenged, to prove directors exercised their required duty of care.

- Minutes of directors meetings are legally required to be taken and preserved.

Attendance

'The board's role is to provide entrepreneurial leadership of the company within a framework of prudent and effective controls' (FRC's 'Guidance on Board Effectiveness'). Many boards meet regularly in something approaching formality and, most, more often, informally, to take both short and long term decisions. Only directors have a right to attend board meetings, and although others may be present to give reports, answer questions etc., they should take no part in the decision-making process. Although there is no explicit legal requirement for directors to attend board meetings, directors cannot abrogate their legal liability for the company's actions. Since directors have a collective responsibility for board decisions whether present or not, for their own protection they should regard attendance as mandatory. Indeed the internal rules may require attendance as CA85 Table A reg.81 states that any director who fails to attend board meetings without reason (or permission of the board) for six months can be removed from the board by the other members.

The Secretary has no right of attendance, although if he is regularly excluded from board meetings he should consider whether he is comfortable with that – after all he is a company officer and potentially liable as such. In addition, a vital part of the role should be to compile a record of the board's decisions. If the Secretary is not present, someone else needs to do this since compilation and retention of board minutes is a specific legal requirement.

Administration

Meeting administration starts with setting meeting dates – possibly looking at least six months ahead (with a larger company / board, perhaps twelve months or more) on a rolling six-month basis. Despite directors already knowing the dates well in advance, specific notice of each meeting with an AGENDA should be sent to all entitled to attend (say) five working days prior to the meeting. Even if it is known in advance that a director will be unable to attend, an agenda plus supporting papers should still be provided – not least since directors (including non-executives) must keep themselves updated on all subject matters, reports etc. concerning the company.

Case study: Keep updated

During the case brought against non-executive directors following the collapse of Barings Bank after the devastating losses caused by Leeson's illegal trading in Singapore, the Court stated that 'directors, collectively and individually (have) a duty to acquire and maintain a sufficient knowledge of the company's business to enable them to discharge their responsibilities'.

Being sent (or worse have tabled) a mass of documentation for decision with no time for consideration is hardly likely to create a situation where directors have *sufficient knowledge* to be able to make informed decisions.

The effective meeting

The Harvard Business Review has suggested that in order to achieve an effective board meeting:

- an agenda is essential (with updating of current matters under consideration conducted in advance);
- there should be no more than seven participants;
- it should not last longer than an hour (to facilitate which the meeting should be conducted standing);
- electronic devices should be banned; and
- Chairmen should seek opinions from all, as some members may not speak unless asked.

It might also be wise to add:

- (other than in an emergency) interruptions should be prohibited;
- minutes should be published within 5 working days; and
- members' copy minutes must be kept confidentially and securely.

Agenda

A well-prepared agenda can assist the efficient execution of a meeting, although experience indicates that the production of very skeletal board agendas (often with hardly any advance notice) is widespread. Such an agenda may be adequate, but it often provides no detailed guidance regarding each item requiring a decision. A detailed agenda can help members prepare themselves adequately for the meeting. Proper (e.g. say five working days) notice (supported by the requisite documentation) should be provided so that members have time to consider items requiring decisions. They may also wish to conduct their own research – directors are expected to be pro-active.

Composition

A meeting's length tends to be proportionate (sometimes dispropor-tionate!) to the number of people present. If that number is swollen by persons whose contribution is unnecessary, the meeting's effectiveness may be diluted and its duration extended needlessly. Effective contribu-tions (concise yet comprehensive) should be sought. Setting a time limit for the meeting may encourage this and may minimise time being wasted on trivia. Conversely applying such a guideline too strictly may mean thought and discussion is curtailed. Every director has a right to be heard on every subject – and each has a vote. The chairman also has a vote and often under the Articles (or by agreement of the board) may have a second or casting vote if there is stalemate. The latest model Articles for an LTD grant the chairman a casting vote but companies not using these Articles need to clarify the situation – in advance of it being necessary.

Considering the data

Reports, etc., should accompany the agenda or a note regarding late or delayed submission (with a date of expected arrival) should be appended. Tabling a bulky or complex report at a meeting is to be avoided – since decision-taking on its contents could be uninformed and in breach of a director's inherent obligations.

Case study: Acting recklessly

In *Gwyer & Associates and anor v London Wharf (Limehouse) Ltd & ors,* a director of a company in financial difficulties made no effort to ascertain the interests of and effects on his company before voting on a board resolution. The Court held he was negligent and in breach of his fidu-ciary duty to exercise his discretion independently and *bona fides* in the company's interests. The Court also stated that where a company was on the brink of insolvency the directors owed a duty 'to consider as para-mount' the interests of the creditors.

On occasion, because of time pressures it may be impossible to provide directors with enough reading time before a decision is needed. In that case a synopsis highlighting the main points and effects could be presented.

Example: Summary sheet for board reports

Organisation name _____ Standard covering sheet _____

Report title_____ Date of report _____

Author/sponsoring dept _____

Date to be considered by meeting _____

Subject matter _____

Recommendations

1 _____

2 _____

3 _____

Synopsis of facts / contentions supporting recommendations

_____

Synopsis of facts / contentions contesting recommendations

_____

Implications for organisation if not proceeded with*

_____

Implications for organisation if not proceeded with NOW*

_____

Capital expenditure implications _____

Skill / personnel implication_____

Safety implications _____

*Questions posed to delineate the impact (and timing) of the recommendations of the report and as a guide to those asked to make a decision when they may not have had a chance to study the report and consider such implications.

Notes:

1. Where there are time constraints and the matter is material, it may be practicable, rather than holding a meeting, to obtain approval of all the directors by means of a written resolution. This entails drafting a resolution and sending it to each director asking them, should they agree, to sign and return it. The individual signed copies should be preserved in the minute book. Such a procedure needs to balance the need for urgency with the overriding principle that each director should be given as much information as possible and have the opportunity to requisition an emergency meeting of the board to *discuss* the matter prior to decision/commitment.

   Alternatively the board could conduct their business by using the telephone or teleconferencing facilities, although it might be best if these methods of arriving at board decisions were referred to in the Articles to avoid any challenge to the validity of decisions arrived at in this way and/or that all such decisions are subsequently recorded in writing with each director signing their agreement.

2. The term *material* may need to be defined. This could range from *contracts in,* to *contracts NOT in, the ordinary course of business* – although the word *ordinary* will also need definition. Financial and / or other limits (e.g. potential liability) should be set where appropriate.

The chairman

The role of the chairman is key to both board and company success. A chairman needs to have attributes that *make things happen*, such as:

- vision, to move the meeting towards the attainment of its aims;

- perception so that almost by instinct and certainly from a process of sound leadership and active listening he is aware of the aspirations and preferences of each member;

- good communication skills so that this vision is easily communicated to board members;

- enthusiasm to motivate members so that they believe in plans and in their own ability and that of their teams to perform and achieve them; and

- the ability to delegate, to force decision making and accountability down the chain of command, not so that someone at a low level is left *carrying the can* but to widen their horizons, make them aware of the issues and encourage them to make suggestions.

Good chairmanship:

i) agrees the aims, values and ethos of the board and the company;

ii) (with the Secretary) sets the agenda for each meeting, ensures relevant data is prepared and provided to directors in sufficient time in advance of each meeting so that content and possible effects can be considered;

iii) demonstrates genuine and effective leadership and is always available for guidance;

iv) inspires and motivates directors and employees;

v) interfaces with owners, authorities and the media to promote the company's interests;

vi) ensures new directors undergo meaningful induction and regularly evaluates the performance of all directors;

vii) oversees the work of sub-committees of the board and ensures committee-chairmen mirror the board chairman's performance and approach;

viii) ensures all directors contribute, their ideas are heard and there is rapport between them in sharing common goals;

ix) encourages all directors to speak their mind and to listen to any objective criticism;

x) ensures risks facing the company and its progress are identified and suitable controls are set up (and regularly reviewed) to minimise adverse effects;

xi) implements a reliable information and reporting flow;

xii) plans for managerial and directorial succession;

xi) acts as the spokesperson for the company;

and so on.

Aims

To be effective meetings should have targets. As Sir John Harvey Jones stated in *Making it Happen:* 'you've got to have a clear idea of where you want to take whatever it is you've got'. In order to focus the attention (individual and collective) of members on the subject matter, and to try to avoid a meeting descending into what can otherwise become a meandering discussion, targets should be identified. An agenda for a regular meeting can provide additional short-term aims, even though longer term, strategic aims may be set out elsewhere. An agenda can act as a directing force on the meeting, creating pressure on members to work towards target-attainment. Thus, although a board of directors might have adopted as the overall targets of the company:

- maximising profit to at least £X million in the current financial year whilst not utilising any additional capital;
- keeping employment costs to no more than 25% of gross margin;
- earning Y% return on capital employed;
- achieving output of Z% over previous financial period;
- maintaining quality and service, to levels as defined;

and so on, these are long term strategies, within which it is possible to implement a number of shorter-term alternative actions or tactics. The horizon and timetable of actions of the board are essentially long-term but there will understandably be deviations in the short term. CA06s172 explicitly requires boards to consider (and balance) not only the long term consequences of their decisions, but also the interests of what have been called the company's *stakeholders* – i.e. the company itself as a separate legal entity, its shareholders, employees, customers, creditors and suppliers, as well as society and the environment (see DIRECTORS DUTIES).

Procedural guidelines

The level of formality of the meeting will differ widely according to company custom. For example, it was once fairly common (though not a legal requirement) for board members of companies (particularly some charities who may still require it) to sign a book of attendance, and to address and speak only through the chairman, and some boards still operate a system whereby a director is only allowed to speak once on a subject. Whilst this latter restriction may assist in forcing members to marshal their thoughts and arguments it may prevent subsequent constructive thoughts – sparked by the comments of later speakers. Ideally a board should operate as a dynamic – ideas from one person creating reactions and new ideas from others – tantamount to *brainstorming*. Restricting a director's input to just one opportunity to make their points can stultify such creativity – second thoughts can be valuable.

Decisions reflect the collective responsibility doctrine of board work and once everyone has had their say, (every director has a right to be heard on every subject) the chairman should summarise arguments, before taking the *sense* or decision of the meeting – usually by consensus, but if necessary by vote. The following guidelines may be helpful, although boards operate in different ways and they need to be customised to fit specific requirements.

Example: Guidelines aimed at improving meeting efficiency

Requirements to be issued to all meeting members and those submitting information to be considered at the meeting

A. Timetable

1. A timetable for all required to attend and to submit data to and draw information from the meeting will be prepared on a rolling six-month basis.

2. Other than in the most exceptional instances, the timing of meetings will not be changed and any member unable to attend a meeting must inform the Chairman/Secretary as soon as possible.

3. An agenda with supporting data must be issued at least five working days prior to a meeting.

B. Data required

1. All information and reports for consideration must be made available to the Secretary at least seven working days before the meeting.

2. All data should be submitted with the stated number of copies required. The stated number should be the number of persons entitled to receive the agenda plus any required to be sent out for information, plus, say, one spare for each five persons on the distribution list. Where a number of documents accompany the agenda, colour coding documentation could be considered.

3. If data is not available to meet the submission deadline an indication of the availability date must be given, the chairman/Secretary should be informed and a note of the expected date of receipt/issue entered on the agenda.

    Those submitting data late must make every effort to convey it directly to meeting members prior to the meeting with the required number of spares to the Secretary. Asking for data to be tabled at the meeting, particularly if it consists of detailed, involved or lengthy reports, is to be avoided. Unless genuinely urgent it may result in the item being *'left on the table'* for consideration at a later meeting.

4. Documentation will be presented in agenda order.

C. Presentation

1. Every item prepared for the [board / committee] will be required to prepare a standard covering sheet.

2. Subsequent sheets may be presented in the most suitable format.

3. The utmost brevity, commensurate with the subject matter, should be employed. Commentary should be avoided and facts and suppositions, and opposing data, suitably differentiated must be presented clearly.

4. Source(s) of data should be referenced, and a summary used, rather than including such data as part of the submission.

5. The conclusions and recommendations required to be set out on the first page of the report must be clearly evidenced within it.

6. Plain English should be used with jargon avoided. Where jargon is unavoidable, a glossary must be provided.

D. Supporting commentary

1. At the meeting, the report's originator or person responsible for the subject matter should be prepared to speak to the report, to answer questions from other members and generally to assist the meeting to come to a suitable decision regarding its content and/or recommendations.

2. Should the meeting require amplifying documentation this must be provided in the same format as that used in the original report and submitted for the next following meeting.

3. Proposers should endeavour to cover all salient facts in one short presentation.

4. After such proposal and counter-comments, if the subject is of such import the chairman may wish to encourage a short general discussion on the subject, otherwise the next move will be to summarise the content and take the sense of the meeting.

E. Decisions

Board decisions will be communicated externally by the meeting convener and/or the sponsoring member. If approved or referred back for reconsideration the decision will be supported by a copy of the appropriate minute including any conditions, timing, capital expenditure, and so on.

The Institute of Chartered Secretaries has published a code of Good Boardroom Practice.

Board sub-committees

A company's Articles often grant to its board the right to appoint sub-committees either for a specific purpose or for on-going considerations (e.g. a remuneration sub-committee). The terms of reference of such appointment together with initial appointees should be set out both in the board minutes and the minutes of each sub-committee meeting.

Example: Board sub-committee appointment resolution

That [names] be and they are hereby appointed a committee to consider and report on [subject] by [date]. The quorum for the committee shall be [number, normally 2] and the committee shall have all the powers of the board necessary for the purpose of carrying out their enquiry, subject to the rules, resolutions or restrictions that the board may impose on them from time to time. The subcommittee will have the power to co-opt [or *require attendance from* – see below] such further persons that it feels will contribute to the consideration of the matter. Minutes will be prepared and submitted to the board within 7 days from each sub-committee meeting.

Notes:

1. Articles based on CA85 Table A only permit directors to be appointed to a board sub-committee. If a company uses this version, where input/assistance is required from others they should be regarded as being in non-voting *attendance*.

2. Where there are time constraints, it may be more practical (rather than convening a meeting) to obtain approval of all the directors by means of a written resolution (providing this is not prohibited by the Articles), or by teleconferencing. However research indicates that even when linked by CCTV or equivalent the effectiveness of the discussion is not as good as when people are physically face-to-face.

   Electronic communication negates *body language* which can account for as much as 93% of the message.

Briefing the chairman

KEY POINTS

- Those required to take the chair at a meeting may welcome some guidance notes.

- This is particularly true when chairing General Meetings (which may be somewhat more formal than the average board meeting) where specific wording might be necessary.

- Preparing a brief enables calm consideration of all eventualities.

Annual General Meeting

The legalistic overtones of statutorily required meetings, with certain forms of wording to be used regarding proposed formal resolutions may cause concern, where it is the first time someone has to take the chair. Accordingly it may be helpful for the Secretary to provide guidance – or even a complete crib!

Example: Chairman's crib for AGM

Crib for XXth annual general meeting to be held on (date)

At (time) call meeting to order with a few introductory remarks such as...

'Ladies and Gentlemen I welcome you to the XXth AGM of .... LTD/ PLC. I will now start the formal proceedings, following the conclusion of which you will be able to meet members of the board and other executives informally over some refreshments. We have provided displays of our products and services and I hope you will find these of interest.

The notice of this meeting was despatched to all members of the company on (date) and I will ask the Secretary to read it.' *(Secretary reads notice)*

'The first item on the agenda concerns the consideration of the directors' report with the report and accounts for the (12) months ended (date). Those accounts, the directors report and the balance sheet as at that date have been audited by your auditors Messrs (Name) and I request Mr/Ms (name) a partner of that firm of registered auditors to deliver their audit report.' *(Auditor reads report)*

'May I propose that the Report of the Directors, together with the annexed statement of the company's accounts for the (twelve) months ended [date] and the balance sheet as at that date duly audited be received.

Has anyone any questions or comment?' *(Pause)*

(If questions are raised it will be necessary to deal with them and/or if they are of a technical/financial nature it may be preferable to pass them to the finance director to answer. Alternatively answers could be posted on the company website.)

'Following on from your consideration of the report and accounts may I also propose that a final dividend of (amount) per cent, or (amount) pence per share on the ordinary shares of the company payable on (date) be now declared for the (twelve) months ended (date). I call upon (name) to second these proposals.'

'All those in favour please raise your hands *(pause)*. Anyone against?' *(Pause) (Assess and declare result.)*

'I therefore declare the motion carried.'

'Item 2 concerns the re-election of the retiring director(s). The director(s) retiring by rotation is/are (names) and I have much pleasure in proposing that (name) be and he hereby is re-elected a director of the company. I will ask (name) to second that proposal.

All those in favour *(pause)* and against *(pause) (Declare result)*

I declare Mr (name) duly re-elected a director of the company.'

'Item 3 concerns the re-election of Messrs (auditors) as auditors of the company and I call upon Mr (name) to propose that resolution and Mr (name) to second it.

All those in favour (pause) Anyone against (pause)?' (Declare result.)

'Item 4 authorises the directors to fix the remuneration of the auditors and I will ask Mr (name) to propose that resolution and Mr (name) to second it.

All those in favour *(pause)*. Anyone against *(pause)*?' *(Declare result.)*

'Is there any other ordinary business for consideration?'

'I therefore declare this xxth AGM closed. Thank you.'

Notes:

1. Reading the notice of the meeting and / or the audit report is unnecessary – and doing so is rare. However, reading the notice should at least cover the arrival of latecomers; whilst reading the audit report can identify the auditor to the members.

2. Legally members only *receive* the report of the directors and the accounts both of which are *approved* by the board. Even if members purport to reject both, their status is unchanged and they must be filed with CH within the required time limits.

3. Only if the dividend recommended by the directors is *final* do the shareholders have any control over it; they can approve, reject or reduce it but not increase it above the amount recommended. There is no necessity for a final dividend; instead, on their own authority, the directors could pay interim dividends.

4. For PLCs, if more than one director retires by rotation, separate proposals are required for the re-election of each unless a proposal to deal with all such re-elections as a single resolution is first passed unanimously by the meeting.

   Proposals may also be needed to re-elect any directors who have been appointed since the previous AGM. Re-elected directors may wish to express their thanks to the meeting.

5. Other than the proposal of a vote of thanks to the chairman/board it is unlikely that anything else can be discussed by the meeting since notice of such business will not have been given. However, if every member entitled to be present, is present and agrees to waive notice, other business could be considered.

General meetings

For CA06 companies, the word 'extraordinary' in relation to any meeting of the shareholders other than the AGM has been dropped, such meetings being simply referred to as GENERAL MEETINGS. However the Articles for the majority of pre CA06 companies using pro forma Articles from a previous Act (e.g. CA85 Table A) may refer to EGMs. By its very nature (that is not being ordinary and non-controversial) it is more likely that business at such a meeting can provoke greater attention and even disagreement and dissent. This could be the case should the company be experiencing financial difficulties, and unpalatable measures need to be considered. There follows a condensed version of a chairman's brief for an EGM, developed jointly by the chairman and Secretary of a company in serious financial trouble and where the former chairman / managing director had been forced by the board to resign to facilitate a capital restructuring to be put in place in an attempt to save the company. Notice of the EGM having been given, the shareholding former chairman submitted an item for consideration at the meeting. Rather than risk the need to convene a further EGM (and the inherent costs and dilution of effort) the new chairman requested the meeting to allow consideration of the matter (which it did) although the proposal was then voted down. It was fortunate that all members were present, as, had fewer than the holders of 95% of the voting shareholders been present and thus able to waive notice, it is unlikely if that proposal could have been properly put to the meeting.

Example: Chairman's crib for EGM

The commentary and advice to the chairman is shown within square brackets.

[Mr Chairman – I have assumed that voting will be by show of hands in which case a simple majority of hands carries the resolution – i.e. each shareholder has one vote. It is, however, possible under the Articles for any shareholder to demand a poll, in which case the meeting must be adjourned whilst we conduct a poll where the votes in accordance with number of shares held will decide the outcome. If a poll is demanded we also need to appoint tellers. I have prepared three sets of voting slips in case polls are required.

I have also primed several shareholders so that each time you ask for a seconder you should always find someone prepared to do so.

I have prepared a handout which details all the resolutions and proposals to be placed before the meeting (including a synopsis of the additional matter put forward for consideration by Mr K) and will give one to each member as they arrive. This should make it easy for them to follow the business as it proceeds. Call meeting to order at 12 noon]

CHAIRMAN: 'Ladies and gentlemen, my name is [x]. At a meeting held on 4th February, the board elected me its chairman. This extraordinary general meeting was convened by the board by a notice issued on 28th January which I propose we take as read – does anyone object to that?'

[Pause – then, assuming no objection...]

'Subsequently, Mr K, a shareholder holding in excess of 10 % of the shares, as is required by the Articles, requested that a further item of business be considered at this meeting. We will deal with that request later.

Since the first item on the official Agenda concerns myself I shall vacate the chair and ask Mr Y to deal with it.'

RESOLUTION No 1
Confirmation of appointment of 'chairman'
Y: 'Ladies and gentlemen, as you will see the first item on the agenda concerns the proposal to confirm the appointment as chairman of Mr X. Neither this nor items 2 and 3 need shareholder approval nor are they required to be dealt with at a general meeting, but in view of the financial situation of the company and the dissent that has prefaced this meeting, it was thought this would be advisable. Accordingly I would like to propose that Mr X's appointment as chairman of the board be and it hereby is confirmed. Do I have a seconder? All those in favour?

Anyone against? I declare the motion carried and hand the meeting back to the Chairman.'

RESOLUTION No 2
Confirmation of appointment of managing director
CHAIRMAN: 'At the meeting which appointed myself as chairman, a majority of the directors also appointed Mr Z as managing director. I would now like to propose that Mr Z's appointment as managing director be and it hereby is confirmed. Do I have a seconder?

All those in favour? Anyone against? I declare the motion carried.'

RESOLUTION No 3
Confirmation of appointment of Secretary
CHAIRMAN: 'The directors also requested Mr Y to assume the role of Company Secretary in addition to acting as a non-executive director and I would like to propose that Mr Y's appointment as Secretary be and it is hereby confirmed. Do I have a seconder? All those in favour? Anyone against? I declare the motion carried.'

RESOLUTION No 4
Creation of additional share capital, alteration of Memorandum
CHAIRMAN: 'The next two items on the agenda concern the creation of additional share capital, so that the major restructuring of the company can take place. Copies of the formal resolution which must be filed with the Registrar of Companies have been given to you and I propose THAT the share capital of the company be increased from £10,000 to £2,000,000 by the creation of:

a) 990,000 new ordinary shares of £1 each ranking in all respects pari passu with the 10,000 existing ordinary shares of £1 of the company,

AND

b) the creation of 1,000,000 Cumulative Redeemable Convertible Preference Shares of £1

The notice refers to a coupon rate of 10% but the board feels that the rate needs to be left for individual negotiation. Does anyone object to this?'

[Assuming no one objects (and having canvassed all the shareholders and found that no-one currently does), the motion itself can then be put to the meeting.]

'Do I have a seconder? All those in favour? Anyone against?

I therefore declare that resolution carried.'

RESOLUTION No 5
Change of auditors
[I have checked with the retiring auditors who have no objection to making way for the new auditors. They have confirmed that with the steps currently being taken by the board, including the matters that are to be dealt with later in the meeting, they have no intention of lodging any statement requesting that any matters be brought to the attention of the shareholders.]

CHAIRMAN: 'Your Board originally requested ABC to act as auditors, a role they carried out until the end of 2XXX, when it was felt more advisable to appoint auditors located nearer to the company. Messrs ABC have indicated their willingness to resign. As part of the investigation carried out by Mr Z, an audit-type investigation on the activities of the company to 31st December 2XXX was completed by Messrs DEF, and I propose that Messrs DEF be and they hereby are appointed auditors of the company until the conclusion of the first Annual General meeting which must be held within the next few weeks. Do I have a seconder? All those in favour? Anyone against? I declare that resolution carried.'

RESOLUTION No 6
Company strategy
CHAIRMAN: 'The next item concerns the restructuring of the company and the strategy for the next two years, details of which are included in

a report from Mr Z copies of which have been sent to you. The restructuring and 'audit' reports contained within it were prepared very urgently and within a very short time span.

We are asking today for shareholder approval in principle to the plan which entails amongst other things, the conversion of shareholder loans with which I will deal later.

I would like you to confirm your acceptance of this plan with those comments in mind, and without discussion since the matter is so urgent we need to move to the next item. However if any shareholder does wish to make any comments... '

[You will have to play this by ear. Since all the shareholders have already received a copy and we have spoken to several and dealt with a number of their queries, this may go through 'on the nod' – which is hardly surprising bearing in mind the pressure evinced by the shareholders to nominate Mr Z as the replacement MD. You can expect Mr K to object of course but I suggest you request him to put his comments in writing for the attention of the board when it comes to implement the plan. In any event, and as I am sure Mr K knows, the voting strength is overwhelmingly in favour of acceptance.]

PROPOSAL No 7
Conversion of loans made by shareholders into share capital

CHAIRMAN: 'The next item concerns the conversion of loans made by us all to the company as part of our shareholding investment. Previously such loans were counted as shareholders' investments, but the new auditors state that these loans do not constitute part of the shareholders' investment and if they are excluded from that category, the company is insolvent and should cease trading. We need everyone to agree today to convert these loans into ordinary shares, and unless this is done, we cannot see that new money can flow into the company which is the only way the company can survive. Thus the directors view this matter as a choice for shareholders – 'convert your loans into shares or the Board will recommend the company be put into receivership'. If the loans are not converted your investment is lost, whereas if they are converted, there is a chance of saving the company. I must stress that as one of the largest investors and, in terms of my shareholder loan, one of the largest creditors of the company I am prepared to convert my loan into shares immediately after this meeting. Any comments?'

[I have forms that will enable shareholders to either a) convert loans into ordinary shares, or b) convert some loan into shares and some into Cumulative Redeemable Convertible Preference Shares (CRCPS) or c) invest new money in Ordinary shares and/or CRCPS. You will need to try to 'insist' that before people leave they sign a form.]

PROPOSAL No 8
Item put forward by Mr K

CHAIRMAN: 'The last item concerns a request made by Mr K for an alteration to the Articles. Before we can consider the item itself (which we have set out on the handout) you will note that the short notice given in respect of this item needs to be agreed. The board think it would be advisable for everyone to agree to consider the item and thus I would propose that proposal (8) be considered by the meeting notwithstanding that short notice was given – those in favour? Any against? I declare the motion carried in which case we may now deal with the proposal put forward by Mr K that the articles of association be changed as set out in the wording of the resolution. Mr K do you wish to make any comments regarding this resolution?'

[You will have to play it by ear but you may like to comment – the board's view being entirely against the proposal – and need to put it to the vote – in favour, against, declare result. We might have a demand for a poll here, although my canvassing indicates little support for a proposal that really could have the effect of restricting the actions of the board in its efforts to save the company.

You could make the point that the chance of saving the company is slim, and it may be the only way forward is to transfer ownership of part or all of the company which would almost certainly mean the offer of additional shares. Since no existing shareholder is willing to put more money into the company it is difficult to see the point of the proposal.]

CHAIRMAN: 'That concludes the business of this extraordinary general meeting.'

Notes:

1. The appointments of chairman of the board, managing director and Secretary are not matters for the shareholders and this was only adopted to test support for the actions of the newly constituted board in a difficult situation. Had such support not been forthcoming, attempts to save the company would probably have been abandoned immediately.

2. The question of issuing convertible preference shares with a variable coupon rate requires legal advice. In fact here, against the advice of a number of people involved, it was put to and approved by the meeting, although the issue was never actually implemented as the board had to invite the lending bank to put the company into administrative receivership within a few weeks.

3. The value of canvassing support, particularly in difficult situations like these, cannot be over-emphasised. Whilst not wishing to stifle fair criticism and comment, the will of the majority needs to prevail (subject to there being no oppression of minority rights) so the company can make progress.

4. Using a handout, particularly as here where there was an extra item of contentious business, can aid attention, and thus the flow of the meeting.

5. The preparation of such a script/crib (providing advice on each item), and the canvassing of support, took several hours but, since the meeting went without a hitch, the aim was achieved. The concept was to try to pre-empt every alternative, or to provide an answer for every possibility and or concern.

Charging assets

KEY POINTS

- Company assets are predominately used within the business but some can also be used as security for working capital.

- Lenders who wish to protect their position can require the company to create in their favour a charge over asset(s) of appropriate value.

- The creation of charges must be made clear to creditors by lodging details at CH.

Borrowing on asset value

The creation of a charge over an asset, or the acquisition of an asset subject to a charge, may entail the company registering details within a set time limit with CH. This *puts into the public arena* details of the charge so that information is made available publicly (and particularly to creditors) that assets appearing in the accounts, which might otherwise support a creditor's debt (should the company fail), have actually been taken out of the asset pool available. The assets over which the creation of a charge requires registration are:

- the securing of debentures;

- a charge on uncalled capital;

- a charge evidenced by an instrument which, if executed by an individual would require registration as a bill of sale;

- a charge on land or any interest in land;

- a floating charge on the undertaking of the business or its property;

- a charge on calls on share capital made but not paid;

- a charge on a ship (or a share in a ship) or aircraft;

- a charge on goodwill or intellectual property (including any patent or trade mark, registered design, unregistered design right, copyright or any licence in respect of any such rights);

- a charge on book debts.

Administration

In order to register a charge a company must file with CH:

- certified copy of the mortgage or charge;

- form MR01 or MR02 (see CA06s860);

- a filing fee (currently £15 if filed electronically, or £23 for hard copy).

A statement detailing the beneficiary of the charge, whether it is a floating or fixed charge and/or whether there are any restrictions on the use of the asset for further borrowing, must also be filed. If a fixed charge is created over any land, ship, aircraft or intellectual property (e.g. patent, trade mark, registered design, copyright or design right) registered in the UK, a short description of the registrable property must also be filed.

Charges should be filed within 21 days of creation. If the charge is created within the UK the 21-day time limit commences the day it was created. If the charge is created outside the UK the time limit commences the day after the instrument is received in the UK. If the company attempts to file details after 21 days the documents may be rejected by CH, and the company must obtain clearance from the Court. Assuming the Court accepts the reason given for the delay, it provides a note of clearance, which is then submitted to CH with the original documents.

On acceptance, CH issues a unique reference code to make it easier to locate the charge in its records. This should be of assistance as there have been previous instances of CH having difficulty identifying the correct documentation when companies have wished to register discharges of charges registered pre1990.

A certificate of filing confirming that a charge has been entered on CH records is then issued. These certificates are made available to anyone inspecting the company's records with the warning that they cannot be relied on for the accuracy of the charge itself.

It is the responsibility of an officer of the company to register the charge, and under CA06 the officers are liable if they do not do so – although such failure is no longer a criminal offence. In practice it is often the lender who files the charge as it is in their best interests to ensure the item is registered swiftly – and properly. If so, the company should ask for a copy of the CH certificate.

Effect of late and/or faulty registration

In the event of late registration, the charge is voidable against a liquidator or a person who acquires an interest in the property subject to the charge until it is properly registered, although the charge remains valid between the company and the creditor. If incorrect details have been registered the company can submit a corrected version.

Release of charge

As required by CA06s872, and with confirmation that the debt for which the charge was given has been paid or satisfied, and/or that the property charged has been released from the charge or has been sold or otherwise disposed of, CH accepts the form and places the detail on the record. The charge itself however remains as part of the record – the discharge effectively cancelling the entry.

Discharging a charge in respect of a loan that has been repaid is often overlooked and it has been estimated that a third of all the charges registered at CH are in respect of loans that have been repaid. Failing to notify CH that the money has been repaid and the charge discharged could damage the company's credit worthiness.

Note: Since it is possible that personal information (e.g. a private address) could appear on the public record (being included within the documentation being filed) it is permissible to obscure such data under CA06s859G and in order to make this clear, wording explaining what has been done should be included as part of the filed data.

Classes of shares and class meetings

Ordinary shares

Ordinary shareholders have no right to any payment (dividend) in respect of their shareholding – or to any repayment of capital if the company is insolvent and fails – they are the real entrepreneurs or risk-takers. Conversely if the company is successful and profitable their returns could be considerable.

If the board feels the market price of the company's shares is too high, subject to shareholder approval or to the Articles authority, it can increase the number of shares either by sub-dividing the existing shares (e.g. for every one £1 existing ordinary share, a shareholder will have four new 25p ordinary shares) or by issuing additional shares (i.e. making a *bonus issue*) in proportion to the shareholders' original holding e.g. one new extra share for every five shares already held. In this instance, although the number of shares increases by 20% (in the absence of any other action) the proportion held by each holder to the total number of shares in issue remains unchanged. The total value of the original holding plus the bonus shares should be the same as the total value of the existing shares before the bonus – each share being worth proportionately less.

If the board wishes to increase the number of shares in issue and, at the same time, raise more capital, provided it has or obtains authority from the existing shareholders, the company could make a *rights issue*. This gives the existing shareholders the *right* to subscribe cash for additional shares at a price that may be a discount to the market price (or audit valuation in an unlisted company) to encourage subscription for the new shares. Shareholders wishing to subscribe, pay the price required and the new shares are added to their original holding. Alternatively the rights to subscribe for the shares themselves may be able to be sold since they may have a value of their own (as they entitle subscribers to obtain shares at less than the market value). Some holders of large numbers of shares in listed PLCs adopt the policy of selling sufficient of their rights in the market in order to generate enough cash to enable them to subscribe for the remainder (known as 'swallowing the tail').

Some companies, wishing to retain control to the existing shareholders, yet extend the capital base of the company issue (say) 'A' Ordinary shares which would rank for dividend but do not have (for example) voting rights. There could also be 'B' and 'C' (etc.) ordinary shares with other restricted rights.

Preference shares

Holders of these shares take precedence (as far as the annual dividend and repayment in a winding up) over ordinary shareholders. Preference shares usually have a stated rate of interest e.g. '7% preference shares of £1' indicating that each year the holders must be paid a dividend of 7p in respect of each share held. The Articles of some older companies specify that if the dividend on their shares is in arrears, preference shareholders have the right to attend the AGM and vote in respect of the number of preference shares they own. They may have similar voting rights should there be a proposal to wind up the company.

Cumulative preference shares

If a dividend payment is missed, most shareholders have no right to recoup this later. Cumulative shareholders however do have a right to recovery of any missed dividend.

Convertible preference shares

Holders of such shares have the right (usually at specified times and sometimes at specified and preset – and possibly favourable – rates of exchange) to convert their preference shares into ordinary shares.

Redeemable preference shares

These shares have a redemption date requiring the company to return the nominal value of the shares at that date (or within a specified period). Thus someone holding '7% Cumulative Redeemable Preference shares 2018/19' would have right to have the shares redeemed (usually at par) between 2018 and 2019.

Non-redeemable preference shares (n-rps)

These shares can neither be redeemed nor converted into redeemable preference shares since this could be deemed to be preferential treatment to the detriment of the creditors. They normally have a stated coupon rate that must be paid, but only if they were also *cumulative n-rps* would holders be entitled to any missed dividends.

Deferred and/or Founder shares

Usually holders of such shares surrender immediate income from dividends on their shares in the hope or expectation that at some set or unspecified date in the future they will share in profits usually at a very advantageous rate – or see the value of their shares increase.

Debenture or Loan stock

These are not shares but forms of guaranteed or secured borrowing. Debentures (with a set annual rate of interest) are usually issued under a trust deed that appoints a trustee for the holders whose responsibilities are to protect the holders rights, and to take action if interest is not paid or there is a breach of any other covenant set out in the trust deed. Debentures are usually backed by a CHARGE over all the assets and undertaking of the business (a floating charge) or over specified asset(s) e.g. freehold property(ies) (fixed charge(s)).

Right of pre-emption

Unless the Articles declare otherwise, usually if new shares are to be issued, they must first be offered to existing shareholders in the proportion that each individual holding bears to the total in issue. This is called a right of pre-emption (or *first refusal*) and is very pertinent if the proportions of shares held are important – e.g. a holder of 75% of the ordinary shares has considerable power since with that proportion of votes they have authority to change the Articles. The moment any additional shares are issued to others, their holding will fall below 75%. If shares are not to be issued to existing holders in accordance with their pre-emptive right, they must first consent to waive the right by resolution in general meeting (or by a written resolution) and, if this varies the Articles, it needs a special resolution (i.e. one requiring 75% approval of those voting either in person or proxy at a meeting or, if passed by written resolution, by 75% of the total voting strength).

Pre-emption rights do not need to be waived for:

- shares for employee share schemes;
- non-participating preference and similar securities;
- any other non-equity securities;

- allotment of shares for a non-cash consideration, and
- allotment of shares under a renounceable letter of allotment.

Payment

The original subscribers to the Memorandum of a PLC must pay for their shares in cash. But shares in an LTD can be issued in exchange for the rights to property, a patent or a new process, or other intellectual property rights, etc. If shares are issued for a consideration other than cash (e.g. as payment for such assets) then the assets themselves must be handed over within five years of the shares being issued. If this does not happen, the allottee is liable to pay cash for the shares (and any premium) plus interest for the period from the issue to the date of the transfer.

If shares are to be issued in exchange for an asset, the value of the asset must be assessed by an expert (i.e. a person qualified to act as an auditor).

Record and title

The issue of a share certificate acts as both receipt for the money subscribed and evidence of title to, or ownership of, the shares. Some Articles state that share certificates are only valid as evidence of title if they bear the common seal of the company. If a company with such a requirement, wishes to dispense with using a SEAL, either the Articles need to be changed or a 'securities seal' purely for use on share certificates should be retained.

Each time new shares are allotted the Secretary must:

- enter the register of members;
- issue a share certificate;
- send (within 28 days) notice of the allotment to CH using form SH01 in accordance with CA06s555.

Single member company (SMC)

If a transfer of shares results in the company having only one share-holder or member this fact and the date of the event must be stated in the register of members for the remaining member (e.g. 'From [date] this is a single member company'). Conversely should a single member transfer some of his shares to someone else, or (a) new share(s) be issued to a second shareholder, then the message 'From [date] this is no longer a single member company' must be written in the shareholder's account.

Where a company not set up as an SMC carries on trading with only one shareholder, after six months the remaining shareholder loses their limited liability protection and, should the company fail, has potential personal liability for its debts.

Meetings

Normally only holders of ordinary shares have the right to attend general meetings of the company. However when there are matters which may affect the interests of holders of various type of shares or loans they may have the right to convene and attend a meeting of their own class of shares. The Articles will normally provide a protection to holders of such shares by stipulating that nothing must be agreed that would affect their interests without their agreement.

If agreement is needed to such a proposal the holders of the shares affected by the proposal have the right to meet to consider the matter. The detailed procedure for convening such a meeting will usually be set out in the Articles but, if not, CA06 states that two or more holders owning 10% or more of the shares of that class may convene a meeting. Legal advice should be taken to ensure the correct procedure and wording is followed so that there is no prejudicial effect.

Example: Notice of class meeting

To: The holders of the [specify] shares of [company name]

NOTICE OF CLASS MEETING
Notice is hereby given that a meeting of the holders of the [specify] shares in the company will be held at [time] on [date] at [place] for the purpose of considering and, if thought fit, passing the following resolution

'THAT this class meeting of the holders of the [specify] of the [company] by this extraordinary resolution hereby consent to the variation of their rights by [specify]'

By order of the board

Secretary   17th October 2XXX

A member entitled to attend and unable to do so may appoint one or more proxies to attend, vote and speak in his/her place. Such proxies should be sent to the Registered Office of the company to arrive not later than 48 hours before the commencement of the meeting. Proxies need not be members of the company.

CA06s334 stipulates that the quorum for a class meeting is 'two persons… holding at least one third… of the issued shares… in question'. If 15% or more of the affected members feel their interests have been prejudiced by the resolution or action they can apply to the court (not more than 21 days after the resolution) and the resolution (if passed) cannot be implemented until the court sanctions it. Legal advice should always be sought if class rights are to be varied to avoid any question of prejudicial action. CH must be advised with 15 days of the resolution.

Company Secretary

The role

Sir John Harvey Jones (when chief executive of one of the largest UK companies) put the role of the Secretary into perspective when he said 'in many ways the appointment and role of the Secretary is key for the company – more vital than that of many directors – not least because of the increasing weight and scope of legislation and the increasing criminalisation of the activities of officers of the company...the Secretary needs to be dynamic'.

Such an appointee is the company's:

- *guardian*: ensuring fulfilment of compliance with an ever-increasing range of legislation as well as protecting its statutory books, assets, reputation etc.;

- *facilitator*: easing communication between board and management;

- *recorder*: taking and protecting the legally required minutes of board and general meetings;

- *confidante*: supporting all members of the board and particularly the chairman; and

- *chief administrative officer* of the company (i.e. being a legal officer of the company with all the attendant responsibilities and liabilities that description entails).

Former Master of the Rolls, Lord Denning described the Secretary as 'chief administrative officer' of a company, and stated 'he regularly makes representations on behalf of the company and enters into contracts on its behalf. He is entitled to sign contracts – all such matters come within [his] ostensible authority'. Since then the role has gained an increasing prominence – not least to ensure compliance with obligations under corporate governance. The Secretary must be fully aware of all legal requirements affecting the company, its officers, its employees and its agents. Sir John again: 'I always work with a positive board system, by which I mean I don't allow silence. After discussing each subject I ask each member of the board what their opinion is and why – this includes the Secretary as I have always believed that his views should be heard.'

The importance of the role is determined by the fact that unlike directors, there are restrictions on those to be appointed Secretary of a PLC. Thus CA06s273 states a PLC's Secretary must be:

- a barrister or a solicitor, etc.;

- a member of the several accounting institutes;

- a member of ICSA; or

- any other person that the directors think capable of undertaking the duties.

Whilst the last option may seem to be a dilution, the previous classifications provide criteria for the required (or expected) skill, experience and expertise of the person undertaking the role. The appointment should provide a neutral viewpoint at the board meeting since the views of the Secretary may be more objective than that of directors some of whom may be more interested in *fighting the corner* for their own department, sublimating their company-wide obligations.

Although the ultimate responsibility for all the acts of the company rests with the directors, the Secretary as a company officer has a fiduciary duty to put the company's interests before his own.

The above encapsulates the challenge for those companies that decide not to appoint a Secretary. Whilst a director is expected to take risks to drive the company forward; the Secretary should aim at keeping the company legal. Companies need both *risk taker and driver* and *keeper of the company's conscience and compliance officer.*

Responsibilities

There are now over 3.5 million UK companies and no doubt over 3.5 million different job descriptions for Secretaries. The following checklist sets out the main corporate responsibilities.

CHECKLIST: A Company Secretary's corporate duties

✓ **Ensure compliance with company law**. The Secretary should know the requirements of company law – and ensure compliance with those requirements. (The danger of an LTD operating without a Secretary is obvious. Interestingly, the Republic of Ireland's latest Companies Act not only makes the post of Secretary compulsory, it also requires that person to sign a declaration acknowledging the legal duties and obligations of the role.)

✓ **Understand and interpret the requirements and obligations contained in the Articles** and guide the board on these, recommending when and how the Articles should be updated or revised.

✓ **Maintain statutory registers**. This entails keeping updated the various statutory books and, for a company limited by shares, dealing with share registration work.

✓ **Update and protect the company file with CH**. Although the board is ultimately responsible, it is normally the Secretary who advises CH within specified time limits of changes in directorate, charges over assets, changes in members etc., and of any other matters affecting the corporate nature of the company at the appropriate time, as well as filing the annual CONFIRMATION STATEMENT and the company's accounts.

✓ **Liaise with shareholders**. The extent of this responsibility will depend on individual companies – in some, the directors take on this role, however in most the Secretary is responsible for the documentary contact with shareholders – i.e. notice of general meetings, preparation and despatch of annual report, dividends etc.

✓ **Ensure legally required documentation is prepared.** This is a wide-ranging responsibility since much of what is required is derived from obligations under commercial, employment and other laws. Familiarity with the obligations of such laws is essential.

✓ **Convene company and board meetings.** The Secretary can only do this at the board's direction. To ensure the board fulfils its legal duties he should ensure that board meetings are held regularly and are quorate. He should attend board meetings.

✓ **Compile (legally required) MINUTES of board meetings and subcommittees** – not only to preserve the record of control, but also to have available documentary evidence which might be needed as a defence in any actions against directors (e.g. to be able to prove they exercised their duty of care and took account of the interests of the company stakeholders as required by CA06).

✓ **File accounts, returns/statements and other forms etc. on time**. Increasingly the obligation to file such items within specified time limits is being backed by rigorously enforced fines. Repeated failure to file on time can lead to directors' disqualification.

✓ **Carry out instructions of board.** As the chief administrative officer the Secretary may have the prime role for interfacing with management. Alternatively executive directors may take this role – whoever takes it needs to comply with the exact requirements of the board.

✓ **Act as board / chairman's confidante.** The Secretary (particularly where he is not also a director) may be aware of internal developments of which directors are not aware and thus can provide a valuable communication conduit to and from the chairman / board.

✓ **Act as chief administrative officer.** This responsibility will vary depending on individual organisations, nevertheless the Secretary is often the source from which management first learn of and are required to implement decisions.

✓ **Protect the company's assets**. It is the Secretary's duty to protect the statutory records and the board confidentiality. It may be logical to make him responsible for other aspects of corporate/asset security.

✓ **Oversee legal matters.** Often the Secretary may be the only executive with some experience of the law – or at least aware of such developments. Increasingly legal requirements are penetrating all company activities and someone must undertake this role and responsibility.

✓ **Oversee the arrangements permitting inspections** of certain records of the company providing access to statutory and other bodies.

✓ **Ensure compliance generally** – with all contractual and commercial law, health and safety law, environmental law, employment law, and so on.

Many Secretaries additionally take responsibility for insurance, pensions, property, security, employment and/or financial matters. This is a vast obligation – particularly given the amount of legislation currently being enacted.

Board meeting duties

Much of the Secretary's basic work may revolve around convening, servicing and supporting the work of board meetings. Directors have an obligation to ensure that this work is carried out appropriately bearing in mind that board meetings provide evidence of the reasons for and the decisions taken by the board – which could provide valuable evidence should there be a DERIVATIVE claim.

Case study: How not to do it

The comments made by inspectors following their investigation of the Phoenix / MG Rover collapse puts the role into perspective. The report highlights many breaches by that company, including the following that one would have expected to have been avoided by an effective and involved Secretary. The company:

- convened board meetings without notifying all directors entitled to be there;

- did not take minutes of board meetings at which important matters were 'decided';

- created false minutes (e.g. directors were shown to be present when not only had they not been told of meetings but also, in some cases, they weren't even in the country);

- allowed directors to vote on matters in which they had an interest;

- allowed directors to benefit from decisions in which they had an interest;

- did not approve minutes at subsequent meetings, and so on.

One commentator stated that 'it would seem to offer an open and shut case for the directors of MG Rover Group to be disqualified for life'. Having paid themselves around £42 million during the time the company was failing, the 'Phoenix 4' directors (as they were known) plea-bargained agreements not to be involved in running a UK company for (respectively) 6, 5, 5 and 3 years which many would think was getting off pretty lightly particularly considering the company's auditors – Deloittes – were subject to a £3 million fine for *significant misconduct* in their professional standards.

In terms of board administration the Secretary should:

1. Generate an AGENDA and notice of meetings in liaison with the chairman.

2. Ensure board composition is in accordance with the Articles; board members are properly appointed, have declared interests (and that any restrictions on those with any such interests – e.g. in the Articles – are known and observed).

3. Ensure all data for consideration by the board accompanies the agenda or there are dates by which it will be ready and distributed. Accompanying data is best presented in Agenda order.

4. Convene meetings in good time. There is no legal requirement regarding the amount of notice due to be given of a board meeting but to allow the directors to be properly briefed at least (say) five days' notice with data should be given. The Secretary should compile and update a timetable of future meetings.

5. Ensure, if a QUORUM is required to be present before the meeting can commence, that at least members satisfying that requirement will be present.

   Checks would also need to be made to ensure that, if required, there is a disinterested quorum, i.e. that any directors with interests in third parties are excluded from discussions affecting those third parties if required by the Articles (see 8).

6. Record apologies for absence and note any late arrivals or early departures so that it can be shown who was present when each decision was taken.

7. Have available any statutory and other registers that need to be inspected and/or signed (e.g. the registers of seals, director's interests, etc.).

8. Ensure that any notifiable interests of directors (where these might affect the capacity of the director to vote or form part of the quorum) are updated.

9. Check members have all the documents required (and have spares available).

10. Arrange meeting's supports, provision of refreshments, note-taking aids, protection against interruption, etc.

11. Ensure the chairman adheres to and does not overlook any agenda item.

12. Ensure those who speak and vote are entitled to do so.

13. Ensure the meeting takes required decisions and that these are clear and clearly understood by all present – and that those required to carry out the decisions are clearly identified. The FCA states that they

would like to see evidence that directors challenged matters before decisions were taken (i.e. not simply acquiesce to proposals).

14. Ensure the appropriate voting power is reflected when votes are taken. In some joint venture companies, in the event of an equality of votes, directors nominated by one of the partners to the joint venture have enhanced voting rights.

15. Record the sense of the meeting in notes that will become the base of the first draft of the minutes.

16. Prepare minutes, have them approved in draft by the chairman, re-draft as necessary and eventually distribute to the members for approval by them at the next following meeting.

17. Keep the minutes secure. Minutes must now be preserved for only 10 years but many commentators feel it should be *life* of the company as it is for minutes of meetings held up to October 2007.

18. Make the minutes available to members, the auditors (and, if required, during an investigation following an accident, by the HSE).

19. Ensure action is effected as required by the meeting and reported on at the appropriate time.

20. Anticipate the level of support available, and any antipathy or opposition to, matters due to be considered by the board and brief the chairman accordingly.

21. Be proactive.

Authority

The Secretary is a company officer and, in the event of culpable non-compliance, is liable with the directors for fines and other penalties. He can have several types of authority:

- *Actual* – by delegation from the board (via specific requirements set out in the Articles/ board minutes etc.);

- *Ostensible* – since many documents require the signature of the person holding the post of Secretary at that time;

- *Derived* – from what has gone before and been accepted both internally and externally;

- *Express* – in that the Secretary is appointed to hold office under law, by the members.

Unfortunately, it is not always the case that legislative and contractual requirements have been complied with and a newly appointed Secretary should never assume that everything required to be done has been done.

CHECKLIST: On appointment

✓ **Check authority of appointment.** A note of the appointment should made in the board minutes, recorded in the register of secretaries and notified to CH within 14 days of the operative date (form AP03).

✓ **Check the Articles (and, for pre CA06 companies, the Memorandum), any changes thereto and compliance therewith.** Articles of LTDs should be reviewed at least every three years (PLCs every year) to ensure they reflect changed circumstances. Within a group, if possible, it may be helpful to give all subsidiaries the same Articles. The Articles should support the directors – not restrict their legitimate activities.

✓ **Check entries in statutory books** (registers of directors, secretary, members, those with SIGNIFICANT CONTROL etc.) are up to date. These entries can either be held in hard copy in a combined register, or electronically via a computer package (although this may not be cost-effective for a group of fewer than, say, 10 companies), or the records can be held only at CH.

✓ **Locate the Certificate of Incorporation.** This Certificate records the exact name and number of the company that must be used where required, as well as its date of incorporation. If the company's name (or its type of registration – e.g. LTD to PLC) is changed, a fresh Certificate is issued by CH confirming the new name – but its number is never changed. The certificate should be kept safely but no longer needs to be displayed. It may be required to be produced (e.g. to a finance house, should the company wish to borrow money) to prove its formation and existence.

✓ **Check disclosure of corporate details including NAME.** A company's name is the embodiment of what it is and does – and may have a value in its own right. As such it needs to be protected and used. The way in which it is used is subject to controls and the Secretary needs to be aware of these controls and requirements. Whether the name needs to be protected as a trade mark should also be addressed.

✓ **CONFIRMATION STATEMENT.** Check filing is up-to-date and note the due date of the filing.

✓ **Ensure the Accounts are filed within the time limits.**

✓ **Locate and secure the minute books.** Minutes of general meetings of the shareholders/guarantors must be held at the registered office and made available for inspection and copying by them. Minutes of board meetings can be kept anywhere and can be inspected by directors, auditors and the HSE only (i.e. not by shareholders or guarantors). The security of the board minutes (particularly of copies held by board members) should be checked.

✓ **Locate and secure any SEAL.** The seal (optional since CA89, subject to the Articles) is the binding signature of the company. It should be kept safely and ideally (since the record can be helpful in the event of later dispute) its use recorded.

✓ **Ensure directors with interests with third parties have declared these** and brought / bring their declaration(s) up to date.

Maintaining a 'Registrar's' file

When filing items with CH, not only should a copy of every form filed be kept, but also a receipt should be obtained. With forms filed electronically this should be automatic as CH email a confirmation, but for companies filing hard copy, a receipt can be obtained by sending in duplicate a covering letter referring to the item enclosed (see REGISTRAR OF COMPANIES). Alternatively a duplicate of the item itself could be sent for receipt stamping and return. Provided a reply paid envelope is also enclosed CH affix an adhesive bar code to the item as a receipt. Some time ago CH acknowledged that over an 18 month period around 200 accounts submitted had been lost internally so a receipt may be essential evidence that at least the item was received by CH. Both a copy of the item sent and of the receipt should be added to the Registrar's file as a permanent record of what was sent and when.

Joint, deputy and corporate company secretaries

Joint Secretaries can be appointed with each having joint responsibility and liability. Unless the company's Articles allow, all so appointed will have to sign documents requiring the Secretary's signature. Details of the appointees must be filed at CH in the normal way. A company's Articles may also permit there to be a deputy or assistant secretary. In such a case should the Secretary be unable to act (or the position falls vacant) the role can be filled by a deputy or assistant.

A corporate body can act as a Secretary as can a partnership. If a partnership is used:

- in an English or Welsh company all the partners are joint secretaries of the company
- in a Scottish company the partnership itself is the secretary.

Confirmation Statement

Required details

The details required to be covered can be confirmed in a two-page form displaying only the company's name and registered number and the confirmation date. When introduced in 2016, since the requirement to advise CH of persons of SIGNIFICANT CONTROL had at that date already come into effect, it was unlikely that many companies would be able to file only this two-page CS initially. Where a company cannot confirm there has been 'no change', or that any of its required filed information is up to date, the two-page CS alone is insufficient and the relevant pages of the second part of the statement need to be completed. Unfortunately this comprises over 60 pages. It is divided into 5 parts and allows a company to update information that, in most cases, should have previously been filed. Where an entry has to be made only in part of the main statement then only those pages need to be filed.

Part 1 (A1 and A2)

The company's classification code (SIC): these pages must be completed if there has been a significant change in the company's principal business activities meaning its SIC may have changed. If the SIC cannot be determined then a statement of the company's 'principal activity' can be inserted.

Part 2 (pages referenced B1 and B2)

Statement of capital – these must be completed only if there has been a change in the shares issued (or their details) including statements if shares are held in more than one currency. Particulars of rights (e.g. voting, dividends, participation in a capital distribution, redemption details) attached to each class of share must also be given.

Part 3 (C1, C2 and C3)

Trading status of shares. In the majority of private LTDs there will have been no change in that status, however if the company's shares have been admitted to trade on a market, this must be declared and details provided in D1. Conversely, C3 allows a company whose shares are now traded on a market to claim exemption from these requirements.

Part 4 (D1 and D2)

Shareholder information change. This requires disclosure not only of shareholders at the Statement date (in alphabetical order) but also any changes since the previous filing. It also requires disclosure of anyone who holds 5% or more of the shares and who was not shown as such on the previous filing

Part 5 (E1 – I3)

Information re the Persons of Significant Control (PSC). Potentially requiring the completion of a considerable number of pages, this is not just a 'snapshot in time' (i.e. details as at the date of the return) but requires information setting out any and all changes to the data that have occurred during the 'confirmation period' (i.e. since the previous return). There are a number of subsections.

E1: Statements that there are no persons of significant control or that the company has not yet completed its work to find out if there are.

F1: Entries required regarding all individual PSCs including 'ons' and 'offs'. For an individual's birth date only the month and year will be disclosed in the public records; in addition, full private address details are not needed.

F2: This page is not part of the publicly available record and requires in respect of all those disclosable, their full dates of birth and addresses (unless the subject has a CA06s790ZF exemption from such disclosure).

F3: Statement re the nature of an individual PSC's control (e.g. ownership of shares, voting rights, right to appoint directors, or right to exercise significant influence or control – referred to below as 'the required data').

F4: Statement re the nature of control by a firm over which an individual has significant control (i.e. the required data).

F5: Statement re the nature of control on a trust over which an individual has significant control (i.e. the required data).

(There follow 5 pages if additional space is required.)

G1: Relevant legal entities (RLE) disclosure. Data is required of any RLE which can exercise significant control (i.e. the required data – RD)

G2: Disclosure required of the nature of the control by an RLE (i.e. the required data)

G3: Statement re the nature of control by a firm over which any RLE has significant control (RD)

G4: Statement re the nature of control by a trust over which any RLE has significant control (RD)

H1: Statement of any 'other registrable persons' (ORP). An ORP could be a corporation sole, a government department, an international organisation whose members include two or more countries or their governments) and/or a local authority/government body, etc.

H2: Statement re the nature of control by an ORP (RD)

H3: Statement re the nature of control by a firm over which the ORP has significant control (RD)

H4: Statement re the nature of control by a trust over which the ORP has significant control (RD)

I1: Statement re additional individual PSC statements. This enables a company to advise if there is a so-far unidentified registrable individual, or that the required particulars of an identified registrable person have not been confirmed, or that it has served notice regarding disclosure but this has not been complied with by an identified person. It also enables the company to advise if it has (or if or a Court has lifted) a restrictions notice under CA06 paragraph 1 Schedule 18.

I2: Statement re additional RLE statements. This enables a company to advise that there is a so-far unidentified registrable RLE, or that the required particulars of an identified registrable RLE have not been confirmed, or that a served notice regarding disclosure has not been complied with by an identified RLE. It also enables the company to advise if it has (or it or a Court has lifted) a restrictions notice under CA06 paragraph 1 Schedule 18.

I3: Statement re additional ORP statements. This enables a company to advise that there is a so-far unidentified registrable ORP, or that the required particulars of an identified ORP have not been confirmed, or that served notice regarding disclosure has not been complied with by the identified ORP. It also enables the company to advise if it has (or it or a Court has lifted) a restrictions notice under CA06 paragraph 1 Schedule 18. There are a further 30 pages of continuation sheets.

Filing

The forms are available on the CH website which also provides guidance on completion. If filed in hard copy it costs £40 (£13 if online) to file an initial CS although filing subsequent statements (e.g. if it is desired to show an updated situation to the public) within a year is free. Form CS must be filed within 14 days of the record date (that is the anniversary of the made up date of the previous CS.

Derivative claims

KEY POINTS

- CA06ss260/9 introduces a new right for shareholders to sue directors.

- The right can be exercised if a director has failed to act in the best interests of the company, and/or that the company has suffered loss because of a director's 'actual or proposed act or omission involving negligence, default, breach of duty or breach of trust'.

- Any such legal action must first gain Court permission.

Taking action

Company owners have always been able to sue directors for failing to act in accordance with the provisions of their company's Articles – the rules under which the company is required to be directed. A breach means that those responsible were acting *ultra vires* (beyond their powers) – and they can become personally liable for any resulting losses suffered by the company. If directors allowed the company to act outside its objects clause (formerly set out in the Memorandum – now in or deemed to be in the Articles) this was also *ultra vires*. CA89 diluted the last offence by allowing the members retrospectively to authorise acts in breach of the objects – although directors who breached the requirements could still be held liable for any losses.

Prosecuting actions against directors alleged to be acting *ultra vires,* is not an easy process but CA06 makes it easier. If the claim is successful, it is the company (not the member initiating the action) that benefits, at the director's expense. To some extent the right to initiate such claims has changed the previous situation that a director was not normally held liable for making a wrong decision provided it was made in good faith, to one where a director can be held liable for an act (or omission) even if it is made in good faith and the person taking the decision does not benefit from that decision. With hindsight everyone can make impeccable and correct judgements, but directors have to take decisions on what is known at the time – responding to many pressures – not least, under CA06, taking account of the interests of the company's *stakeholders*. Since, at least in theory, it is now easier for members to take legal action, making a contemporaneous record of all decisions and their reasons (i.e. detailed MINUTES), may assume an even more important facet of company administration.

Obviously in companies where all the members are directors, the possibility of derivative claims may be fairly remote (although there can be considerable dissent and enmity in family-owned and directed companies!). However where there are outside members (i.e. shareholders not on, or represented on, the board) the possibility of a derivative claim could be far more likely, as the number of instances where a director could be accused of failing to act in the best interests of the company/ members could be considerable.

Case study: Equality = loggerheads

In what is believed to be one of the first derivative claims to be listed there were two shareholders each holding 50% of the shares. *Kiani v Cooper* were at loggerheads, with one of them having an interest in a third party to which it was proposed the company should make some payments. The Court permitted the claimant to process the claim.

Disgruntled shareholders actions

One can imagine a scenario where an individual shareholder angry at some action or perceived inaction of a director initiates a claim; or a situation where a shareholder thinks they might benefit from a payment to desist as a result of them threatening to take such action. However, to bring a derivative action, a shareholder must firstly apply to the Court for the right to initiate it. Only with Court permission, can the action proceed. Traditionally, Courts have always been loath to interfere in the internal activities of companies and perhaps this is the reason the number of such actions remains much lower than was initially expected – and feared.

The Court will not allow the claim to proceed if:

- the act (or omission) complained of has since been ratified by the company; or

- it is unreasonable (e.g. the act complained of is such that a person trying to promote the success of the company would not make such a claim).

The Court has discretion taking into account the views of independent shareholders and:

- whether the person bringing the claim is acting in good faith;

- the relevant importance of the claim to a person trying to promote the success of the company;

- whether the matter the subject of the claim is likely to be authorised by the company;

- whether the member could bring the claim in their own right; and/or

- whether the company itself had already decided not to bring such a claim.

Notes:

1. Unless they are charities, banks etc., companies whose turnover is less than £10.2 million do not need to have their accounts audited. Directors of such potentially exempted companies might find it prudent to consider whether retaining the independent view of the results might help dissuade potential derivative claimants.

   Indeed the very fact that there are independent persons reviewing company and board actions may deter disgruntled shareholders.

2. In the event of the Court finding a derivative claim to be unreasonable, costs can be awarded against the claimant. Conversely if the Court feels it was a reasonable case, it can award costs even if the claimant is ultimately unsuccessful.

Directors: appointment, induction and evaluation

KEY POINTS

- Board members have collective responsibility for the whole company.

- A manager promoted to the board must sublimate his department's interests to the company's overall interests.

- A director thus may have to take a decision diametrically opposed to the interests of their own department.

- Directors have a fiduciary duty to the company, so must put its interests before any other – including their own.

Numbers

Articles often state that there will be a minimum number of directors, for example, two – compulsory for PLCs – and may specify a maximum number (seven being very common). If it is wished to appoint directors in excess of the maximum the Articles must be changed. Since there is no legal requirement for a maximum it may be preferable to remove it completely. A director appointed in excess of a specified maximum could find themselves personally liable for the actions they take on behalf of the company.

If the number of directors falls below the minimum stipulated, the remaining director(s) can only continue to act if they are allowed to do so under the Articles – their power usually being limited to filling the vacancy or convening a general meeting. Unless the members ratify any other purported acts, the remaining director(s) could be personally liable for actions taken whilst the minimum was breached.

The appointment of alternate directors (see DIRECTORS – TYPES) is only possible if the Articles permit it. The appointment of an alternate adds to the number of directors, so it too must not breach any maximum set by the Articles.

Eligibility

1. Both real and corporate persons can be directors. However, there must be at least one real person on every board and there are now restrictions on the appointment of corporate directors.

2. The minimum age is 16. There is no upper age limit.

3. A person cannot be a UK director during a period of disqualification – either in the UK or in any overseas jurisdiction.

4. A person cannot be a director during any period they are sectioned under the Mental Health Act or are an undischarged bankrupt (unless the Court permits).

The Mental Health (Discrimination) Act section13 changed the model Articles accompanying CA06 by removing the provisions regarding termination of a director's appointment because a Court Order has been issued. Such a change will be automatically effected for companies adopting the newly amended Articles.

However, companies who have already used these pro-forma Articles as a base for their Articles should pass a Special Resolution amending them. The aim is to ensure that on recovery, a directorship can be resumed.

5 . The company's auditor cannot be a director.

6. Appointees must sign a consent to act as a director – which must be held by the company.

7. Individual Articles may prohibit other persons from being directors (e.g. in a company set up to own and run a block of flats, director-ships may be restricted to residents).

8. Directors of companies operating in the financial services industry may require FCA approval.

Before making such an appointment, checks should be made that the person is who they say they are and has all the qualifications and/or experience claimed.

Case study: Check it out

Patrick Imbardelli was chief executive of the Asia Pacific region of the Inter Continental Hotel Group. Just before he was to be promoted to the main board of that worldwide company he had to resign when it was discovered that the three University degrees he claimed were false.

Many might feel that his claimed degrees were probably unnecessary to perform his job well – but he lied. The essence of company/director/ employee relationship is mutual trust and confidence – obviously this is lacking if lies are told. Under the Fraud Act 2006, lying to get a job is regarded as fraud, punishable by up to 10 years in jail. In a research paper *'The untouchables: protecting your organisation from leadership risk'* (published by HireRight, a due diligence company), it is suggested that few businesses check career and qualification statements claimed by applicants for senior positions although this is surely negligence?

Directorship aspects

All directors are of equal status with no distinction between executive and non-executive directors, or between a director properly appointed and a shadow director. The board usually has power under the ARTICLES to make additional appointments – at a properly constituted and convened board meeting. Since ultimately directors are appointed by members, the Articles usually require those so appointed to retire at the next general meeting and seek confirmation of their appointment. There should be a minuted Board resolution, for example:

'It was unanimously agreed that Mr J Bloggs be appointed a director of the Company with effect from [date]' or, if the appointment is required to be

made immediately, 'It was unanimously agreed that Mr J Bloggs be and he hereby is appointed a director of the Company.'

Personal details: name (and any former name), date of birth, private address or (if the director does not want a private address to be subject to public scrutiny, a service address) must be recorded in the company's Register of Directors and form AP01 (AP02 for corporate directors) signed/authorised by a serving officer of the company must be sent or electronically submitted to CH within 14 days of the effective date.

Although, if a service address is supplied, the residential address is not made publicly available, CH is obliged itself to keep a note of it and to disclose residential addresses if required by the Court.

Any changes to these details must also be entered in the register and advised on form CH01 within 14 days. On termination of the appointment the effective date must be entered in the register and filed with CH (using form TM01) again within 14 days.

Notes:

1. Realistically the protection of non-disclosure of personal addresses may be limited. For example, if someone asks CH for an old annual return, the private address of a person who was then a director (unless he has since moved) may be available.

2. Married female directors (and Secretaries) are required to disclose their maiden names and any previous married surnames.

3. Whilst dates of birth may still have to be notified to CH, the actual day of birth is not part of the publicly available data (to try to prevent identity theft).

Register of directors' share interests

This Register is no longer required to be kept by LTDs.

Register of directors' interests in contracts/third parties

CA06ss175-187 requires directors to notify their company of any interest they may have in contracts (or proposed contracts) between the company and a third party. Interests are defined are either general or specific.

- *General* – a director has an interest in all matters concerning a named third party. Such a statement should be made upon the director's appointment and/or when it occurs, and/or when it ceases.

- *Specific* – a director has an interest in a particular contract. Such a declaration must be made at the first board meeting that considers the proposed contract, or on the director acquiring or becoming aware of the interest. There is no requirement for the company to keep a register of such interests but many might feel it prudent to evidence that they have informed the company, not least since failure to notify an interest is punishable by fine. It may also be a defence should there be an investigation under the Bribery Act (see AUTHORITY CONTROL). As well as using this register as a document of record it may be advisable for it to be available at every board meeting so that the members can see if any director has an interest (or new interest) in any matter under discussion

To compile such a register directors could be asked to state on appointment as well as annually (or more often) thereafter (whether or not there have been any changes) whether they have any interests in third parties that could conflict with those of the company. At the same time directors could be asked to confirm that they are not currently disqualified not only in the UK but also in any overseas jurisdiction.

Example: Appointment undertaking

To [Board of company – name] _____

Name of director designate _____ Date _____

I confirm that:

- I am willing to act as a director of [company]

- I am not currently disqualified from acting as a director under either UK law or the legislative process of another country.

- Neither I nor any connected person have any interests with third parties with which the company may do business *

- I and/or a connected person have the following interests in third parties with which the company does or may do business [give details]*

Delete as applicable

Signed _____

Notes:

1. CA06ss252-4 defines connected persons as *spouse, civil partner, (and any person with whom the director lives as partner in an enduring family relationship), child or stepchild (up to age 18), parents and any company or body corporate in which the director has a voting interest of 20% or more.*

2. Not all directors involved in failed companies are disqualified and to provide such track-record information, business information/credit agency Experian maintains a database showing the names of directors previously involved in such companies.

3. Obviously circumstances change and it may be prudent to ask for further disclosure on occurrence (when it could be entered in a Register of Directors interests) and by completion of an updated form, annually (say at the first board meeting each new financial year).

4. As a result of the Bribery Act, some companies also require a statement of all instances of providing entertaining and being entertained in a quarterly declaration. Alternatively (or additionally) this could be achieved by entries being made in any register of directors' interests.

Example: Declaration of entertainment

To (Board of company – name) _____

Name _____ Date _____

During the last [period under review] I have been involved in the following instances of entertaining:

Provided to suppliers, clients, customers, others (please specify)

_____ (date, occasion, guest/organisation, amount)

_____

Enjoyed as a guest of suppliers, clients, customers, other (please specify)

_____ (date, occasion, guest/organisation, amount)

_____

It may be appropriate to provide some practical guidance as to what should (or should not) be disclosed – see GIFTS.

Induction

For newly appointed directors, the Secretary should ensure they understand their role and its parameters, as failure to appreciate the relationship and the need to clarify the relationship to third parties may be dangerous.

Case study: Who is the main party?

When signing a contract on behalf of his company a director should check that it is clear that the contract is with the company and not him personally – or he could be liable. Thus in *Hamid (H) v Frances Bradshaw Partnership*, H signed a contract bearing the trading name (but not the company name) of a company of which he was a director. He was found to be personally liable for the contract since there was no indication he was signing on behalf of the company.

Ideally there should be a process by which new directors can be made familiar with the company and the board activities. This can be considered in two parts – firstly from a relationships viewpoint, and secondly from the personal familiarisation viewpoint. The FRC's *'Guidance on Board Effectiveness'* defines an effective board as one that:

- provides direction for management;
- demonstrates ethical leadership;
- creates a performance culture;
- makes well-informed and high-quality decisions;
- is accountable;
- thinks carefully about its governance arrangements; and
- creates the right framework to help directors meet their statutory duties.

Experience indicates that whilst most of these are, almost instinctively addressed by most boards, the last item may be overlooked.

CHECKLIST: Directors induction – 1

Preparation

✓ Set up a budget to cover board appointment induction.

✓ Appoint a senior director to oversee (or mentor) the process.

✓ List shareholders/guarantors and provide this to the new director possibly arranging meetings with major holders.

✓ List all advisors and scope and areas of work.

Provide

✓ Details of any shareholders' agreement.

✓ Declaration of any person(s) of SIGNIFICANT CONTROL and the nature of the control.

✓ Commentary on and copy of strategy of company.

✓ Copies of minutes and supporting papers.

- ✓ Copies of accounts.

- ✓ Summary of key factors and suggested methods of achieving.

- ✓ Current budget (and performance to date with commentary explaining variations).

- ✓ Banking arrangements, charges, covenants etc.

- ✓ Details of current products/services and developments.

- ✓ Promotional and advertising plans.

- ✓ Details of all locations and status (freehold, leasehold etc.).

- ✓ Details of any outstanding legal actions.

- ✓ Staff details, newsletters, works council minutes etc.

- ✓ Organisation chart(s).

- ✓ Ethical and/or corporate social responsibility statement.

- ✓ Relationship with non-executives/executives/Secretary.

- ✓ Personal details of such directors and guidance to areas of operation.

- ✓ Monitoring of the performance of both the board and individual members.

- ✓ Details of board member appointed to mentor the newcomer.

Many directors are promoted from the company's own management team. However accepting a directorship requires the subject to take a quantum leap from operating as a manager and it is important that those making such a leap fully appreciate what is now required of them. Directors have personal legal liability for their companies' activities. Literally *the buck stops in the boardroom* and thus those in the boardroom need to know for what they have responsibility. If any answers to the questions in the following checklist are *no* – personal and/or corporate research should fill the gap(s). Almost certainly this will be ongoing since many aspects are constantly changing – it can be helpful for a brief précis of legislative and other changes to be presented at each board meeting.

CHECKLIST: Directors induction – 2

Legal obligations

Does the director understand the legislative environment under which the company operates e.g?:

✓ the basis and outline of company law?

✓ the latest commercial legislation, including competition law?

✓ outline requirements of employment law?

✓ general requirements of other legislation specifically affecting the company?

✓ the internal operating rules of the company (e.g. the Articles of Association)?

✓ has the chairman checked the scope of such knowledge?

✓ that the board are responsible for the information required to be regularly filed at CH?

Finance

Does the director understand:

✓ the management and published accounts and ancillary data?

✓ that he has joint personal responsibility for the figures?

✓ the method by which queries should be raised?

✓ that since he must always be confident of the future solvency of the company he should not allow credit to be taken on when it might not be paid on the due date or within a reasonable time thereof?

✓ that commitment to expenditure on behalf of the company should only be in accordance with the regularly reviewed authority/risk chart?

Board work

Does the director realise that:

✓ he has a fiduciary duty to the company and must always put its interests first and foremost (sublimating his own and his departments' interests)?

- ✓ for the company's success, its aims and the means to attain those aims must be delineated (and updated regularly)?

- ✓ he has an implied obligation to attend board meetings – and to contribute to the discussion (which infers that he should be satisfactorily briefed on all matters)?

- ✓ he should always declare an interest in any third party with which the company is dealing?

- ✓ he should always exercise his decision-making process independently of other directors (even if this means he is in a minority of one)? (The FCA expects directors to 'challenge' decisions, not simply to acquiesce in them.)

- ✓ minutes should be read and agreed (or objected to and corrected) and not passed without consideration?

- ✓ his role is proactive not reactive – he must make things happen?

- ✓ the performance of every board member should be regularly and formally assessed?

- ✓ he should insist (except in emergency) that at least two working days are allowed between the receipt of items (other than routine matters) and a decision time?

- ✓ he should insist decisions are properly minuted and that any requested dissent is included?

- ✓ if there are matters of which he is unaware (both in and outside the board room) that this should be made clear and he must take steps to obtain the information?

Morality

Has the director:

- ✓ been given a copy of the codes of gifts, ethics, corporate governance and/or any other similar requirements?

- ✓ shown that his knowledge of such items is adequate?

- ✓ been told that bribes, inducements etc. must not be offered or made by any person on behalf of the company or received (and that he could be personally criminally liable if this occurs)?

✓ been briefed on the obligations of the Modern Slavery Act, Taxation requirements etc.?

✓ if he becomes aware of wrongdoing, been told that he should take immediate steps to ensure it ceases, errors are rectified and appropriate sanctions applied?

Accountability

Does the director realise that:

✓ he is answerable to the shareholders for the activities and actions of the company and its results?

✓ he is expected to take risks but only after a proper assessment of those risks and their potential outcome?

✓ contingency and disaster recovery plans should be prepared and updated covering all major eventualities?

✓ he is answerable to the various regulatory authorities for the activities of the company and its employees?

If unable to answer 'yes' to any of the above questions, it might be in the director's own best interests to research the item.

Listed PLCs are required to ensure those appointed to the board undergo a process of induction part of which process could use the above – a non-authoritative (and non-exhaustive) checklist. Whilst it may be tempting for directors of non-listed PLCs and LTDs to feel they can ignore the above, since under company law there is no differentiation between the types of companies or the obligations of their directors, they too are assumed to be able to answer 'yes' in all cases.

Responsibility

A board of directors acts as an entity with shared (collective) responsibility for all the company's activities. Irrespective of his executive responsibilities for a particular discipline, a director must take decisions, and share in the overall decision-making process in the interests of the company. This could mean he must even support a board decision that is detrimental to the interests of the discipline he heads. Once the decision has been made, even a dissenting director must accept it and work to make it happen. If he finds it impossible to support a material decision and cannot persuade the other directors to change their views, his only recourse may be to resign.

Evaluation

Listed PLCs are required to ensure that the performance of each director is evaluated each year and the recommendation for boards of FTSE350 companies is that such evaluation should be sourced externally at least every three years. The effectiveness of the board as a whole as well as that of individual members should be monitored. This could include examining:

- the skills within the board available to deal with the identified challenges facing the company;

- the validity and quality of board discussions and decisions dealing with such challenges;

- the means by which, as well as quality of, timely information is made available to the board to enable it to make informed decisions;

- the procedures by which board decisions are communicated and promulgated;

- the effectiveness of each individual and the way in which they inter-relate to one another;

The FRC's 'Guidance on Board Effectiveness' recommends that boards should commission an outside body to judge their effectiveness. For boards not wishing to pay for such external facility, determining the answers to the following might be applicable:

CHECKLIST: Evaluation

In the past year has the director:

✓ contributed to (and to what extent*) and worked towards implementing the decisions arrived at by the board?

✓ contributed (*) effectively and validly to the corporate strategy decision-making?

✓ assisted (*) in the formulation of the aims and purposes of the company and board and worked to the implementation of these?

✓ helped (*) ensure that short-term decisions do not impede progress to the long-term strategy)?

✓ helped (*) formulate/update, promulgate and ensure adherence to an internal code of ethics, as well as its own constitution (i.e. the Memorandum and Articles) and, if a listed PLC, the listing agreement?

✓ promoted (*) the corporate entity and developed products/services for the future?

✓ updated his own skills and knowledge and made them available at board level (and through board members and management at all levels)?

✓ motivated (*) the team to perform well and monitored results?

✓ applied controls over the commitment of the company to contracts, etc., ensured adequate authority control over all purchases?

✓ displayed a comprehensive understanding of the financial records and reports of the company?

✓ assisted (*) effectively in the expansion of the company based on well-researched, well-prepared, and well-considered, plans?

✓ developed contingency plans to protect the company's earning capacity in the event of a downturn or change in demand, and the effects of possible disasters affecting operations?

✓ helped (*) protect the corporate entity and the products/services from criticism, attack and loss as far as possible?

✓ ensured there is adequate comprehension of all new legislative enactments affecting the organisation?

✓ made effective contributions (*) but with a properly independent attitude at all board meetings?

and so on.

Corporate directors

Corporate directors (i.e. entities other than real persons) are no longer permitted other than in:

- UK listed and quoted PLCs;
- Larger PLCs and LTDs in group structures; and
- Charitable companies and trustee companies of pension funds.

Directors: employment status

Employment test

Although directors may be paid via the company's payroll, with PAYE and NI contributions deducted, this does not, of itself, make them employees. However, given their considerable potential corporate liabilities, it is arguable that some kind of balance might be achieved if executive directors had the protection of employment legislation. Obviously this is a decision that can only be made by an individual – whose taxation position might need to be considered. If this is required, to avoid a successful challenge, evidence should support the dual relationship.

Case studies: Judged to be an employee/director

In *Pemberton v Claimstart t/a Parkin Westbury & Co*, Mrs Pemberton owned 33% of the shares of the company of which she was a director and Secretary. The company was put into receivership, and following her dismissal by the Receiver, she claimed unfair dismissal. The EAT held that being a shareholder did *not* preclude her from also being an employee and suggested companies could ask the following questions:

- Is the employment salary determined by the board?

- Is the salary commensurate with responsibilities?

- How much remuneration does the director receive via dividends (i.e. do they draw the bulk of remuneration via dividends or salary)?

- Are directors listed as employees in the company's *wages book*?

- Have their earnings increased in the last three years (if so it would suggest employment)?

- How are directors' salaries assessed?

- Did the board meet in the ordinary course of business or not? If not then that would suggest there was no genuine employment relationship between the parties.

In *Stack(S) v Ajar-Tec Ltd (A)* the Court of Appeal stated that S who had agreed to work for A for nil wages until the company was profitable enough to afford to pay him, was an employee, even though he was also a shareholder (and had received dividends as such) and was a director.

Similarly in *DBIS v Knight* the EAT held that even though a sole share-holder/director had waived her salary (to try to ensure the company's survival) she was still an employee – and entitled to redundancy pay when her company failed.

To avoid disputes, the dual (director/employee) or triple (owner/director/employee) relationship with the separate legal person that is the company should be clearly evidenced. If an executive director has virtually the same relationship with their company as that of an employee (which is probably the case for executive directors of the vast majority of LTDs) and also wishes to be an employee, clarity is essential.

Keeping separate records of the decisions of what could be loosely said to be those exercising strategical control (shareholders or guarantors), tactical control and fiduciary duty (directors and other officers) and administrative control and duty of fidelity (employees) might aid the identification of the true (multi-faceted) relationship.

Service contract

If the director is to be an employee, the service contract should address requirements under employment law. The duties to be undertaken by directors for the company are customarily controlled by and set out in a document termed a *service contract* or *service agreement* negotiated between the parties on an individual basis – and which must be made available for inspection by owners for two hours each working day. Whilst this will specify most of the normal details to be enjoyed by the average employee, it may not contain all the items required to be included in a contract of employment. Indeed it will often contain restrictions on the work that can be undertaken immediately after its termination which may be more restrictive than those for an ordinary employee and include a *garden leave* (i.e. enforced idleness) clause.

Clarifying the relationship

To evidence a dual relationship of officer and employee ideally a contract should specify

- that the subject of the contract is an employee as well as a director, and

- that it is the *principal statement* required under the Employment Rights Act 1996 as well as being the service contract required to be displayed under company law.

An example of wording is given below but legal advice should be taken to ensure appropriate drafting of the clauses – and their relationship to the company and director.

Legal precedents

Although there have been a number of cases which found that share-holding directors were **not** also employees, in the main these have now been overtaken by the following:

Case studies: Determining twin/triple relationships

In both *Bottrill v Secretary of State for Trade & Industry* and *Fleming v Secretary of State* the Courts commented that 'the fact of majority share-holding [of a director] was no more than a relevant factor in determining whether [he] was also an employee… there was no rule of law which said that a majority (controlling) director could not [also] be an employee'.

In *Heffer v Secretary of State for Trade & Industry* the EAT stated:

- a limited company is a distinct legal entity separate from its shareholders and directors;

- a director of a limited company may enter into and work under a contract of employment with that company;

- a shareholder of a limited company may enter into and work under a contract of employment with that company.

In *Nesbitt & Nesbitt v Secretary of State for Trade and Industry* even though the Nesbitts between them held 99.9% of their failed company's shares they were found also to be employees and thus could claim redundancy payments. Neither of the Nesbitts had received dividends or directors fees.

In *Clark v Clark Const. Initiative Ltd* the EAT set out relationship guidelines:

- If there is an ostensible contract of employment, the onus is on the other party to prove that it is not what it appears to be, rather than the director being required to prove it is. So the absence of a written contract could be an argument against employment (since employees have a legal right to a contract of employment).

- If the director works in accordance with what would normally be expected of an employee, this could be a strong argument in favour of them being employed by the company.

- The mere fact that the director has a controlling shareholding does not prevent him also having a contract of employment (although it may raise doubts).

- Taking a salary rather than dividends is an argument in favour of employment.

- That the person founded and built the company will not prevent them also being an employee.

- That the person had financial arrangements with the company – had loans from, or made loans to it, or gives guarantees, will not normally be of assistance in determining whether there is an employment relationship.

In *Neufeld v A&N Communications in Print Ltd (in Liquidation)* Neufeld was originally an employee, but then became a shareholder and a director. He was then made managing director with 90% of the shares. He gave guarantees in respect of the company's liabilities. Although there were no written contracts between the three directors and the company, Neufeld, despite his large shareholding, continued as part of the sales team – working as a salesman. When the company went into liquidation, the EAT found that he was an employee.

Administration

Some companies not only set out the relationships in a joint service/ employment contract, as mentioned above, but also insert a clause which, in the event of its termination, grants to the company a power of attorney giving it the right to act as if it were the director. Thus, the company would then be able to sign a resignation letter and any other documents which, in the event of a dispute, the director would no doubt refuse to sign to retain greater bargaining power. Granting such power should not restrict the right of the director to take action under the service contract, for breach, and possibly, under the *contract of employment*, for unfair dismissal. Alternatively the situation could be clarified in the Articles, with authority by which directorships can be *resigned* being included. Legal advice should be taken.

Example: Sample draft contract

This Agreement is made this day of 2XXX, between [the company] and .... (the executive).

It is hereby agreed that:

1. The company shall employ the executive as [title, list of duties, etc.] and the executive shall serve the company commencing the day of 2XXX (the commencement date) for a rolling period of a maximum of three years so that (unless either party shall have given written notice of termination of this contract) the period shall be extended by a further one year on each anniversary of the commencement date. This contract is the *principal statement* required under the Employment Rights Act 1996 as well as a service contract.

   The appointment of the executive as director and employment of the executive shall otherwise continue until the occurrence of

   a) three months from the date on which either party shall give to the other three months notice of termination in writing. For the purposes of employment legislation the date continuous employment commenced was [date], or

   b) the passing by the shareholders of a resolution removing the executive as a director, or

   c) summary dismissal as a result of gross misconduct committed either as a director or as an employee.

The executive hereby grants a power of attorney in favour of the company authorising it to sign the required forms evidencing such removal as resignation from the post of director, and all ancillary matters, notwithstanding any rights the executive may have under this agreement.

2. The executive shall during the continuance of this agreement faithfully serve the company and use his utmost endeavours to promote the interests of the company and its shareholders, giving it at all times the full benefit of his knowledge, skill and ingenuity, and shall perform all his duties as may from time to time be assigned or vested in him/her by the board of directors of the company (the board).

3. The executive shall during the continuance of this agreement devote the whole of his time and attention to the duties of the appointment

(unless prevented from so doing by illness). He shall not, and shall cause his spouse and immediate family not to, directly or indirectly enter into, or be concerned in any manner (other than with the consent in writing of the board or as a minority shareholder in a company quoted on a public stock exchange or bourse) with any company or organisation deemed to be (at the discretion of the board) a competitor of the company.

4. The duties covered by this agreement shall be mainly carried out at the head office for the time being of the company, but the executive will be expected to travel to all company locations and elsewhere on company business and may be required to relocate within a [250 mile] radius of [London].

5. During the continuance of this agreement the company shall pay the executive (monthly) at the rate of £XXXXXX per annum or such other rate as may from time to time be agreed by the Board and will provide (at the cost of the company) a private motor car to the equivalent of [exact terms of allocation and use could be inserted here.]

6. In addition to remuneration, the executive will be entitled to reimbursement of all travelling, hotel and other expenses properly and reasonably incurred in the exercise of these duties and supported, as far as possible, by VAT receipts (if possible made out in the name of the employer) and invoices.

7. The executive will be entitled to [ ] paid days holiday in each year (plus public or Bank holidays) at such times as may be agreed by the board. At least 20 days each year must be taken within the holiday year.

8. In the event of the executive falling sick and being unable to perform the duties, the company will continue to pay the salary for a maximum of [ ] days in any one year. Should incapacity exceed such a period, further payment(s) will be at the discretion of the board. [It may be advisable to specify the relationship between Statutory Sick Pay and salary – e.g. whether the company will pay only SSP or top it up to the normal pay.]

9. Should the executive become unable (by reason of ill-health, imprisonment) to perform the duties adequately, or fail or neglect to perform the duties, or breach any of the provisions of this Agreement, then the company may forthwith determine this Agreement without notice as previously stipulated.

10. The executive shall not, without the consent in writing of the company, divulge to any other person, firm or company, and shall use his best endeavours to prevent the publication to any other person, firm or company of any information concerning the business or its finances or any of the secrets, dealings, transactions or affairs of or relating to the company. Since the executive is expected to concentrate on running and developing the business he/she is expressly prohibited from making plans to set up or join a competing business during his time with the company.

11. The executive acknowledges receipt of the company's codes of gifts, ethics and anti-bribery and undertakes to abide by the requirements thereof.

12. The executive undertakes to notify the company immediately of interest he may have in a third party with which the company does business, and of any change to such interest(s) and to advise the company immediately of any directors disqualification order made against him either in the UK or elsewhere.

[13. The executive acknowledges receipt of the company's Stock Exchange listing agreement and undertakes to abide by the requirements set out therein.]

14. The whole interest of the executive in any inventions emanating as a result of his employment shall become the absolute property of the company without any payment being due to him.

15. Upon the termination of this Agreement (whether by effluxion of time or otherwise) the executive shall not (without the express written permission of the company) for a period of six months thereafter be connected with, or take part in the management of, or advise or direct, another business whose activities could conflict with the activities of the company. In addition the executive will not for a period of six months from such termination, solicit or take away any staff, custom, or business under the control of the company at the time of the termination.

16. If the executive resigns in order to join a competitor or to set up in competition with the company, the company stipulates (and it is expressly hereby agreed by the executive) that for a period of six months from the date of such resignation he will not work for that competitor and will remain on 'garden leave'.

The principle behind this clause is to provide protection for the company in respect of up-to-date knowledge gained by the executive during employment. As such the company requires that, should a period of 'garden leave' be implemented it is expressly understood that during such leave, the executive will:

- take any accrued holiday to which he is entitled;

- have no right to carry out any work for the employer;

- not approach or enter the premises of the employer (other than at the specific and previous request of the employer);

- not contact any employee or customer of the employer by any means whatever;

- not work for or advise a competitor, or set up as a competitor of, this organisation;

- not represent himself to any third party as being or still being an employee of the employer.

The provisions of the Contracts (Rights of Third Parties) Act 1999 are specifically excluded from this contract.

17. The Company's disciplinary policy (a copy of which is attached) applies.

18. It is a fundamental term of this contract that all data, inventions, research and/or customer contacts whether listed or not etc., are and always remain the property of the company. Any person, during or after employment, using for personal or another person's gain or passing to another person any such details or data (without the previous written consent of the company signed by at least two directors) renders such a person (and any other person involved) liable to legal action.

19. If wishing to work on company records/correspondence/data remote from the normal work location (particularly if the executive uses their own equipment), the director should firstly obtain prior permission to do so from [the Chairman]. Full details of the data being worked upon will be recorded by the [director] with (if necessary) regular updates of developments. In the event of termination of employment for whatever purpose, all such information will prior to the last day of work be transferred to the employer with confirmation from the director of its entirety. It is expressly understood that should there

be any concern from the employer regarding full transmission of all such data, access will be provided to the director's equipment. Failure to comply could lead to legal recovery action.

20. Adversely commenting upon the company's products and/or services and/or personnel or agents in any media or forum whatever during or after termination of the appointment, which results in loss occasioned to the company could lead to legal action for recompense.

21. Any notice or other document required to be given under this agreement shall be deemed to be served if it is sent by recorded delivery:

- by the company to the executive at his/her last recorded home address; or

- by the executive to the company via the chairman or Secretary at the registered office of the company.

Signatures of parties _____

Witness _____

Notes:

1. This draft must be customised and legal advice should be taken.

2. It should be treated as a deed and it would be preferable that the subject director did not sign on behalf of the company.

3. The requirement for the subject not to work for a competitor for a set period after termination of employment (so that personal knowledge and/or contacts become out-dated and of less relevance) means the company has to continue payment for the *garden leave* period.

4. *Payment* in respect of garden leave periods must include all non-cash benefits in respect of the period (e.g. car, health cover, etc.) whilst holiday entitlement should be taken. Only the cash equivalent of any pre-leave accrued holiday should need to be paid.

5. The exclusion of the Contracts (Rights of Third Parties) Act attempts to prevent someone not immediately involved in the contract being able to circumvent its clauses (see below).

6. Clause 19 has been inserted to enable the company to recover data etc. particularly should the termination not be amicable (see below).

Case studies:

Regaining company data

In *Fairstar Heavy Transport NV v Adkins & others* the Court of Appeal granted a company authority to access emails stored on its former MD's personal computer. The records related to transactions concerning their business which they needed to assess potential liability regarding a claim.

In *Eurasian Natural Resources Corp v Judge* it was stated that the only way for a company to access all its documents held personally (in whatever format) following a person's termination would be to insert such a right in the appointment documentation.

Third party rights negate garden leave

When a husband, subject to a contract's six-month *garden leave* clause, resigned to join a competitor, his employer enforced the clause. However his wife, successfully exercised *her* rights under the Contract (Rights of Third Parties) Act to insist that his employer gave him work to do at home (thus partially negating the effect of the garden leave clause) because she didn't want him 'getting under her feet' with nothing to do at home!

Get the wording right

In *Ranson v Customer Systems plc*, whilst he was still in employment, the employee made plans for a competing organisation that he would operate after he left. However such preparations were held not to be a breach of any fiduciary duty he had to the company. His (old) contract of employment did not prohibit such activity.

Protecting the company

In a survey regarding breaches of company security, over 60% of employees admitted that they had stolen confidential documents, customer databases, details of contacts and/or potential sales leads from their employers. Of those who made such an admission, 50% said they believed that sales leads and contacts belonged to them and not to the company. A separate survey revealed that 33% of directors admitted stealing corporate information from their companies. The onus is very much on the company to ensure that employees including directors realise that such theft is unacceptable.

Although such a clause (18 above) may be effective in terms of employees and directors the situation regarding Agents of the company is somewhat different.

Case study: Agents rights

In *Cureton v Mark Insulations Ltd* an agent worked on behalf of the company and built up a customer database. Because the EU Database directive stipulates that whoever builds a database is its owner, when they parted company, he did not have to return it to the company.

(It might be wise to insert in the Agency agreement that any database built by the agent, reverts to the principal on termination of the agreement and/or that the principal needs a copy of the database updated every 6 months.)

Directors: duties and liabilities

The seven explicit duties

Traditionally directors' duties of directors have always been implied, however, CA06 sets out director's duties explicitly. Although most should be easily recognizable as already being implied (and even taken for granted), they might be thought not to pose too many challenges to directors, however they set criteria against which directors can be judged particularly by shareholders who might wish to initiate a DERIVATIVE claim. It is arguable that if these seven duties were met in their entirety, there should be no need for corporate governance codes.

a) Directors must act within their powers (s.171)

Directors must act in accordance with the Articles that are now the company's Constitution. Directors of LTDs that decide to operate without a Secretary should ensure someone knows the Articles requirements (including any objects clause deemed or actually transferred from the

Memorandum) to ensure the directors do not breach these and risk personal liability.

Case study: Twin breach

In *Smith v Henniker-Major* a director acting on his own purported to pass a board 'resolution' at a board meeting of which he had deliberately failed to give his colleagues notice. Not only did his failure to inform his colleagues of a board meeting breach company law (since all directors have a right to receive notice of every board meeting no matter who initiates it) but also the company's Articles stipulated that the quorum for valid board meetings was two directors. The Court stated that the 'resolution' was a worthless piece of paper. Further, since he had acted *ultra vires* the Articles, if he implemented the 'resolution' and the company lost money, he would be held personally liable.

b) Directors must promote the success of the company (s.172)

Directors must promote the company for the benefit of and in the interests of the company's members whilst taking into account the interests of others – collectively called 'stakeholders'. The directors also need to be aware of the consequences of their decisions and the desirability of the company maintaining a reputation for high standards of business conduct. Thus the law requires directors to consider:

- the long term consequences of all decisions;
- the interests of employees as a result of the decisions;
- the need to foster the business relationships with suppliers, customers and others;
- the impact of the company's operations (and thus their decisions concerning those operations) on the community and the environment;
- the desirability of the company maintaining a reputation for high standards of business conduct;
- the need to act fairly as between members of the company.

The challenge for boards inherent in these requirements can perhaps best be illustrated graphically. Whilst many of these obligations have been required for some time, some are novel (at least in terms of corporate legislative requirements).

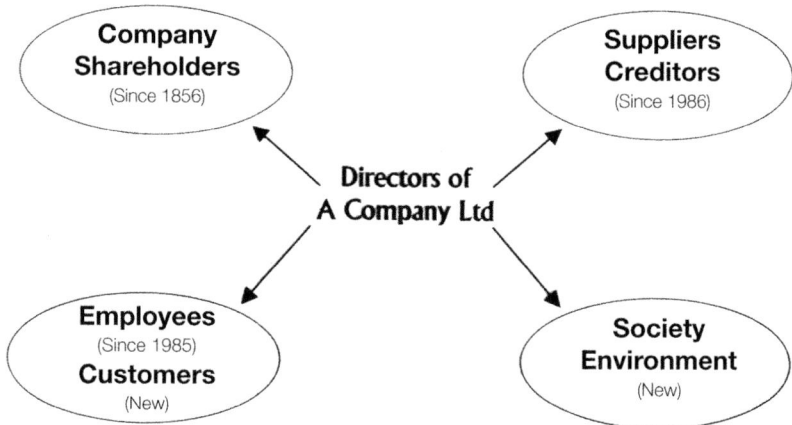

Of course some of these responsibilities are not new. Directors have been required to consider the interests of:

- the company itself and its shareholders since CA1856;
- suppliers and creditors since the Insolvency Act86; and
- employees since CA85.

However for the first time under corporate law directors must take account of the interests of their customers, the environment and society as a whole. Of course it may be that in taking decisions some such interests may be diametrically opposed. Further, if challenged, how could directors *prove* they did consider these various interests and, presumably, reconcile such conflicts. So that there is some documentary evidence that the board is aware of the obligation, it may be that (perhaps at the first board meeting after start of *every* financial year – and the first meeting after a new director joins the board) there is a minute such as *'The board reminded themselves of the seven duties of directors set out in the Companies Act 2006 and confirmed that in taking decisions they would continue to take account of these duties and bear in mind the disparate interests of the company's stakeholders.'*

c) Directors must exercise independent judgement (s. 173)

A director must vote according to his own personal views – even if this results in him being in a minority of one. A director placed in such a position, should require that his dissent (and the reason for it) is noted in the minutes. If including his objection in the minutes is resisted the director should write a note to the chairman (and keep a copy) objecting to his dissent not being recorded.

Case study: Investigation required before decision

In *Gwyer & Associates and anor v London Wharf (Limehouse) Ltd & ors,* a director made no effort to ascertain what were his company's interests (when it was approaching insolvency) before voting (*with the crowd*) on a board resolution.

The Court held he was not only negligent, but also in breach of his fiduciary duty to exercise his discretion independently and *bona fides* in the interest of the company; and that where a company was on the brink of insolvency the directors owed a duty 'to consider as paramount' the interests of the creditors (see WRONGFUL TRADING).

---

d) Directors must exercise reasonable care, skill and diligence (s. 174)

These key words were uttered by Judges in deciding cases brought under to earlier legislation. The test here is that the director should act with the degree of care skill and diligence that would be exercised by a person with the general knowledge skill and experience reasonably expected of a person carrying out the functions such as those carried out by the director.

Case studies:

Must take care – and perform to expected level of own skill

In *Dorchester Finance Co Ltd & anor v Stebbing and ors,* the three directors of the company were all qualified accountants. Two directors, X and Y, were non-executives who left the running of the company to Z. X and Y often signed blank cheques for Z's use, and made no enquiry of how such funds were used. The company failed owing a considerable sum to the creditors.

The Court found that both X and Y had not only failed to apply the necessary skill and care in the performance of their duties but also failed to perform **any** duties as directors. In addition, Z had failed to exercise any skill or care as a director as well as misappling the assets. All three were held liable.

The Court ruled that a director in carrying out his duties must:

- Exercise 'the degree of skill that may reasonably be expected' from a person of his knowledge and experience. Thus in considering liability for wrongful trading a Court might consider a director who is a qualified accountant to have a higher degree of culpability than those without such training because of his expected knowledge in the corporate field.

- Take such care that a man might be expected to take on his own account.

- A question that could be asked is 'Would I be so cavalier concerning these funds, if this was my own cash rather than it being that of my company?'

- Exercise the powers granted to him in good faith and in the interests of the company of which he is a director.

Must be diligent

In the *D'Jan of London* case where a director claimed he signed without reading it, an insurance proposal form that contained a blatantly erroneous statement about him, the Court stated that directors must be 'diligent person(s) having … the general knowledge, skill and experience that may reasonably be expected of a person carrying out the same functions as are carried out by that director in relation to the company'.

The Court held that although the director could be excused some liability as the mistake was 'not gross. It was the kind of thing that could happen to a busy man, although that is not enough to excuse it', he had to contribute £20,000 to the loss suffered by the creditors of his failed company. The judge stated that although it was unrealistic to expect a director to read everything he had to sign, he had to exercise some judgment; here the proposal consisted of only a few sentences.

e) Directors must avoid conflicts of interest (s. 175)

However a director will not breach this rule if:

- the conflict has been authorised by the directors at a meeting where there is a disinterested quorum: and
- for an LTD, it is not specifically prohibited by the Articles; or
- for a PLC, the directors have specific power in the Articles to allow it

CA06s182 requires directors to declare any interest (direct or indirect) which is already in existence. Obviously in allowing a colleague to retain a conflicting interest, the other directors would have to take the decision bearing in mind their own fiduciary duty to the company.

Under CA06s184, interests are required to be brought to the attention of the directors, hence the suggestion that a company maintain a 'register of directors' interests' to be available for inspection on every occasion when board decisions are made involving such interests.

Secondary legislation under CA06 stipulates that all companies formed before 1st October 2008 must obtain shareholders' consent giving the directors permission to authorise such conflicts. If such consent amends the Articles it would need to be a Special Resolution.

Case study: 'A house divided among itself'

In *British Midland Tools* (BMT) v *Midland International Tooling* (MIT) four directors of BMT secretly decided to set up MIT in competition with BMT. One of the four resigned and started setting up MIT. His three colleagues, who remained in office with BMT, then enticed employees to join MIT, and poached BMT's customers for MIT. The Court held that the three directors who remained in office had a duty to the original company to stop the enticement and poaching and were liable for not taking such action.

f) Directors must not accept benefits from third parties (s. 176)

However the benefit could be accepted if it cannot reasonably be regarded as one that gives rise to a conflict of interest. It might be prudent to request that any benefit received from a third party – even if not giving rise to a conflict – should be entered into a 'register of directors' interests' (available at each board meeting) so that other board members are advised/reminded of the interest.

g) Directors must declare any interest in proposed transactions with the company (s. 177)

Such declaration can be either a specific (s184) or general (s185) notice but a director does not have to make a declaration if the interest cannot reasonably be regarded as likely to give rise to a conflict.

The fiduciary duty

A director owes a fiduciary duty to his company. If, as well as being a director he is also an employee, he has a duty of fidelity. Directors are required:

- *To act at all times in the best interests of the company.* Defining what are the best interests of the company can be a matter of opinion but nevertheless this is an obligation and a balance or choice may need to be made between the short term and long-term interests.

- *To act fairly between members of the company.* Thus directors must not unfairly prejudice the interests of a minority shareholder. Their decisions must be for the benefit of the company and in the interests of the shareholders as a whole (decision in *Re Smith & Fawcett*).

Case study: Minority protection

In a case concerning the taking private of a listed PLC – Essar Energy – the FCA stated that following a board vote in favour of such a proposal, any majority holder trying to buy out the remaining investors and delist the company would have to obtain the approval of at least 75% of the votes cast in a ballot – and, additionally, a majority of the independent shareholders would also need to be in favour. (Presumably the fact that the company was listed would have been included within the Articles. If so delisting would require a special resolution – 75% of those voting in favour – to effect the change to the Articles – which would then need to be filed with CH.)

- *To act as a trustee in respect of the company's assets.* A director must act without any additional purpose which would affect the main and overriding interests of the company (even sublimating his own interests).

- Directors have powers under the company's constitution but must use those powers for the proper purposes of the company (*Smith & Fawcett*). A director should not make a secret profit without the consent or permission of the company members (*Regal Hastings Ltd v Gulliver*).

- *To exercise the best degree of skill and care depending upon his personal knowledge and experience.* Historically a director could not be made liable for a judgmental error. He was expected to 'give of his best' and be judged in this respect on his level of experience. He could, however, be penalised if he was found to have acted negligently (see DERIVATIVE CLAIM).

- *To declare all and any interests and to act honestly and reasonably, particularly where his own interests may be in conflict with the interests of the company.* Only if not proscribed by the Articles and agreed by a disinterested quorum of the board (for LTDs) or only if specifically permitted by the Articles and agreed by a disinterested quorum (for PLCs) may any personal profit made by a director by virtue of his appointment, be retained by him. On appointment and on later occurrence a director must immediately declare any and all interests to the board. Failure to disclose an interest can result in personal penalties – on summary trial to a fine of £5000 (unlimited if on trial on indictment). A director also found to be in breach of his fiduciary duty could be subject to further penalties.

Case studies: Must act in his company's best interests

In *Item Software (UK) Ltd v Fassihi & Ors,* a director was secretly setting up a new company to trade in competition with the company of which he was sales director. He sabotaged contract negotiations between his existing company and a third party, so that he could divert the latter's contract with Item to his new company. The director was held to have:

- breached his fiduciary duty by sabotaging the negotiations for this own benefit; and

- failed to tell the company of his breach.

The Court described the director's actions as 'fraudulent concealment' and stated that if a director appropriates business for himself then he has a duty to account to the company for any profit. The director was ordered to pay damages both for the sabotage and his failure to disclose the breach.

In *Tesco Stores Ltd v Pook,* a senior manager fraudulently arranged for payments on false invoices and received a bribe from the *'supplier'* for doing so. The Court held that directors and senior managers (i.e. company officers) because of their fiduciary duty, have an obligation to disclose any breach to the employer and advise it of secret profits. Pook was in breach of this requirement and therefore had to pass the bribe to Tesco as well as the fraudulent receipts.

To ensure the company acts in accordance with the requirements of laws affecting the company: The Accounting Practices Board suggested that boards should compile a register of all the laws and regulations with which their companies are required to comply. Compiling such a register is merely an administrative chore – the underlying purpose is for a complete set of the company's obligations to be generated, promulgated (to encourage compliance) and policed (to deal with non-compliance). It would of course need constant updating and many would consider it a virtual impossibility to ensure compliance with such a mass of legislation (which is also constantly changing).

Directors' fraudulent activities

Corporate fraud is on the increase. It has been stated that 60% of all UK companies are losing as much as 5% of turnover to fraud and theft (and that relates only to known frauds and thefts!). The impact is felt directly on the bottom line. For a company earning 10% profit on sales, sales of ten times any amount lost to thieves will have to be generated simply to regain the pre-theft *profit-position*. Under the Fraud Act the offences include:

- making a false representation (including something as basic as lying on a job application which few have appreciated even though several applicants have been jailed for such breaches);

- failing to disclose information where there is a legal duty to do so; and

- abusing one's position.

Since a director must, by virtue of his position, safeguard and protect the shareholders' assets, any dereliction of this duty is fraud. Similarly if he makes gain by abusing his position (or causes the company loss by so doing) that is also fraudulent. CA06s175 allows a director to seek authorisation from the board to exploit personally some property or opportunity even though there may be a conflict between his interests and those of the company. In an LTD, this can be done provided there is nothing in the Articles banning it. However directors of PLCs can only do so with specific authorisation allowing it in the Articles – if not, the

Articles would need to be changed for it to be permitted (i.e. the specific authority in a special resolution of the shareholders would be needed).

Whilst a director is an officer of the company and acts as its agent they are separate persona – the director being a 'natural' person and the company being an 'unnatural person'. A director cannot seek to make the company liable for his activities even if they were undertaken by him in the name of the company.

Case studies:

Not in my name

In *Bilta (UK) Ltd (in liquidation) v Nazir & ors*, all four directors of Bilta were involved in a scheme with a third party to create false transactions (in the company's name) that would enable it to over claim VAT fraudulently. The directors argued that the liability for their fraudulent activities was that of the company as 'they were [only] acting in its name'. This was not accepted and the liquidator was entitled to seek financial contributions from those involved in the fraud. In addition, by involving the company in their fraud the directors had damaged the company and thus were in breach of their fiduciary duty to it.

Similarly in *R v Sale(S)*, S was the sole shareholder and director of a company which by bribing Network Rail employees had received the benefit of lucrative contracts. S was found guilty of corruption but defended the seizure of the value of the contracts from the company by contending that it was the company, not himself, who had benefited. It was held that there was such a close link between the legal persona of the company and the real person that both had acted in the corruption and both should be held liable.

Note: The Government has suggested that boards of directors that fail to prevent or stop their employees from committing fraud could be made criminally liable for the offences. In 2017, the Justice Minister stated *'companies must be held to account for criminal activity that takes place within them'*. One option under the proposals would hold a company liable unless it can demonstrate that it took all reasonable steps to ensure fraud did not occur.

Settling the company's liability

In *HMRC v O'Rourke* (O'R), O'R was finance director of LW & Co Ltd during the 11 months between the company's incorporation and it being placed into administration, it owed HMRC over £200,000 in unpaid NI contributions. Under the Social Security Administration Act 1992, a company officer has personal liability to pay NICs if through his *'fraud or neglect'* such payments were not made, O'R was found personally liable for the company's debt.

General aims/responsibilities of the board

Collective

A board acts as an entity with shared responsibility for all the company activities. Thus, irrespective of whether a director heads a discipline in the company, he must take decisions, and share in the decision making process, in respect of all matters concerning the company as a whole. This can mean supporting a board decision which is actually detrimental to the interests of the discipline he heads – or to him. Once the decision is taken – even if he voted against it – any director not in favour of the proposal must sublimate his personal preferences and work to implement the decision with his best endeavours. If he cannot accept the decision, resignation would seem to be the only alternative.

Individual

The items of a corporate nature expected of a director could include ensuring:

- company strategy is formulated, known widely and adhered to;

- the aims and purposes of the company are promulgated internally and externally (e.g. to shareholders, advisers, media, etc.) and updated as necessary;

- tactical decisions and actions take the same general direction as the strategy of the company (i.e. ensuring short term decisions do not hamper or impede long term strategy);

- the formulation, promulgation and adherence to an internal code of ethics covering GIFTS etc.;

- the company complies with its own constitution (i.e. the Articles) and, if a listed PLC, the listing agreement etc.

- there is a company spokesperson to promote the corporate entity and its products/ services at all times;

- the appropriate blend of skills is available at board level (and through board members and management at all other levels), that people at all levels know what is expected of them, are motivated to perform well, and warned and disciplined when performance or actions are not as required;

- there are adequate controls over the commitment of the company to contracts, etc., and adequate authority control over all other purchases (e.g. using a delegated authority chart – see AUTHORITY CONTROL);

- the financial records and reports of the company are prepared in accordance with legal and accounting requirements, and that such reports are filed with authorities within time limits;

- products and/or services are developed so that continuity of earning power of the organisation is on-going;

- the company is developed on well-researched, well-prepared, and well-considered, planning;

- there are disaster recovery plans to protect against risks damaging its earning capacity (e.g. in the event of a downturn or change in demand, and/or the effects of possible disasters affecting operations);

- the corporate entity and the products/services is protected from public criticism, attack and loss as far as possible; and

- the company pays the appropriate amount of tax on its profits.

Taking precautions

As the corporate environment becomes more and more onerous for those charged with running corporate bodies, an obvious question is 'how can directors negate their liability'? They cannot, but they may be able to minimise or restrict their exposure:

a) By keeping aware

In an increasingly litigious society, boards need to be aware of the liabilities they have and how this scenario is changing. Secretaries should make themselves aware of developments, keep up to date on the law, its interpretation, the range of liabilities – and the level of compensation awards being made, and advise the board accordingly.

b) By formulating rules and procedures

Adequate and effective rules, procedures etc. can provide some measure of defence in that the company could be shown to have recognised the problem and to have taken reasonable steps to try and eradicate it. Thus the company should try to ensure that:

- all rules regarding trading, recruitment and relationships as well as attitudes and actions towards employees during employment are clear regarding fair treatment; whilst rules outlawing price-fixing, slavery and exploitation, tax evasion, and bribery have observance at all times;

- all employees have read and understood the rules and that all procedures etc., are regularly checked, reviewed and policed and always adhered to;

- immediate action is taken once there is any question of an accusation or suspicion that there is a breach of such rules and sanctions are applied against everyone in breach;

- all safety rules are adhered to, specifications regarding maintenance are compiled and inspections carried out in accordance therewith; adequate protective measures are in place and observed; and risk assessments are prepared and updated;

- all reports of problems potentially affecting safety, as well as concerning bullying, discrimination, harassment, stress etc. are immediately investigated, policed, and rectified;

- all employees are advised of their responsibilities for their own and their colleagues' safety, and the protection of their employer's assets; and

- everyone is constantly reminded of the need to adhere to rules, procedures etc., to think before acting or speaking and to consider the implications of liability claims, etc.

To ensure that dangers, poor procedures or attitudes etc., are reported it may be advisable to stipulate that anyone aware of such activities should report to a named person and that everyone making a disclosure (providing it is made in good faith) will not suffer any detriment. The adoption of a whistleblowing procedure (compulsory for listed PLCs) is recommended.

Example: Whistleblowing policy/procedure

1. [As stated in its general compliance policy] [the organisation] operates within the country's laws and regulations and expects all employees to co-operate in this by strictly adhering to all policies and procedures.

2. Every employee is expected to advise [specify a named person or position] should (s)he become aware of any matter or act which seems not to be in accord with the general aim set out in 1 above. Specifically all employees are expected to make such notification immediately they become aware:

   a) of the breaking or proposed breaking of any law or regulation by an employee, director or any other person acting on behalf of the organisation;

   b) of an organisation's procedure or policy being broken;

   c) of any wrongdoing;

   d) of any matter which seems likely to harm an employee, customer, supplier, member of the public, the environment etc.; and

   e) of any possibility or suggestion that one of the items set out in (a) to (d) has occurred and is being covered up.

3. Assuming these requirements have been met (i.e. the initial report must be to [specify] rather than to an outside body), the [organisation] undertakes to hold the employee harmless and to protect them from any personal claims and from any victimisation, harassment or bullying occasioned as a result of their acts. The aim is that the career of any notifying employee should not in any way be harmed or hindered as a result of their act (whether the item reported proves to be true or not provided the reporting was carried out in good faith).

4. The action of any employee against someone who has made disclosure under this policy (and as a result of such disclosure) whether they are affected by the disclosure or not, will be regarded as gross misconduct.

5. Anyone, including an elected safety representative, who becomes aware of a hazard or dangerous occurrence is expressly required to notify [specify] before making any other report – e.g. to an outside body – not least so that immediate action can be taken to remove any hazard/occurrence.

6. Failure to notify when reasonably aware or certain of an occurrence covered by 2 above is regarded by the organisation as misconduct. Failure to notify internally before notifying externally is usually also regarded as misconduct. Only if an employee has reasonable grounds for believing that no notice will be taken of an internal report may contact be made to an outside body in the first instance.

Note: If the organisation has a compliance officer, then it may be logical to insert the name of that person in such a clause. However in safety reporting it may be important that a person is designated for this purpose on each site, so that urgent investigation and rectification can be implemented.

A person making a disclosure in accordance with the above principles should be protected (in the event of any action being taken against them) under the Public Interest (Disclosure) Act. If dismissed in such circumstances and the disclosure is agreed to have been in the public interest there is no limit on the compensation that may be awarded.

c) By obtaining an indemnity

Many directors already have an indemnity – possibly without knowing it. If a company uses Table A of CA85 as part or whole of its Articles, it will almost certainly have retained regulation 118 which provides a standard indemnity clause for company officers. It can only be utilized by persons acting within the law, and such an indemnity only has value whilst the company is solvent. There is nothing to stop a CA06 company incorporating that regulation in its Articles.

d) By effecting insurance cover

Directors and Officers (D&O) insurance cover could be effected. Care must be taken to check the extent of such cover. It is against public interest to insure an illegal act so if the matter itself is illegal even with the cover there may be no payout – other possibly than the costs of the defence. Before D&O cover is purchased the board should check they have authority – it would be prudent to insert the right to effect the cover in the Articles.

The penalties?

Obviously some of the potential breaches referred to above are fraudulent in which case the offenders could be prosecuted under the Insolvency, Fraud, Modern Slavery or Bribery Acts and those found guilty could be jailed for up to 10 years (see WRONGFUL TRADING), disqualified under CDDA86 for up to 15 years and fined.

Case study: Disqualified and fined

In *R v Owide,* the director was disqualified for 7 years in 2000. However he continued to run a number of businesses (for doing so, having already been disqualified, he would have unlimited liability). In January 2004 he was disqualified for a further 5 years and fined £200,000 (to be paid within 18 months or he would be imprisoned for another 18 months).

Directors: payments, loans and interests

Payments

Mainly due to the excesses of some directors the question of the payment of directors is rarely far from the headlines. It is perhaps inevitable that having considerable power over their companies some directors can be tempted to over-reward themselves. As economist J K Galbraith stated 'the salary of the chief executive of a large corporation is not a market award for achievement. It is frequently in the nature of a warm personal gesture by the individual to himself".

Under the Enterprise and Regulatory Reform Act 2013, shareholders of listed PLCs must (by ordinary resolution, colloquially called having their 'say on pay') approve their directors' remuneration policy at least every 3 years; and any payment inconsistent with that policy can be recovered by the company from the recipient. Any director who authorises a payment in breach of the 'say on pay' resolution can be made personally liable for it unless they can prove they acted honestly and reasonably. No payment for loss of office can be made unless that payment conforms to the most recently approved remuneration policy – or has been specifically approved by the shareholders. There have been a number of PLCs' AGMs which have seen 'shareholders revolts' concerning 'over-compensation' of directors and there is a continuing anger at the 'fat cat' syndrome particularly in the financial services industry. Despite this furore the perceived overpayment of those in charge of large companies continues.

In the UK there seems to be a far wider gap between the earnings of those who direct companies and those at the sharp end who carry out their instructions. A number of initiatives have suggested that a multiplier concept be used – the MD being paid X times the amount of a shop floor operative. This actually happens in the John Lewis partnership where the Chairman is paid not more than 75 times the earnings of a shop floor partner. In some companies the actual multiple of shop floor pay to top job is now in excess of 400. In 2004 the multiple was 68 – if it was 68 in 2004 why should it have jumped to 400 13 years later?

Often the argument for excessive pay of listed companies' directors, is that it is a reflection of the share price. The actions of directors can affect the share price, but so too can market forces entirely outside their control – and if rewards are linked to an increasing share price, what happens when the share price goes down? Given the widespread concern as such payments, it seems likely that there will be some kind of legislation or control.

Disclosure

Generally, all *value* given to directors must be disclosed in the company's ANNUAL REPORT. *Value* includes all benefits in kind, and all payments, goods or benefits given to the director and persons *connected* to him. It also includes anything provided for a person as an inducement to them becoming a director as well as anything paid to them following cessation of a directorship. Any sums given to a third party for the benefit of the director must also be disclosed.

Connected persons include:

a) husband, wife or civil partner of a director;

b) a partner in an enduring family relationship with a director;

c) a director's children or step-children (from the relationships set out in (a) or (b)) up to age18;

d) the director's parents; and

e) bodies in which the director has a 20% or more holding.

Payments to a body to which any director has been seconded must also be disclosed.

Loans

CA06ss197-214 stipulate that, subject to a £50,000 limit, a company can make a loan to a director to carry out the work of the company. Loans can also be made to cover a director's costs in defending himself in a civil or criminal proceedings or in an investigation re negligence etc. (where, if guilty, the loan must be repaid and, if innocent, presumably, any loan should become a grant).

Other than loans for the above purposes, a company is only allowed to make loans to its directors and/or connected persons up to the following limits (larger amounts need the specific permission of the members):

- a loan or quasi loan up to £10,000;

- a credit transaction £15,000; and

- a loan in the ordinary course of the company's business (e.g. if part of the company's business is to lend money to allow the purchase of an individual's main residence) – no limit.

If a director borrows money in breach of the Act (e.g. to the detriment of the creditors) he can be required to repay the amount. Thus in *Currencies Direct Ltd v Ellis*, a former director of a company was required to repay a loan made to him whilst he was a director.

Indemnities

Although a company may not indemnify its directors (or anyone else) against an illegal act, under CA06ss.232/237/238 indemnities can be granted but must be recorded and kept in a register at the Registered Office or SAIL. Any such indemnity must be retained for at least one year from termination or expiry of contract. Companies must make the records available for free inspection by its members within seven days of a request. Directors and Officers liability insurance can be effected and paid for by the company provided this is disclosed in the directors' report (s236). If director(s) have been negligent, or have defaulted on required actions or breached their duties, such acts can be ratified by a majority of the members (disregarding any votes of the subject director, s239).

Interests

CA06s175 states that directors (and connected persons) must avoid conflicts of interest. However a director will not breach this requirement if:

a) the conflict has been authorised by the directors (at a meeting where there was a disinterested quorum); and

b) (for an LTD) it is not specifically prohibited by the Articles; or

c) (for a PLC) the Articles give directors specific power to allow it.

When a disinterested quorum is asked to permit an interest to subsist, they should check that they do not breach their own fiduciary duty to the company. S182 requires that a director must declare an existing interest (direct or indirect). Since under s184 interests are required to be brought to the attention of the directors, a company could maintain a *register of directors' interests* to be available for inspection at every board meeting. Obviously there should be an element of realism concerning interests – being entertained (and providing the same) at this level is very common-place, the difficulty may be in differentiating between what is *run of the mill* entertaining as an opportunity to discuss business and a situation where the value of the benefit is such that to a reasonable outsider it could suggest that a *bribe* is being offered (to get or be given business).

Bribery Act guidance indicates that unless it is intended to persuade someone not to act 'in good faith, impartially, or in accordance with a position of trust', normal business entertaining does not breach the Act.

- Under s176 a director must not accept benefits from third parties. However, if the benefit cannot reasonably be regarded as giving rise to a conflict of interest, it can be allowed. It might be prudent to request that any benefit received from a third party – even if not giving rise to a conflict – should be entered into a *register of directors' interests*.

- Under s177 a director must declare any interest in proposed transactions with his company. Such declaration can be either specific (s184) or general (s185) but a director does not have to make a declaration if the interest cannot reasonably be regarded as likely to give rise to a conflict.

On notification of an interest, the Articles may stipulate a range of controls, e.g.:

- the interest (or the directorship) cannot continue;

- the director cannot take part in any vote concerned with the third party (and may even be required to leave the room during any discussion);

- the director cannot be counted as part of the quorum for that part of the meeting;

- the director can vote providing the interest has been previously declared (or does not exceed a stated value);

- any profit made by him as a result of such interest must be given to the company;

- any profit made by him must be declared and the board can decide the outcome; and

- any profit made can be kept by him.

Case study: Costly non-disclosure

The FCA fined a non-executive director over £150,000 for 'using her positions to better herself'. Although she was a consultant for a fund manager, when she also became chair of two investment committees of mutual insurance companies, she sought work for the fund without disclosing her interest in the fund.

WARNING

The Companies Act 2006 (Commencement No 5 Transitional Provisions and Savings) Order 2007, stipulates that all companies formed before 1st October 2008 must obtain shareholders' consent giving the directors permission to authorise such conflicts. Although it is not stipulated that this needs to be a Special Resolution (thus amending the Articles) this course might be safest.

The General Counsel of the London Stock Exchange FTSE 100 Companies has a guidance paper for those companies that wish to amend their Articles by way of a general power for directors to authorise conflicts of interests. The paper gives guidance to the wording of an amendment, best practice on directors authorising conflicts, and how to review previous authorisations.

Directors: removal

KEY POINTS

- Directors cease to hold office by resignation, disqualification, and death, or by forcible removal under law.

- For good administration, resignation should be evidenced by a signed letter of resignation, entry made in the Register of Directors, and completion of form TM01 filed within 14 days with CH.

- Great care is essential if the removal is involuntary.

Resignation

A resigning director should be asked to sign a letter of resignation stating the effective date and confirming he has no claims against the company. Under the pro forma Articles accompanying CA06 it states that a person *'ceases to be a director as soon as a notification is received by the company stating that the director is resigning'*. If a director has resigned but refuses to sign a letter of resignation, particularly if there has been antipathy, in order to gain certainty and clarity, the process of forcible removal (see below) might be better followed.

Disqualification – external removal

A person will be disqualified from acting as a director, if he:

- has been declared bankrupt (unless the Court permits him to continue to act). Under the Enterprise Act 2002, a director who becomes bankrupt through no fault of his own (i.e. he is not deemed to have acted irresponsibly) can retain personal assets up to £20,000 and regain eligibility to act as a director in one, rather than three, years;

- has been convicted of WRONGFUL or FRAUDULENT TRADING under the insolvency Act 1986;

- is sectioned under the Mental Health legislation. He should be removed from the board whilst sectioned. The model Articles accompanying CA06, state that a director can be removed if a registered medical practitioner gives a written opinion that the director has become physically or mentally incapable of acting as a director and the condition is likely to last for at least three months. However, The Mental Health (Discrimination) Act section3 changes those Articles by removing the provisions regarding termination of a director's appointment because a Court Order has been issued (so that a director, if and when recovered, would be able to resume his duties);

- has been disqualified under CDDA86; or

- has been responsible for the persistent late filing of documents at CH, or because his conduct makes him unfit to act and the Court has made a disqualification order.

Disqualification means that he cannot act as a director of *any* UK company during the disqualification period. Following a disqualification order, CH sends termination form(s) to every company of which he is a director, requesting he resigns his directorship(s). If the director does not act, CH may seek the assistance of the other directors of those companies to effect his removal.

Case studies: Mismanagement = disqualification

In *Secretary of State for DBIS v Aaron & ors* directors of an investment services company were disqualified for miss-selling SCARPS (Structured Capital at Risk Products). They were in breach of the FSA Code of Business Principles and Rules in not bringing the high level of risk to the attention of potential customers. As well as being liable for mismanaging a company, directors can be disqualified if they are not sufficiently concerned with regulatory requirements i.e. 'conduct as a director makes [him] unfit to be concerned with the management of a company' (CDDA86s6).

A number of directors of *Surety Guarantee Consultants* were involved in and found guilty of a fraud, but one, Williams (W) claiming ignorance, was not found guilty. Subsequently it was disclosed that W did know of the fraud and did nothing to stop it. He was fined £25,000.

Forcible removal – internal

A director can be removed by his company taking the initiative and forcing the issue. However, the forced removal of a director can result in publicity which the company may wish to avoid, so it is more common for there to be a negotiated settlement contingent on the director tendering his resignation. If not, the process of compulsive removal must be followed.

CHECKLIST: Compulsory removal of a director

Check:

✓ The Articles for the board's powers of removal with or without recourse to the shareholders.

✓ The director's attendance record. Under regulation 81 CA85 Table A, a director can be removed if he is absent without permission of the rest of the board for six months from board meetings held in that period, and the directors so resolve.

✓ The provisions of the director's service contract (see below and DIRECTORS – EMPLOYMENT STATUS)

✓ If the director is due to retire by rotation at a forthcoming AGM, voting against his re-election may be arranged. In this case the director would probably have a right of action for breach of contract, whilst the legality of such a move needs to be checked.

CA06 rules

If none of the above are available, removal can be effected under the following legal provisions:

- Notice is given to the director of the intention to remove him at a general meeting at least 7 days before the date on which notice of the meeting must be despatched.

- The director may within those 7 days lodge with the company any representations against his removal.

- Called *special notice*, the reasons for the intention to remove and any director's representations against must be given to all shareholders entitled to attend with the notice of the general meeting.

- At the meeting, the director must be allowed to put any representations to the meeting (even if he is not a shareholder) before any vote is taken.

- Although it needs special notice, the resolution to remove is an ordinary resolution, requiring only a simple majority of the votes cast in person or by proxy at the meeting.

- Removing a director in this way does not necessarily prejudice any subsequent action for breach of contract.

Notes:

1 . There must be a members meeting to consider removal – it cannot be processed using a written resolution.

2. Only the company law procedure for removal is available to a *right to manage* guarantee company.

3 . On a director ceasing to hold office, CH must be advised on form TM01 within 14 days, and entries must be made in the Register of Directors.

4. The company can retain to itself a power of attorney in directors' service contracts, with the sole purpose of enabling it to *resign* the directorship in the event of a disagreement. The legality of such a power should be checked and the Articles' requirements reviewed.

Such a device – even though it may be quite legitimate – would not prejudice any action the director may have for breach of contract.

Forcible removal – external

For a number of breaches, directors can be disqualified under CDDA86. There are around 4,500 disqualification actions each year. The maximum disqualification period is 15 years, although those operating under financial services legislation can be banned for life by the FCA. Currently, however, the latter can only be banned from operating in the financial services sector and unless also banned under CDDA86 could continue to act as director of a non-financial services company.

Case study: FCA has sharp teeth

Jonathan Burrows was a city-based fund manager earning around £1 million p.a. He was caught defrauding a train company of around £43,000 over a number of years by 'fare dodging' on his journey from the south coast to London. The FCA barred him from working in the City of London 'for life' because of his 'lack of honesty and integrity'.

It is more than ironic that by comparison most of the directors responsible for multi-billion pound financial service company failures (had they not been bailed out by taxpayers' money) many of whose actions breached basic company law, seem to have walked away without injury or penalty. At least Burrows repaid the money he stole.

Directors: types

Executive

All directors are either executive or non-executive although there is no legal distinction between them – or their liability. An executive director is authorised to carry out day-to-day functions including entering into contracts, managing employees and assets and generally executing the decisions of the board made collectively by its members. An executive director may be an employee as well as an officer and, if so, the paperwork concerning their appointment should reflect this (DIRECTORS – EMPLOYMENT STATUS). Although an executive director usually has specific managerial duties (e.g. a sales director heading up the selling side of the business); when acting as a director, all departmental issues and priorities should be sublimated to the interests of the company as a whole.

Executive directors must have an intimate knowledge of the organisation and its employees and their capabilities when pressing for initiatives and exercising judgement on strategy and tactics. Companies do not stand still – they either expand or shrink. If a company is to prosper, the development of tomorrow's products and services may be almost as important as the delivery of the current products and services. Whilst successes are obviously to be sought and welcomed, analysis of failures can be important as a guide to avoid repeating mistakes.

Promotion to the board (i.e. from internal management) may be viewed as a reward but is also a challenge to help the company prosper and to drive it forward as part of the top team. The FRC's *'Guidance to Board Effectiveness'* states 'an effective board should not necessarily be a comfortable place'. Company law expects directors to take risks to drive the company forward, but equally an expectation of executive directors is to ensure that risks are identified and there is action and planning to ensure rapid and positive recovery response should risk occur.

Non-executive

Most company boards consist predominantly – for LTDs very often exclusively – of persons working full-time in the company, i.e. executive directors. Since it may be difficult for them to retain objectivity and a long term view of the challenges facing the company, it has become increasingly common to appoint directors without executive responsibilities. Drawn from senior management (and often retired former directors) from the same or different industries as the company, their purpose is to provide executive directors with advice drawn from such experience. Since they do not depend for their living on their work for the company as do most executive directors, the theory is that such non-executive directors should be far more objective (being a *critical friend*) regarding the progress (or lack of progress) of the company, and, in essence, requiring answers to questions the executive directors may least want asked. It may also be easier for non-executive directors to question the appropriateness of certain actions – thus in the Guinness illegal share-price support scandal of the early 1980s, the *wrongdoing* of certain of the executive directors, was eventually challenged by the non-executives. Should the actions complained of continue, the theory is that the non-execs. should find it easier to resign in protest, with possible attendant publicity (the *noisy exit*).

However, non-executives have exactly the same responsibilities – and potential liabilities – as their executive colleagues. Both the Institute of Directors and the Stock Exchange are in favour of the extension of the non-executive director concept, whilst draft proposals from the EU would require a majority of non-executive directors on the boards of listed PLCs. The Non-Executive Directors Association (NEDA) promotes the concept.

Despite such pressure, any marked extension of the numbers of non-executive directors seems unlikely in the light of recent cases where regulatory authorities have attempted to make non-executive directors liable for actions or inactions of the board equally with the liability of the executive directors. Thus the non-executive directors of Equitable Life (who were each being paid on average less than £20,000 p.a.) were collectively to be sued for £3.2 billion since it was alleged they failed to exercise due care when the company granted too-generous guarantees to policy holders. Ultimately the action was dropped, but the possibility of such actions epitomises the potential liability of the non-executive. Few may be willing to risk unlimited personal liability for such relatively low rewards – particularly as a (usually part-time) non-exec. is likely to know far less of the detail of what is going on in the company than their (full time) executive colleagues – and wrong-doing initiated by or with the connivance of the executive directors can easily be concealed. Conversely to meet the required increased numbers of female directors many such appointments are non-executive. A survey by the Audit Committee Institute disclosed that:

a) Only one company (out of more than 700 in the FTSE All-share index) did not have a non-executive director; and

b) Six had fewer than three non-executives.

Case study: Executive and non-executive directors' identical liabilities

The imminent collapse of Queens Moat Houses PLC was avoided by the creditor banks providing ongoing financial support to avoid its liquidation mainly since had it failed, the massive bad debts would have affected the banks' own balance sheets. All board members (which included three qualified accountants) were disqualified as directors for a variety of periods – ten, eight and seven years – whilst the former deputy chairman, Martin Marcus was also fined £250,000. Finally the non-executive chairman, John Bairstow, who founded the company and originally built it into a major hotel chain, was disqualified for 6 years.

The judge stated 'had Mr Bairstow performed his duty as director and chairman of QMH properly, he would have been aware from the information available to him that the profit figures given to the banks were seriously unrealistic'.

John Bairstow commented 'It seems that all directors, including non-executives, are deemed liable for any accounts whether they had any involvement or not.'

Exactly so – knowledge expected of the chairman of a listed PLC!

Company law (which expects directors to take risk) conflicts with charity law (which restricts risk-taking). Further, in charitable companies, unpaid and non-executive trustees often form the entire board. Since someone must execute the decisions of the board, this would seem to pose a dilemma. Even if the person ultimately executing the board's decisions is not recognised as a director, they may be so regarded under company law (in any event they are almost certainly an officer). Very often of course it is a General Manager or Chief Executive of the charity who acts in this way and in fact recommends actions to the (non-executive) board who, following his recommendations, so resolve. This can put such persons in a position of power vis-à-vis the non-executive board. The advice given to the Association of Chief Executives of Voluntary Organisations was that if a person acted in this way he was almost certainly a *de facto* or shadow director. Such charities could consider reconstituting themselves as Charitable Incorporated Organisations. The FRC's *Guidance on Board Effectiveness* urges non-executive directors to 'devote time to developing and refreshing their knowledge and skills… to ensure they make a positive contribution to the board'.

As this book went to press, it was announced that action to disqualify the nine former directors and trustees of the failed charity Kids Company is to commence. In addition the colourful founder and chief executive Camila Batmanghelidjh may face similar action if she is classified as a *de facto* director. It has also been mooted that, since the charity became insolvent, action could also be taken against the directors for personal financial liability.

Chairman

Boards are usually more effective if there is a person who is 'first among equals' and thus Articles usually require board members to elect one of their number to be chairman. Although often described as such in the media, the chairman is not *company* chairman but chairman of the *board,* and indeed, depending on the wording of the ARTICLES, may be appointed only *for the time being.* Further, the chairman of the board is not necessarily the person that takes the chair at members' meetings. It would be embarrassing if the board chairman tries to take the chair at a members' meeting only to be required to vacate because a member, referring to the Articles, points out that they state that the members present may elect one of their number as chairman and there has been no such election! Actually in such a situation it might be preferable to change the Articles, since the chairman of the board is the logical person to chair general meetings – an elected non-director shareholder is hardly likely to know sufficient detail of the day to day operation of the company to be an effective chairman.

Whether the chairman has a second or casting vote needs to be determined. In the CA06 pro forma Articles for an LTD, it is stipulated that before any person is given a casting vote all the directors must approve the suggestion – i.e. it should be decided at the first board meeting.

Managing director

In many organisations the functions of chairman and managing director are combined and vested in one person. In the past there has been criticism of listed PLCs where these appointments were held by a single person, critics inferring that the concentration of power in one person was detrimental to the overall control of the company. However, since research suggested that the financial results of companies where the two roles were performed by one person were generally better than companies where the functions were split opposition to the dual relationship has been dropped! Where there is a separate managing director function, it may be more usual for the chairman to be non-executive and to interface with external parties, leaving the managing director to ensure other board members and management who report to him carry out the requirements of the board and their own responsibilities – i.e. essentially an internal role. However, it is difficult to be precise about this since companies operate in different ways and the range or scope of the individual duties of such appointees may ultimately depend on their personalities.

Legally the managing director may be in a different position to other directors and his powers, responsibilities and the provisions of any re-election applicable to him need to be checked. In some LTDs a proportion (often a third) of the directors are required to retire *by rotation* at each AGM and, if eligible and they wish, seek re-election at that meeting. A managing director, however, is often excluded from this requirement – indeed under regulation 84 of Table A CA85 only non-executive directors are required to retire by rotation. Where the chairman is non-executive, the MD is the senior director or chief executive officer (CEO) and is usually responsible for developing strategy for approval by the board, communicating it down the chain of command, ensuring it is followed and delivered so he can report on progress to the board. One of his most important duties is overseeing the financial state of the company and ensuring the delivery of information regarding this to the board. At all times directors must know that the credit the company is taking on will be paid on the due date or within a reasonable time thereof.

Alternate

Only if the company's Articles permit, a director can appoint an alternate to act in his place. An alternate director acts as a full representative for the appointee and, as a director, has the right to receive all data and information sent to other directors. Because board work is as much about the *chemistry* of the members working together, usually the Articles stipulate that any such appointment can only be made subject to the approval of the board. All the requirements applying to the directors apply to the alternate.

Historically there have been relatively few alternate directors but this situation could change quite dramatically as a result of the extension of maternity leave and the pressure on boards generally (and PLCs in particular) to increase female representation on boards. If during a director's (potential) year long maternity leave, she is not present in the workplace and does not attend board meetings etc., she could be said to be failing to comply with her director's *duty of care* under company law. It is hardly constructive (although possibly safer) for her to resign, and preferable for her to be able to appoint an alternate to act on her behalf during such leave. If the Articles do not allow for the appointment of an alternate director, they would first need to be altered. The Articles should also be checked to ensure the appointment (which must be treated in the same way as any new APPOINTMENT to the board) does not breach any *'maximum number'* of directors. Alternatively there could be a provision in the contract whereby the director could temporarily resign her directorship for the period of the maternity leave, and be re-appointed on return.

Associate, local, regional, divisional, etc.

It is quite common for companies to allow – even encourage – senior employees (not appointed to the board and not registered at CH) to use job titles which incorporate the word 'director'. The use of such a title indicates that the company is granting to the person a high level of authority – commensurate to that of a director. Although executives using such titles are not legal directors, if they use the title in such a way as to suggest that they are, they could be deemed to have *'held (themselves) out to third parties that they are a director'* (i.e. someone in control of the company) and be judged accordingly. In any event, almost certainly persons using such titles would be regarded as officers of the company – and potentially liable as such – even though they may have had no say in decisions impacting such responsibilities – or knowledge of the company's liquidity. Conversely the company will almost certainly be bound by actions they take 'as a director'.

Courtesy titles

There are many executives, again not legally appointed, who use titles such as *'Director of [xxxx].'* to indicate their perceived (or actual) level of authority. Such titles can be given to a person who is not a board member and in a number of cases have been given to those who are not even employees – thus in the Guinness case, the company's Finance Director was an independent consultant. In the event of company failure an insolvency practitioner could argue that such people *'held themselves out to be directors'* and thus those using such titles could also be sought to be held liable as a director. Conversely, since most third parties would be excused for taking such titles at face value and assuming the person using the title has the authority to bind the company, this could prevent the company distancing itself from any commitment entered into by the 'director'.

Case study: Described as a 'director', hence a director

In *SMC Electronic Ltd v Akhter Computers Ltd* an employee was allowed to use the title 'Director of Power Supplies Unit Sales' and signed a contract in such a capacity on behalf of his company. The Court held that the company could not repudiate the contract as it was reasonable for the other party to assume in dealing with a person using such a title legitimately, that they were dealing with someone with power to bind his company.

De facto

At the opposite end of the spectrum to non-directors calling themselves directors, are those who, in reality, are directing the activities of a company but do not so describe themselves and have no wish to advertise the reality of the situation to the outside world; indeed they often wish to conceal their input altogether (sheltering behind *front men* appointees). However if the fact of the matter (from the Latin *de facto*) is that they are directing the company's operations, they may be regarded as directors.

Case studies: *De facto* directors

In *HMRC v McEntaggart (M)*, since M had been disqualified and could not act legally as a director, he repeatedly gave instructions to his wife who 'acted on his instructions' meaning that under CDDA86s15 she was liable and had to pay £73,000 to HMRC.

HMRC also successfully claimed £154,000 from M since – although disqualified – he was found to be a *de facto* director. (A director acting whilst disqualified has unlimited personal liability for his actions in relation to the company.)

In *Secretary of State for Trade & Industry v Holler*, the company had become insolvent and the husband/father had been disqualified. However his wife and elder son acted as if they were directors, taking decisions and requiring actions as directors. They were found to be *de facto* directors and both were disqualified. A second son was found not to have been part of the company's corporate governance and therefore not a *de facto* director.

The judge offered the following guidance to help determine whether a person was a *de facto* director:

- Was the person part of the corporate governing structure (if so he was probably a *de facto* director).

- A distinction must be made between someone who participates in collective decision making at board level (who would be a director) and someone acting purely in management (who would not be).

- The decision is to be determined objectively on the basis of all relevant facts.

- A person may be a *de facto* director even though there is no day-to-day control of the company's affairs and/or he is involved in only part of its activities.

- Factors such a family relationship may be relevant.

Conversely in *Holland v The Commissioners for HMRC and anor* it was held that a sole director of a holding company which was itself the (then permitted) sole corporate director of a number of subsidiary companies was not a *de facto* director of the subsidiary companies. It was said that to become a *de facto* director the individual himself (not a corporate director which is a separate legal person) needs to have done something in relation to the affairs of the relevant company.

Nominee

Major shareholders who wish to exercise some control over the board and/or shareholders of (for example but not exclusively) joint venture companies often appoint their own nominee(s) to a board. Directors nominated in this way owe obligations to two separate bodies (the company itself and their principal) and need to take care to avoid a conflict of interests. Their fiduciary duty requires them to put first and foremost the interests of the company of which they are a director and to act independently. If they allow the person who appointed them to dictate their actions and those of the board, that person could be a shadow director.

A nominee director may have enhanced voting rights (e.g. a vote exercised by a nominee may rank greater than the combined votes of all other members). This could mean the relationship would need to be disclosed in the SIGNIFICANT CONTROL register and notified to CH. Of course if the principal exercised control over the nominee, the principal could be deemed a shadow director.

Shadow

CA06s251 defines a shadow director as '*a person in accordance with whose directions or instructions the directors of the company are accustomed to act*' – that is someone not a director but who is effectively controlling board decisions. The need to define and control such individuals reflects a continuing concern at a tendency of some major shareholders, creditors or others (e.g. customers) controlling and directing the company (without any liability) whilst sheltering behind the appointed board (who could be liable). Without requiring such shadow directors to be recognised, the impact of the Insolvency Act 1986 (i.e. making directors personally liable to contribute to any shortfall due to the creditors in the event of their WRONGFUL or fraudulent trading), would be negated.

The definition of a *shadow* can cover a number of relationships – but there are exceptions. Thus, if a major creditor, instructed (or *suggested*) that the board should carry out a certain act on a one-off basis and the board did so, that person would probably not be a shadow director – as *accustomed to act* implies a regular, or at least repeated, relationship. But if such control was ongoing (i.e. such *suggestions* were made repeatedly, and the board usually complied) a shadow directorship would probably exist. Similarly if a major customer regularly required the board to act in a certain way and it often did so, the customer could be judged a shadow director. A company doctor – a person brought in to try to assist the company's survival – would almost certainly be a shadow director (if not properly appointed to the board) simply because of the control they would need to exercise – the Court of Appeal's decision in the case of *Tasbian Limited* where a company doctor negotiated with creditors, countersigned all the cheques and set up a new corporate organisation.

CA06S251(2) excludes from being a shadow, those who act in a professional capacity – auditors, solicitors, bank managers, even if the board regularly complied with such advice.

In *Deverall* the Court of Appeal stated that the words *'directions or instructions'* needed to be interpreted objectively and could include both words and conduct. There was no need to show that there was an expectation that the comment would be complied with. Neither was it necessary to show that the board was subservient to the shadow. Courts will therefore seek to determine whether a person was a shadow director or not, by establishing the extent of their control or influence. The Court said that they would 'look behind the paperwork' at the reality of the situation. Presumably this would mean that repeatedly framing board minutes as 'X suggested and the board decided' would not necessarily prevent X being classified as a *shadow*.

Case studies:

Liable and penalised

In *Re Mea Corporation, Sec. of State for Trade & Industry v Aviss and anor,* A was director and sole shareholder of a parent company with two subsidiaries. B, who had been disqualified, was not a director of any of the companies but, with A, required all monies received by the three companies to be placed in a central fund.

On B's instructions, large amounts were paid from this fund to companies outside the group in which A had a substantial interest, despite the protests of the directors of the subsidiaries (which protests might help protect their positions – since acting in accordance with the instructions of a shadow director is itself an offence).

A was held to be a shadow director of the subsidiaries and B to be a shadow director of all three companies. Both had failed to respect the 'separate legal identities' of the three companies. A was disqualified for seven years and B for 11 years.

De facto or shadow?

The difference between the two can be blurred but essentially both can apply to someone who is exercising control over those who are properly appointed. In *Re UKLI; DBIS v Chohan(C) & ors,* C had formerly been a director of UKLI, resigned but continued to act as if he were a director telling those who were directors what to do. This led to the collapse of the company owing £48 million to its creditors. C was found to be a both a de facto and shadow director at various times and was disqualified for 12 years.

If a company becomes insolvent, the insolvency practitioner(s) appointed will seize as many assets as possible to try to satisfy the creditors. If it is felt that the directors have been guilty of WRONGFUL trading there is a possibility that their personal assets could also be seized. The existence of *de facto* or *shadow* directors would obviously be of interest to the insolvency practitioner since if such person(s) can be proved to have been giving the board instructions or requests, they could be held financially liable in the same way as the legal directors.

Full personal details of a shadow should be entered in the Register of Directors and filed at CH (which would regularise the position) and any contract between the company and the shadow must be made available for inspection and the location notified to CH. If it is not possible to legitimise the directorship, for example, because the director refuses to sign his 'consent to act', or the board refuses to act, those officers aware of the situation should consider their own positions since they too have obligations – and personal liability – particularly if they act in accordance with the wishes of the shadow. It might be safest to bring the matter to the attention of the auditors. Since an audit certificate is required to cover the Report of the Directors which must state the names of all directors during the period) the auditors should refuse to sign, thus putting the company in breach of its filing obligations. Alternatively the situation could be reported to a regulatory authority.

The person in breach is liable for both an initial and a daily fine (which continues until the breach is remedied). If a Secretary (or anyone else) has tried unsuccessfully to legitimise the matter internally first and then reports it externally, should a sanction be applied against him, his personal position might be protected by the Public Interest Disclosure Act (the 'whistleblowing' Act). He could claim unfair dismissal for whistleblowing – in respect of which there is no limit on compensation.

If the board of a subsidiary company is accustomed to act in accordance with the advice or instructions of employees (e.g. directors or senior management) of the parent company there is a possibility that the latter could be shadow directors of the subsidiary. It may be preferable to make the parent company itself a director of the subsidiaries (although of course there must still be at least one natural person on the board). Any personal liability, in the event of failure of the subsidiary, that could otherwise have attached to such senior staff by reason of them acting, however unwillingly, as shadow directors, might then be borne by the parent company. Of course, this negates part of the usual reason for setting up a subsidiary in the first place. Under current law there is nothing to stop a holding company allowing a subsidiary to go into insolvent liquidation whilst the parent has no obligations to the subsidiary's creditors – unless it has guaranteed the subsidiary's debts or had exercised direct management of the subsidiary (see VEIL OF INCORPORATION).

By the very nature of the control being exercised by a shadow director, their details should be entered in the register of persons of SIGNIFICANT CONTROL and advised to CH which adds even more pressure for the relationship to be regularised.

Sole

1992 Regulations allowed companies to be set up with just one owner – a single member company. LTDs can have one director. Thus it is legal for an LTD to have the same real person as sole shareholder (or guarantor) and sole director. However if the sole director is killed or is no longer able to act, so too is the owner and there is no-one able to appoint someone to replace the director. The company will be unable to continue to trade until the ownership of the share(s) is determined – a process which could take several weeks or months during which time the company could fail.

This is to a limited extent overcome by provisions in the CA06 pro forma Articles which allow for the personal representatives of the deceased shareholder or guarantor to appoint a new director (presumably without awaiting grant of Probate or Letters of Administration). Secretaries required to deal with such *personal representatives* would need to check their right to act and might require those representatives to sign an undertaking to 'hold the company harmless' for any liability incurred as a result of the company acting in accordance with their instructions.

The situation becomes even more difficult if

a) there is no Secretary – and potentially no officer who can act

b) the company is a guarantee company with a single guarantor who is also the sole director. When a sole shareholder dies at least the shares still exist and the question is one of ownership. When a guarantor dies the guarantee dies with him and the company would have no members.

Although some world-wide jurisdictions allow a *reserve* director (for use in the above situation) to be appointed, this is not permissible under UK law. Legal advice would be needed re the possibility of a sole shareholder/director being able to appoint a successor *in the event of my death (or other incapacity)*.

Silent or sleeping

Directors have a duty of care from which they cannot be absolved. If a person accepts the appointment of director they accept liability for the actions of the company. If they fail to attend board meetings or to find out on an ongoing basis what is going on in their company they still have liability. A director cannot delegate his responsibility for operating the company. Ignorance of what is going on is no excuse.

Case study: Sleepwalking into liability

On the board of *Lexi Holdings Plc (in administration) v Luqman & ors* were two active directors (brothers L and W) and two *'sleeping'* directors (their sisters Z and M). With W's knowledge, L stole around £60,000 from the company. Judgement was originally obtained against both L and W for the amount stolen, but not against Z and M (even though it was clear they had breached their fiduciary and common law duties to the company). However, the Court of Appeal (since Z and M knew of L's previous convictions, and of the creation of a fictitious directors' loan account, and of loans made in contravention of the Companies Act) held that Z and M were in breach of their duty of care. As directors they had an obligation to seek advice about such matters and to inform the auditors – they could not simply *do nothing*. Z was fined just under £42,000 and M just under £37,000.

This judgement referred to the case of *Re Westmid Packing Services Ltd (No 2)* which set out the principle that any director who allows himself to be 'dominated or bamboozled by [another director]' breaches his own duty as a director. Each director must be prepared to be independent – and each has a duty of care.

Dividends

KEY POINTS

- A shareholder's investment can be rewarded by capital growth and/or by dividends.

- Dividends can only be paid out of profits.

- Final dividends can only be authorised by the shareholders.

Taxation

Corporation tax is a complex subject and the advice of the company's auditors/tax advisers should be sought when considering the payment of a dividend so that the effects of the payment and corporation tax on the financial results are fully appreciated. Dividends are received by shareholders as a net amount and, until 5th April 2016 were *accompanied* by a tax credit – 10% of the grossed up dividend which a shareholder could use to offset part of their personal tax liability. However, dividends are now simply paid net and the taxation is a matter for individual shareholders who are allowed (at present) to receive £5,000 worth of dividend income without a tax liability. Where dividends in excess of £5,000 are received within a tax year, a shareholder will pay tax at 7.5% within the 20% band, 32.5% within the 40% band and 38% within the 45% band.

Thus in paying a dividend on 800 shares in Bloggs Products Ltd at a rate of 5.6p a share, a net payment of £44.80 is due to a shareholder. The shareholder would receive a dividend voucher showing this amount as the net payment.

Ability to pay

Companies can only pay dividends from earnings – not out of capital. However, should a current period's profits be insufficient to pay the amount recommended, any previously undistributed profits (that is the balance of revenue reserves arising from the accumulation of profits from previous years) can be used in part or whole for this purpose. Listed PLCs cannot pay a dividend unless the net assets (as defined) of the company exceed the aggregate amount of their paid up share capital and undistributable reserves by at least the amount of the proposed dividend (in other words after the payment of the dividend there would still be a net asset surplus).

Striking date

An effective date for payment of the dividend must be set, together with a date from which members will be entitled to it – the dividend striking date. Shares in listed PLCs can be bought and sold at any time but only members on the register as at the striking date are entitled to the dividend. Whether, when share ownership changes around the time of the striking date, the previous holder or purchaser of shares is entitled to the dividend is a matter for them, not the company, to determine. Shares are quoted *ex. div.* (or without the dividend) in the market once the striking date has passed. Since the previous owner may still be sent the dividend, they may need to account for it to the new member. If the share is quoted *cum div* it means that if it is sold the purchaser will get the benefit of the dividend. Whether a share is quoted *ex* or *cum div.* obviously affects its price.

Voucher

In paying a dividend, the company has to prepare a dividend voucher and a cheque or note of an account credit, such as the following:

Dividend No 4 Bloggs Products Ltd 3rd July 2XXX

The attached cheque is in payment of the FINAL DIVIDEND for the financial year ended 31st March 2XXX at the rate of 5.6p per share on the 800 Ordinary shares of £1 registered in your name on 15th June 2XXX and payable on 3rd July 2XXX.

J Bloggs, Company Secretary _____

Name and address of shareholder _____

Reference	Holding	Net dividend
oyup12/g	800	£44.80

This voucher should be preserved safely. It will be accepted by HM Revenue & Customs as evidence of a dividend payment.

(Dividend cheque)

Bloggs Products Ltd   3rd July 2XXX

(Valid 12 months)

Ordinary shares dividend warrant

PAY A. Shareholder £44.80 Account payee only

For and on behalf of Bloggs Products Ltd

(Autographical signature)

Dividend payment No. 4. Signed: J Bloggs

Notes:

1. The form of the dividend cheque should comply with the latest requirements of the Association for Payment Clearing Services

2. The cheque is stated to be valid for 12 months as many shareholders fail to present dividend cheques for a considerable time. Although cheques are usually said to be stale after 6 months, discretion remains with a bank whether to accept or refuse a cheque which is older than 6 months unless it is stated to have a longer life.

3. Companies prefer dividends to be paid by bank transfer direct to the accounts of their shareholders (i.e. via BACS) which is less expensive than sending the dividend and tax voucher to the shareholder's address.

Share accumulations

To encourage the extension of private investor shareholdings, some listed PLCs offer their shareholders the option of taking new shares in place of their dividends or allowing the shareholder to invest the dividend in additional shares (a process which the company carries out on the shareholder's behalf). Under this concept the value of the existing shares in the market on the dividend striking date is used as the price of the new shares. This value is then applied to the dividend generating a number of new shares that can be purchased using it. Members can simply nominate to receive up to that number of shares in place of part or the whole of the dividend with any unused dividend being carried forward to the next dividend payment and added to the amount then available for the same purpose. Although they pay the market price for the shares, shareholders avoid paying stamp duty, which would normally be part of the acquisition cost. Whilst this an effective way of building a greater stake in the company, with two dividend payments each year, shareholders gradually accumulate a large number of share certificates. Most companies allow shareholders to amalgamate their share certificates by sending in the various certificates for exchange for one. This is usually a free service although some Registrars do charge.

Communication

Sending dividends to members provides an opportunity for company/ shareholder communication. Details of discounts available on company products or services can be included, as can vouchers redeemable in the outlets of the company, notification of changes of address and even requests to be placed on the company's internal mailing list. These links may aid shareholder loyalty, which could be valuable should there be a hostile takeover bid.

Timing

The London Stock Exchange (LSE) sends listed PLCs a Dividend Procedure Timetable each year. If it follows the LSE's dividend timetable, a company does not have to notify the LSE in advance provided the Secretary advises the amount of the dividend, the striking and payment dates (which should not be more than 30 days apart) and a note of whether there is any share:dividend exchange.

Refusal to pay dividends

Should a company be profitable and yet dividends are not being paid (without good reason – e.g. to accumulate funds for expansion or capital investment), other than an action to remove the directors, the only recourse of a shareholder would be to the Court since this might be classed as abuse of a minority particularly if the directors are paying themselves what might be deemed excessive salaries/bonuses.

Special dividends

Occasionally perhaps because of a specially good trading period generating unexpected profits, or the sale of an asset realising an above expectations price, a company may wish to pass the benefits on to its shareholders by paying a special dividend. The same rules as set out above regarding payment and taxation apply. For this reason the company may opt instead to issue paid up shares instead of a dividend – advice should be taken. The perceived wisdom is that recognising the shareholder's interest in this way may encourage them to be loyal to the existing directorate should there be a hostile take-over bid. Whilst this may be the case, should the bid be particularly favourable, the board may find that such loyalty may not actually count for much.

Obviously a generous dividend policy should affect the value of the shares. Companies can also force an increase in such a value by purchasing their own shares on a buy back process.

Waiving a dividend

A shareholder can waive receipt of a dividend payable to the other share-holders. This should be effected by a *deed of dividend waiver* which the shareholder must enter into on an entirely voluntary basis. It would be best to take legal advice and for the deed to address what the company is allowed to do with the waived dividend.

'Out of touch' shareholders

Losing touch with shareholders is a recurrent problem particularly for listed PLCs. There are two aspects to be addressed:

a) **Dividends**. Obviously if dividends are paid other than by BACS transfer, any dividend cheques will not be presented. Such payments should be held by the company to the order of the shareholder. However all dividends that are more than 12 years old revert to the company and the shareholder (should they re-emerge) will have lost their value.

b) **Acquisition**. A similar difficulty of communication occurs should an offer be made for the shares. However after a set period of non-response a successful offeror can compulsorily acquire the shares of any missing shareholder with the proceeds held on trust should he emerge. After 12 years the proceeds must be paid into Court pending any later claim should the shareholder re-emerge.

Financial year end

KEY POINTS

- A company must choose the date to which its accounts will be made up (i.e. its financial year end or accounting reference date ARD) and notify CH.

- Failure to notify CH means the company's first ARD will be the last day of the month of the anniversary of its incorporation.

- There are restrictions on changing an ARD.

Significance

After the initial accounts filing, LTDs are required to file their accounts with CH by the end of the ninth (for PLCs, sixth) month after their ARD. End of the month now means the last day of the calendar month six or nine months later, although since listed PLCs must publish their accounts on their websites within four months of their year end they may as well file them with CH on that date. Companies filing their accounts late are subject to fine. Since the preparation and auditing of the accounts can be an onerous task, due regard should be given to selecting an ARD which is convenient for this work, and is also appropriate for the business. A date just after the end of the busiest (and/or most profitable) period may be applicable (e.g. in retailing with a preponderance of pre-Christmas/New Year sales, opting for 31 January might be appropriate), although a great many companies use 31 March thus making their financial years coterminous with the tax and fiscal years.

Change

Between the ARD and the end of the filing period (that is before the end of the ninth (sixth for PLCs) month in respect of those accounts, a company can change its ARD (provided this would not mean an accounting period longer than 18 months). The accounting period can usually be lengthened only once in five years, although the period can be shortened without limitation. Also an accounting period that has been lengthened could subsequently be shortened.

Notification

Once the ARD has been notified, any subsequent change in the date requires form AA01 (CA06s392) to be filed. For CA06 companies, their first accounting reference period must last not less than six but not more than 18 months from the date of incorporation and the accounts must be filed no later than 21 months after incorporation (i.e. no later than 9 months after the anniversary of the company's incorporation).

Forms

KEY POINTS

- Forms to enable filing at CH are available.

- The forms use initial letters derived from the title of the subject matter.

- Although most forms are now filed electronically, for the time being they can be filed in hard copy.

- Electronic filing is available at CH on a 24 hour a day, 7 days a week basis.

The following is a guide to the most used forms which can be downloaded from CH website and/or filed online. There is a process of continually updating forms.

Incorporation and updating

- Application to register a company IN01

- Change of registered office AD01

- Notification of Single Alternative Inspection Location (SAIL) AD02

- Application to change a disputed registered office RP07

- Confirmation Statement CS01

- Election to keep statutory information at CH (that is not to hold the company's statutory records at the registered office or SAIL) EH04

Name

- Exemption of use of *limited* from name NE01
- Change of name by resolution NM01
- Change of name by conditional resolution NM02
- Notification confirming satisfaction of conditional resolution NM03
- Change of name by authority in Articles NM04
- Change of name by directors resolution NM05 (where required by Secretary of State or on company being restored to the register)
- Seeking comments from bodies on change of name NM06

Shares

- Return of allotment of shares SH01
- Notice of consolidation, sub-division, etc. of shares SH02
- Return of purchase of own shares SH03
- Notice of sale or transfer to treasury of shares SH04
- Notice of cancellation of treasury shares SH05
- Notice of cancellation of shares SH06
- Notice of cancellation of shares held by or for a PLC SH07
- Notice of name or other designation of class of shares SH08
- Return of allotment of new class of share by unlimited company SH09
- Notice of particulars of variation of share rights SH10
- Notice of new class of members SH11
- Notice of particulars of variation of class rights SH12
- Notice of name or other designation of class of members SH13
- Notice of redenomination SH14
- Notice of reduction of capital following redenomination SH15
- Notice by court applicants for cancellation of resolution re redemption or purchase of shares out of capital SH16

- Notice by company for cancellation of resolution re redemption or purchase of shares out of capital SH17
- Statement of capital SH19
- Application for trading certificate for PLC SH50

Directors
- Appointment AP01
- Appointment of corporate director AP02
- Change of details CH01
- Change of corporate directors details CH02
- Termination of appointment TM01
- Removal of data of a person not consenting to act as a director RP06

Secretary
- Appointment AP03
- Appointment of corporate secretary AP04
- Change of details CH03
- Change of corporate secretary's details CH04
- Termination of appointment TM02

Persons of Significant Control (PSC) registers
- Notice of registrable individual PSC01
- Notice of registrable relevant legal entity (RLE) PSC02
- Notice of other registrable person PSC03
- Change of particulars of a PSC PSC04
- Change of particulars of a RLE PSC05
- Change of particulars of other registrable person PSC06
- Notice of ceasing to be a PSC PSC07
- Notification of additional matters PSC08
- End date of notification of additional matters PSC09

Manager appointed re Companies (Audit, Investigations & Community Enterprise) Act 2004

- Appointment of manager AP05

- Change of service address of manager CH05

- Termination of appointment TM03

Filing

- Consent form for paper filing of PROOF filing PR03

Accounting

- Accounting reference date – change AA01

- Dormant company accounts AA02

Mortgage/charge

- Particulars of charge MR01

- Charge subject to an undertaking MR02

- Satisfaction of a charge MR04

- Statement that property subject to a charge has been disposed of MR05

Striking off

- Application to strike off DS01

Oversea company (OC)

- OC establishing a place of business in UK BR1

Corrections (see REGISTRAR)

- Original filing failed to meet requirements – corrected form plus RP01

- Fraudulent filing correction RP02A or B

- Original form incorrect RP0

In addition, to coincide with the Insolvency (England and Wales) Rules 2016, CH also revised the identifiers of its Insolvency forms so that Company Voluntary Arrangement Moratorium forms now start – VAM; Company Voluntary Arrangement forms – CVA; Administration forms – AM; Receivership forms – REC; Creditors/Members Voluntary Liquidation forms – LIQ and Court winding up forms – WU.

Charges

Charges are levied by CH for filing some items and are regularly reviewed. Although in most cases late filing could attract a fine, with some exceptions, CH do not levy fines. However where the Conformation Statement and/or Accounts are filed late these can be made subject to both filing penalties and fines; whilst should the offence be repeated fines can be doubled. The level of fines applied by CH effectively pay for much of its operation since it is not allowed to make a profit.

Note: CH constantly update the forms so the latest version should be used.

General meetings

a) AGM

Convening and content

A PLC must give 21 clear days notice (20 working days for a traded company) of its AGM to all its shareholders. An LTD must give14 clear days' notice (CA06s307) or such longer period (e.g. 21 days) that its Articles require. *Clear,* for English and Welsh companies, means the day of the meeting and the day the notice is deemed served are in addition to the required period. For companies registered in Scotland, the day of the meeting can be counted as one of the notice days.

LTD shareholders can waive the whole or part of the notice period for (E) GMs provided the holders of at least 90% (unless the ARTICLES require a higher percentage – up to 95%) of the voting rights agree. For PLCs, notice of the AGM can only be waived if there is unanimous consent of every member. Notice of (E)GMs can be waived in whole or part provided 95% of all the votes are in favour.

To avoid claims that insufficient notice has been given, it may be prudent to give in excess of the minimum notice periods. Since items sent by first class post are not deemed to be served until 48 hours later, this period should be added to the calculation of the *days notice* required. Notice is not normally validly served on a day on which there are no postal deliveries (that is weekends and Bank Holidays).

Business

At the AGM the following business must be transacted, although this is not exclusive, and, if it is timely for other matters to be considered, there is no reason why such items should not be included in the notice of the meeting and dealt with at the AGM.

- Receipt and consideration of the accounts and balance sheet and audit report.

Use of the word *approve* is best avoided. There is a widespread misconception that a company's members have the right to approve the report and accounts, but this is the *board's* duty and right. The report and accounts are presented to the AGM (words such as *receive* or *adopted* are often used). Even if the members purport to vote not to *approve* them, it has no effect – the accounts and report must still be filed with CH within the required time limit.

- Approval of any DIVIDEND on the shares. Normally the authorisation and payment of interim dividends is the prerogative of the board and needs no approval from the shareholders. However, shareholders have the right to approve, reduce or reject a final dividend recommended by the board; although there is nothing to stop the board paying an interim (or second, or more, interim) dividend(s) on their own authority, and not proposing a final dividend in respect of that period's trading at all.

- Election or re-election of directors. Some LTD company ARTICLES require a proportion of its directors (a third is customary) to retire by rotation at each AGM. The Articles may require only non-executives to retire. Those who are the longest serving must retire and, assuming they are eligible and wish to do so, can put themselves forward for re-election.

Directors appointed since the last AGM must also retire at the next following AGM and (if they wish and are eligible) can seek re-election. Retiring by rotation is on the decrease for LTD (and unlisted PLC) companies. However, under the Listing Agreement directors of FTSE350 companies are required to retire and seek re-election each year.

- Election or re-election of AUDITORS. The auditors usually hold office until the conclusion of the next following AGM.

- Agreeing the Auditors remuneration – a duty normally delegated to the directors. Companies whose turnover is less than £10.2 million are not legally required to have their accounts audited (unless they are charities or are subject to FCA requirements) although of course the owners (and the directors) may understandably wish to retain this external check.

Preparation

The AGM is usually the only occasion in the year when the company could be said to be *on show*, and where members who are not directors may attend. Hence attention needs to be given to the meeting's presentation. Preparations should be monitored by the board / Secretary on a regular basis.

CHECKLIST: Preparation for AGM

Item Responsibility

- Decide date and time   Board

- Visit venue, check facilities   Sec./board

- Book venue (6/12 months ahead) – check:
    - room and overflow facility
    - air conditioning/ventilation
    - acoustics/amplification

- accommodation including catering/toilet facilities
- notice boards/room directions
- tables for signing in

- If product/photo display required   Marketing dept:
  - display tables or electronic equipment

- Stipulate to venue management: Sec.
  - timetable for arrivals
  - serving tea/coffee
  - lunch (if required)
  - likely departure

- Delegate items to staff: As allocated
  - greeting arrivals (especially 'speakers')
  - ensuring arrivals sign in (taking attendance cards)
  - ushering to seats
  - care of registers & proxies
  - acting as teller(s) (in event of VOTING AND TAKING A POLL)
  - care of statutory books, service contracts, minute book
  - liaison with catering
  - spare copies Annual report, publicity handouts

- Arrange *'speakers'*   Sec.
  - *'tame'* members (and back up in event of absence), who will actually propose and/or second the various resolutions to avoid it looking like too much of a one-person show (i.e. the chairman's)

- Anticipate and prepare for any hostility   Chairman
  - liaise with advisers (see VOTING)
  - preparation of and answers to awkward questions

- If chairman is new to running formal meetings:
  - preparation of chairman's crib (i.e. a script to cover each part of the meeting – BRIEFING THE CHAIRMAN)   Sec.

- Promulgate timetable and checklist   Sec.
  - briefing on preparations, likely problems etc. (i.e. a meeting scenario) for board and advisers

- Liaison with: Finance director
    - auditors (have a right to attend and may wish to read their Audit Report)
    - solicitors, stockbrokers (for listed PLC) Sec.
    - public relations (and, through them, media representatives) Corporate P.R.
    - Company registrar (including printing of Sec. DIVIDEND cheques, and arrangements for granting authority to post)
- Make transport arrangements Transport mgr.
    - for directors, staff, guests, major shareholders etc.
- Arrange for:
    - display of products/tour of premises Director (either actual or electronic)
    - press release (if required, draft and agree with chairman in advance, possibly amending should this be required following the meeting). Corporate PR
    - publication of voting results on company website Sec.

Administration

Notice

The NOTICE and AGENDA of the meeting are usually included in the ANNUAL REPORT although there is no requirement for this and they could be sent separately, which some listed PLCs now do, particularly if a letter of invitation to the meeting accompanies them.

Letter of invitation

With the formal notice, a number of listed PLCs, particularly those with large numbers of private shareholders send a semi-personal *letter of invitation* to shareholders to attend the meeting, which can explain the logic and reasoning behind business proposed to be transacted at the meeting – e.g. reasons for (and detailed wording re) a change to the ARTICLES etc.

Intention and attendance cards

Some companies with large numbers of shareholders send *attendance intention* and *admission* cards. Shareholders are urged to return the *intention* cards in advance of the meeting to help provide an estimate of the number of likely attendees, which is useful for security, accommodation, catering etc. Using *admission* cards on arrival can aid swift admittance, and also assist identification when there is a need for increased security. Obviously no shareholder without a card should be barred from entry – processing their admittance may simply take longer.

Questions

Shareholders can ask questions at the AGM. However, shareholders of *traded* companies cannot ask questions which are:

- undesirable in the company's interest or the meeting's good order:
- only answerable by interfering with the preparation for the meeting;
- answerable only by disclosure of confidential information; or
- already answered in the frequently answered questions (FAQ) section of the company's website.

Questions do not necessarily have to be answered at the meeting. The chairman could state they will be answered later and/or posted on the FAQ section of the company's website.

Proxy

Proxy cards will have been sent with the meeting notice and should be lodged with the Secretary or the share registrar. They should be checked and an analysis of the support for and opposition to each resolution passed to the chairman before the meeting. The proxy cards themselves must be available at the meeting not least so those processing attendance can cross-reference them with the attendees' lists, in case of the attendance of a member who has already lodged a proxy. Whilst there is nothing to prevent this, obviously the votes must not be counted twice. A change of address notification should form part of the proxy card.

A member of a company can appoint more than one proxy (giving each rights in respect of a portion of the shares).

Several PLCs have changed their ARTICLES OF ASSOCIATION so that voting can no longer be effected by show of hands but only by poll thus ensuring all resolutions reflect the true voting strength.

Although the Articles of some older companies (particularly guarantee companies) may state that they do not allow proxies to be appointed (or, if they do, stipulate that the proxy must be a member of the company) such restrictions are no longer valid, being overruled by CA06s324.

LTDs provide *two-way* proxies allowing members to vote for or against each item of business, but traded companies must provide *three-way* proxies allowing shareholders not only to vote for or against but also to withhold their vote (as a form of protest, but one that does not warrant an adverse vote).

Informal communication

Since such meetings may be fairly formal, board members of some listed PLCs make themselves available for, say, 30 minutes before meetings (and/or for some time afterwards) to meet shareholders. At least one leading listed PLC invites shareholders to send it details of any shareholders' topics for consideration at the AGM. The advantage of drawing any hostility from the more public domain of the meeting in this way should not be underestimated, although directors of listed PLCs must be careful regarding any comments they make, to avoid breaching insider dealing legislation. For most LTDs the AGM is likely to be a less formal event and such informal contact can be achieved relatively easily and with fewer concerns regarding the effect of disclosing confidential material, although competitors may be able to obtain shares (or be appointed a proxy) and attend.

Developments

Some companies have been investigating holding their AGM in more than one location (e.g. using a number of regional meeting points) to save excessive cost / time / travel of shareholders based remotely. Such meeting points are linked by closed circuit television to the central location where the board (and perhaps a high proportion of shareholders) might be present.

Case study: Meeting remotely

In *Byng v London Life* the Court of Appeal held that that a shareholders' meeting could be held in more than one place provided there were *fully functional mutual audio-visual links* in all locations. (See VOTING)

Legal advice regarding this concept would need to be taken, and it might be preferable for the ARTICLES to be changed to permit it and thus negate any challenge to the validity of the meeting. The situation regarding the possible invalidating of the meeting should one or more of the links between the venues fail needs to be addressed.

b) (Extraordinary) General meetings (E)GM)

Definition and description

Under CA06 any meeting other than the AGM is a GM although the Articles of most preCA06 companies (unless changed subsequently) refer to such meetings as EGMs. Obviously for companies who do not hold an AGM, those owning (and who are not on the board of) such companies would not normally meet those that they have appointed to run it – even to discuss routine matters. Should there be no obligation to hold an AGM and/or the timing of that meeting is inappropriate for the consideration of business requiring shareholder decision(s), an (E)GM can be convened. Since October 2007, minutes of AGMs and (E)GMs must be taken and kept for at least 10 years although minutes of meetings before that date must be held for the life of the company and it may be preferable for all minutes to be kept for the longer period.

Convening

An (E)GM can be convened by:

- the board;
- the members in accordance with the ARTICLES;
- members holding 5% of the voting strength;

- the AUDITORS, should they resign and/or feel there are matters which should be brought to the attention of the members; and
- the Court.

Members' request

If the board receive a members' request to convene an (E)GM then it must do so within 21 days of receiving the members' request and the meeting itself must be convened for a date within a further 28 days (that is the meeting must be held within a total of 49 days from the request date). Minutes of the meeting must be taken and made available to the members (should they wish to inspect them) for two hours every business day.

Should notice of the meeting have already been sent out and the members require an amendment to a proposed resolution this should normally be treated as a new resolution and any specific requirements of the Articles must be complied with. The question of notice must also be addressed since unless the required percentage of shareholders is available to waive the normal notice requirements, insufficient notice may have been given.

If the board becomes aware of member concerns which could lead to a request for a meeting and/or a resolution or amendment, it may be advisable to try to discuss requirements in advance, since requisitioning a meeting can be expensive. A shareholder holding more than 10% of the shares in Millwall Football Club's parent company requisitioned a meeting regarding development plans for the club. His proposals were rejected, but convening and running the meeting cost the club over £50,000.

Notice

An (E)GM normally only requires 14 days notice. Traditionally some resolutions relating to specific business required longer notice in their own right, e.g. special resolutions originally required 21 days notice. Subject to individual Articles (which unless changed can require longer notice), notice periods for all resolutions and meetings (other than PLC's AGMs which still require 21 days notice – 20 working days under the Listing Agreement) have been rationalised at 14 days under CA06. However a listed PLC can only convene such a meeting on 14 days notice if its shareholders give it such power each year (e.g. at the AGM). If the shareholders of a listed PLC have so agreed and the company offers to all its shareholders a *facility for shareholders to vote by electronic means* then it need give only 14 days notice of a GM (but not of an AGM where 21 days is still required).

As referred to above, notice periods may be subject to an individual company's Articles and, if the Articles specifically require a special resolution to be subject to 21 days notice that amount of notice must be given unless and until the Articles themselves are changed (or the members waive the longer period of notice). An (E)GM of an LTD can be held with shorter or no notice provided 90% (or any higher percentage stipulated in the Articles) of the voting rights agree.

Gifts, ethics and Interests

KEY POINTS

- CA06 imposes strict controls re: conflicts of interests, disclosure of benefits provided for, or obtained by being, a company director etc.

- Further restrictions regarding 'gifts' and ethical conduct expected of companies are contained in the Bribery and Modern Slavery Acts.

- Additional legislation is being introduced regarding the liability of those operating a company in the event of tax evasion.

- Codes and procedures dealing with such matters need to be adopted, promulgated and policed.

Bribery Act 2010

The definitions of bribery in the Act are:

- giving or offering a financial or other advantage to another person;

- requesting, accepting or receiving a bribe;

- bribing a foreign official; and

- failure by a commercial organisation to prevent bribery by a person who provides services to it.

Organisations are expected to take reasonable steps to ensure all those acting on its behalf and interfacing with third parties neither give nor receive bribes. In order to use the defence that 'we took reasonable steps to prevent it' successfully, an organisation must be able to show that:

- it regularly assesses the nature of bribery risks to which it is exposed;

- prevention of bribery is a top level consideration and the commitment to operating without bribery is clearly communicated to everyone;

- there are adequate policies and practices that cover all parties to a business relationship;

- it has implemented its anti-bribery policies and procedures and these are set out in practical terms (i.e. examples would need to provided); and

- it monitors its requirements to ensure compliance.

Some companies now require regular details of entertaining by submission of a form similar to that in DIRECTORS – APPOINTMENT. Such a form may be required annually (or more often), including details of entertaining provided and/or enjoyed. Normal business entertaining is not prohibited but difficulty may arise in defining such a phrase. Whilst there is no intention of seeking to prohibit corporate activities aimed at building corporate relations and promoting business, it is an offence to provide such 'hospitality' if it can be proved that it was being provided to persuade someone not to act 'in good faith, impartially, or in accordance with a position of trust.'

Organisations can be held to be criminally liable for the actions of people acting on their behalf – e.g. agents. Thus there needs to be considerable investigation – and promulgation of problems to all acting on behalf of the organisation – when it enters into new markets, acquires new businesses and/or forms new joint ventures or partnerships.

Note: Transparency International UK (an international anti-corruption agency and pressure group) has two guides for free downloading. *Diagnosing bribery risk* outlines steps to formulate effective bribery assessments including:

- 10 good practice principles;

- a risk assessment template (with an illustrated and documented example); and

- a bribery risk assessment checklist

and *Countering Small Bribes: Principles and good practice guidance for dealing with small bribes, including facilitation payments.*

Case study: Bribery Act bites

Nicholas Smith, sales director of printing company Smith & Ouzman oversaw the payment of around £400,000 so-called *'chicken money'* to customers in Kenya and Mauritania in connection with the printing of election ballot papers. He was jailed for 3 years, whilst his father, company chairman, Christopher Smith was given an 18 month suspended custodial sentence.

Sweett Group have the dubious distinction of being the first company to be convicted under the Act. They were fined £2.25 million for failing to prevent the company's Cypriot subsidiary from paying £680,000 as a bribe to the vice-president of the Al Ain Ahlia Insurance Company to ensure that it received a £16 million consulting contract related to a Dubai hotel. Sweetts argument that the fine would cause it financial difficulties received no sympathy.

A survey by lawyers Eversheds revealed that 75% of British directors have discovered bribery or corruption in their organisations and 66% of them do not believe that their anti-bribery policies worked – indeed 11% said that they did not think they had done enough anti-bribery training.

Modern Slavery Act 2015

This Act requires businesses whose annual turnover is £36 million or more to identify the parts of their business (particularly supply chains) where there is a risk that 'slavery' (which includes forced or compulsory labour) and/or 'exploitation' (e.g. low wages and/or long hours) could take place.

Businesses must set out what steps they have taken to manage the above risk; carry out due diligence to check the supply chain and business generally; train their employees about the risk of slavery and human trafficking. Finally they must compare the effectiveness of their procedures against appropriate performance indicators. Details of compliance (i.e. a report of their actions to ensure compliance in the year under review) must be included in a published statement, signed by a director and posted on the company's website. It has been estimated that over 70% of UK organisations believe that modern slavery is likely to occur at some point in their supply chain; and that there may be as many as 21 million victims globally. In several UK cities (particularly where there are large immigrant populations) instances of slavery, servitude, and forced labour occur. It may be appropriate to include a clause such as the following in an employee handbook to bring the requirement to the attention of all employees and to remind them of the need to 'speak up' if necessary.

Example: Modern Slavery clause

The organisation wishes to trade ethically, paying a fair price for its goods raw materials and services. On no account must anyone working for the organisation or acting on its behalf be in any way connected with third parties providing goods and/or services to it, who are engaged in forced or compulsory labour and/or exploitation (e.g. forcing workers to take low wages and/or work long hours). Anyone being aware that this could be the case should report the matter to [named director]. Being aware of a breach of this policy and not taking such action is regarded as gross misconduct and may also be a criminal offence.

Tax evasion

New legislation is being introduced requiring corporations to prevent anyone acting for them or on their behalf from facilitating tax evasion. For there to be a criminal liability, prosecutors would need to be able to show that the most senior members of an organisation (e.g. members of the board of directors) were involved in the matter. Thus *'a company X Ltd would be guilty of an offence if a person associated with X Ltd commits a UK tax evasion facilitation offence when acting in the capacity of a person associated with X Ltd'*. However, X Ltd would have a defence if it can show that it had *'such prevention procedures as it was reasonable in the circumstance to expect X Ltd to have'*.

Once again for there to be at least the foundation of a defence, detailed guidance would need to be developed and publicised for example:

Example: Tax evasion clause

This organisation is committed to the principle that it should pay the appropriate amount of tax (as reduced by genuine and permitted costs and allowances etc.) on its activities as intended under legislation from time to time determined. The organisation is equally committed to outlawing any deviance from the above principle and regards

a) *any employee operating or acting in the name of the organisation and being in breach of this commitment as being guilty of gross misconduct, and*

b) *any other person (e.g. an agent or consultant etc.) acting in breach of these requirements of the organisation, rendering the relationship and any contract evidencing that relationship null and void.*

Anyone involved in any way with the organisation and becoming aware of activities being carried on in breach of this rule, is expected to report such matters to [named person]. Providing it is made in good faith, the position of any person making such a report will be protected under the organisation's 'whistleblowing' commitment.

Company 'facilitators' (accountants, lawyers, bankers, etc.) who advise their clients regarding devices and/or provide assistance to those clients to evade tax can be subject to unlimited fines.

Codes of Ethics

The chairman of the original committee charged with considering Corporate Governance – Sir Adrian Cadbury – stated ' from a company's point of view, codes of conduct are a form of safeguard for their reputation', although such a safeguard can only operate if those responsible ensure compliance (and can demonstrate how this was achieved) – and apply sanctions for breaches. In a recent survey, loss of, or damage to, company reputation was placed top of a list of risks that could affect a company detrimentally. Those who control organisations are expected to act legally and in a responsible manner and to ensure that all those they employ, or use, act similarly. Companies create wealth and, as a result, become powerful; the danger with such a situation being, as economist J K Galbraith once said, that 'the greater the wealth, the thicker will be the dirt'.

A code can only be as effective as:

- the clarity with which it is promulgated;

- the willingness of those affected to comply with its requirements; and

- the effectiveness of the policing of its requirements and application of sanctions for breaches.

It may be prudent to adopt – and rigorously ensure adherence to – a code of ethics.

Example: Code of Ethics

1. Standards

This [organisation] operates under high quality standards – of products, of services and of customer care, of respect for suppliers and requires such standards to be adhered to at all times in all its dealings.

2. Morality

The organisation will not:

- trade with any regime or organisation regarded as oppressive and/or that does not recognise human rights;

- trade with any weapons producer;

- speculate against its own currency; or

- trade with any supplier or other party indulging in Modern Slavery, and will endeavour to prevent its activities being used for any illegal purposes including exploitation, bribery, money laundering and/or drug trafficking.

The organisation is committed to trading ethically, paying a fair price for its goods, raw materials and services – and paying the correct amount of tax on its profits. On no account must anyone working for the organisation or acting on its behalf be in any way connected with third parties providing goods and services etc. to it, who are engaged in forced or compulsory labour and/or exploitation (e.g. forcing workers to take low wages and/or contribute long hours). Anyone being aware that this could be the case should report the matter to [named director]. Being aware of a breach of this clause, and not taking such action, is regarded as gross misconduct – and may also be a criminal offence.

3. Personal obligations

All employees are expected to:

- be loyal to the organisation in all their endeavours on its behalf;
- be honest and diligent, and maintain high standards of dignity in undertaking their duties and responsibilities and should not:
- act in any manner that will or could damage the organisation's reputation;
- accept, offer or give any bribe or inducement from anyone or to anybody (or any person or organisation acting on their behalf) involved in any way with the organisation;
- permit any activity which might result in a conflict of interests with this organisation, or use any organisational information or material for personal gain;
- seek a position where the company evades taxation properly payable on its profits.

4. Inducements

Other than properly authorised trade and retail promotions, no inducement may be offered to or given:

- to any customer or outlet whereby they will be induced or encouraged to place an order for or take any product or service offered by the [organisation], or

- to any supplier or creditor to obtain improved terms of trade.

Such activity is proscribed by the Bribery Act 2010 and a breach could result in criminal prosecution.

5. Entertainment

i) Whilst it is acceptable to entertain a customer or supplier to lunch or dinner to discuss normal contractual matters, this must be at places and to the limits laid down in the [organisation's] entertainment guide. On no account must the limits and guidelines included in that guide be exceeded without prior written approval of [name].

ii) In the event of any person considering that he needs to entertain or provide a gift for a customer and that the limits are inappropriate (for example the matter concerns an attempt to compensate for previous poor service, quality etc.,) the written authority of a board member should be obtained with an indication of any limitation agreed and that authority should be referred to in the subsequent expenses claim.

6. Hospitality

Employees can accept hospitality from major customers and suppliers in terms of lunches and/or dinners or other similar value entertainment, to a maximum of [number of occasions] per organisation per year. In the event that the value obtained is in excess of that laid down in the company entertainment guide, this fact must be made known to a board member as soon as possible. If the entertainment provided is considered to be in excess of that warranted by the circumstances, the director responsible may need to contact the third party to explain the policy.

7. Anti-competitive practices

This organisation operates in a competitive industry and welcomes healthy competition. On no account may any employee or person acting on behalf of the organisation enter into or agree to enter into an arrangement whereby the effect is to price-fix, arrange collusive tendering, rig bids, split or allocate markets or customers with a competitor, abuse a dominant market position or act in any way which constitutes a breach of the anti-competition legislation and/or is to the detriment of a consumer. Any suggestion of such activity from a third party should be reported immediately to [name].

8. Legal compliance

The [organisation] operates within the [specify] industry and must comply with all laws, regulations and codes of practice etc. It seeks to trade legally, fairly, openly and honestly with all third parties and to give value for money in all its dealings. It requires and expects its employees to carry out their work and responsibilities and to conduct their relationships and dealings with third parties in accordance with these precepts. All dealings must be conducted openly and fairly in such a way that should every aspect of the transaction become widely known (for example in the media) this would not cause any embarrassment, injury or damage to the reputation of the [organisation] whatever.

Attention is drawn to the various codes set out in the company handbook, compliance with which is compulsory.

9. Respect

All employees are required to act responsibly, decently and with due regard for the dignity and rights of others in both business and personal dealings. In many instances personnel (particularly senior personnel) will be seen as acting on behalf of the [organisation], the reputation of which must be protected at all times.

10. Whistleblowing

All employees at whatever level in the [organisation] are encouraged to report any activities which seem to them to be in breach of this code or any other breach of the organisation's rules to [director]. Such reports will be treated as confidential and provided they are made in good faith and not be made with the aim of personal gain, the person making the report should not fear reprisals or detriment.

To try to ensure adherence some companies require their employees to sign such a code; some even requiring the commitment to be updated annually. Of course failing to comply with the requirements set out above could not only result in the application of disciplinary sanctions but also to criminal penalties – including imprisonment.

Whistleblowing

An increasing number of companies (including all listed PLCs who are obliged to do so under the Stock Exchange listing agreement and FCA requirements) have adopted whistleblowing codes (see DIRECTORS DUTIES) so that employees becoming aware of wrongdoing are encouraged to make a qualifying disclosure (QD). A QD is any information which tends in the reasonable opinion of the worker (an objective test in each case) to show a *relevant failure* which include:

- a criminal offence has been, is being or is likely to be committed;

- a miscarriage of justice has occurred, is occurring or is likely to occur;

- someone has failed, is failing or is likely to fail to comply with a legal obligation to which they are subject;

- health and/or safety of any individual has been, is being or is likely to be endangered;

- the environment has been, is being or is likely to be damaged; and

- information relating to any of the above has been, is being or is likely to be deliberately concealed.

Compensation for unfair dismissal because of whistleblowing is unlimited.

Case study: Theft and fraud

Antonio Fernandes was the financial controller of Netcom. His managing director (MD) gave him petty cash slips (for amounts in excess of £200,000) on two occasions without any supporting receipts. When he protested that such claims were almost certainly a fraud on HMRC since they could not be properly claimed as being wholly and exclusively in the proper execution of the MD's duties on behalf of the company, he was told by the MD, and subsequently by the American owners of the company to 'keep your nose clean and pay it'. He refused and was told to resign. When he did not resign, he was dismissed. He was awarded £293,000 compensation.

For a successful whistleblowing claim the matter is now required to be in the *public* interest (not simply a breach of an employee's contract). Conversely, the requirement for claimants to be able to demonstrate that their disclosure was made *in good faith* has been removed under the Enterprise and Regulatory Reform Act 2013 although a tribunal can reduce compensation by 25% if a disclosure was not made in good faith. Unfortunately the term 'public interest' is not defined.

Case study: What is 'public' interest?

In *Chesterton Global Ltd v Nurmohamed* (N), N made a complaint that his employers' results were being falsely manipulated by around £2 million to the detriment of the earnings of around 100 employee managers, but to the benefit of the company's shareholders. Although obviously N had his own interest in mind, he was also found to have been thinking of his colleagues and this satisfied the 'public' test.

Gift policy

Many employees and directors experience a situation where a customer, adviser or supplier wishes to reward them personally for good service etc., and in principle and moderation there should be nothing wrong with this. However it is all too easy, if a gift is substantial, for it to become not so much a *'thank you'* for past service but a bribe seeking to obtain future advantage. Adoption of a gift policy may be helpful both as a guide as to what can be accepted and a way of tactfully refusing larger items. This would also meet the suggestion made by the Ministry of Justice, and quoted earlier, that *examples should be given*. The practical examples (in italics) in the following draft are purely for illustration.

Example: Gift policy

1. Other than at Christmas [and/or other religious/national celebrations where there is a custom that presents are exchanged], employees are not allowed to accept or retain gifts made by any customer or supplier or other third parties, generated as a result of the business relationship. If such gifts are delivered and it seems potentially damaging to the relationship to return them, then, subject to the approval of [director] the gifts may be retained and will be handed to [the Social Club] for use as raffle prizes or disposed of in a similar way. The director will contact the donor and explain what has occurred and why (i.e. it is in accordance with internal rules).

    Practical guidance: A bottle of wine or spirits once a year can be accepted – a bottle every week should not – and must be disclosed.

    Note: Some organisations require declaration of every gift no matter how small.

2. At Christmas [other religious/national celebrations], employees are allowed to accept gifts to a maximum of [amount] per donor. If gifts above this level are received then, subject to the approval of the [director], they may be retained.

    Practical guidance: a gift (or voucher/cash) of value £20 may be acceptable once a year – a gift of £200 or more might not, other than in very exceptional circumstances which should be reported.

3. If multiple gifts are received to mark good service which has been provided by a number of employees, these may be retained and distributed to the employees concerned provided the value per employee does not exceed the guidance laid down in the entertainment policy.

    Practical guidance: A case of wine at Christmas is acceptable but should be distributed between the team. A case of wine every week/ month would not be acceptable and should be reported.

4. The attention of all employees is drawn to the danger of a customer or third party using the previous or anticipated delivery of gifts or inducements as a bribe or to exert pressure to obtain concessions (e.g. orders, better terms, preferential treatment) or any other consideration; or such persons using the threat of or actual publicity concerning the previous acceptance of a gift or lavish entertainment

as pressure to obtain such concessions etc. In all circumstances the response *'I cannot comment further – I must contact [director] to discuss this matter'* should be made.

Practical guidance: Being entertained at a sporting or social activity once a year is acceptable. Accepting such invitations more often/regularly would not be acceptable. An all expenses paid trip to see the Rio Olympics for a week might have been unacceptable, although a day trip to the London Olympics would probably have been acceptable.

5. Any suggestion of using facilities owned, occupied or made available to a third party (for example a holiday villa or other property, concessionary travel, etc.) either on a free basis or for any consideration which seems or is less than the market price, should be communicated to the [director] at whose discretion the matter can proceed or be concluded.

    Practical guidance: Such a scenario is unacceptable, but a short, expenses paid visit, made because it is genuinely necessary to check facilities that might later be used by the organisation (e.g. for a seminar, conference or exhibition etc.) should be acceptable.

6. Any employee feeling unsure about any of the foregoing or that they are being placed in an *awkward* position by a third party, should report the matter to [named person].

This guidance is best summarised as *'if in doubt, shout'*.

Although this is a policy drafted to provide internal guidance, there is no reason why it could not also be distributed to suppliers, customers etc., so that the incidence of them making a gesture that would breach the rules can be avoided thus preventing embarrassment. It is also a method of advertising the subject organisation's wish to act and be seen to act ethically at all times.

Interests

Directors' conflicts of interests are strictly controlled by CA06. The detailed obligations are set out in DIRECTORS: PAYMENTS, LOANS AND INTERESTS. However many companies may wish to restrict executives other than the board from having such interests and thus potential conflicts. Accordingly publication (for example in the employee handbook or similar procedure manual) of guidance regarding the company's attitude to such matters may be advisable. In addition, use of the form referred to above on taking up the position and possibly regularly thereafter could be considered.

Example: Control of conflicting interests clause

1. No-one working for or employed by, or providing services for the [organisation] is to make, or encourage another to make any personal gain out of its activities in any way whatsoever without this being agreed to, in writing and in advance, by [named person/board].

2. Any person becoming aware of a personal gain or interest (or potential gain or interest) as a result of which they would benefit is required to notify [name]. Only if it is agreed by [person/board] will such matter be allowed to subsist.

3. Anyone being in a situation such as is outlined in 2 who fails to report the matter will be regarded as having committed an act of gross misconduct for which the usual penalty is dismissal.

4. Anyone reporting a matter which could involve a benefit being made by or given to another and/or which could conflict with that person's obligations, provided there are reasonable grounds for such suspicion, will be protected.

5. All employees are expected to report any suspicion or knowledge of wrongdoing to [named person].

Inevitably since directors are effectively in control of their company's assets the possibility of them (or their *connected* persons) acquiring such assets no longer required within the company (or selling personal assets to the company) is likely to arise. Whilst assuming that an *arm's length* valuation is obtained, and that since there is nothing in the Articles to prevent such a transfer, such a transaction could proceed, it would be prudent for:

- a disinterested quorum of the board to resolve that the transfer go ahead;
- details to be entered in a register of directors interests;
- the matter to be disclosed to the Auditors.

Prior approval of the members is required if the value of the asset exceeds £100,000 or is 10% or more of the company's net assets (and exceeds £5,000).

Incorporation

CHECKLIST: Incorporation

✓ Decide on NAME.

✓ Apply to CH for clearance of name chosen. If it is required to change an existing company's name, and the date of change is critical, it may be safer to form a shell company with the required name and then for both existing and new companies to pass special RESOLUTIONS exchanging names on the same date. If an original name is preferred, it may be advisable to try and incorporate the company with that name without checking (using the CH *same day web* incorporation service). If the application goes, through, then the name is protected immediately, whereas if it is rejected then little, other than the filing fee, will have been lost. Even checking out a name may allow someone else to slip in first – although this possibility may be, to some extent, prevented by the company NAMES tribunal. Alternatively, a preferred name can be checked for availability/usage using the CH Webcheck service.

✓ Describe activities or objects (if required). Traditionally these details were set out in the MEMORANDUM and it was usual for them to cover virtually every conceivable activity the company could ever enter into to minimise the possibility of the company/board acting *ultra vires*. CA89 allowed a company to be a *'general commercial company'*, i.e. placing no restriction on its activities, although this relaxation was not widely used as finance houses asked to loan money to companies with such objects disliked the lack of control over its activities. For companies formed under CA06, objects clauses are completely unnecessary (other than for charities, CICs, Right to Manage or financial services companies) but, if required, objects clauses must be included in the Articles. The objects clauses of pre CA06 companies are now deemed to be part of their Articles.

Companies without an objects clause may find obtaining a loan difficult as obviously a lender will need to know for what purposes money being borrowed is to be used. Alternatively lenders could require directors' guarantees

✓ Decide location of the company's registered office which must be within its country of incorporation.

✓ Decide whether to keep the STATUTORY BOOKS within the company or at CH.

If CH, advise them using form EH04 and provide details. Alternatively purchase STATUTORY BOOKS in hard copy or electronic version. Registers required are those of:

- members (shareholders or guarantors);
- directors and Secretary;
- holders of substantial interests in shares;
- debenture and/or loan holders (if any);
- CHARGES (although the requirement to keep such a register is being phased out);
- persons of SIGNIFICANT CONTROL; and
- directors' interests in the shares of their company (no longer required for LTDs).

Since, however, companies must be advised of third parties etc., in which their directors may have an interest – and thus a potential or actual conflict – it would be best if the company kept a record of such information. This register (with the word 'share' deleted from its title) could suffice.

✓ Minute books for meetings of both members and directors will be needed as may (optional) a company SEAL and sealing register.

✓ Determine share capital if required (or for a guarantee company the amount of each guarantee). There is no lower limit on the amount of an LTD's share capital, but for a company to be a PLC, a minimum of £50,000 issued share capital of which 25% or more must be paid up in cash. A company formed under CA06 need not have an 'authorised' share capital – the share capital of such a company is decided by the directors (subject to any limitations imposed by the shareholders).

✓ Determine any rights of shares, other than ordinary shares.

✓ Arrange initial subscribers. Formerly every company had to have two shareholders, but CA89 allowed companies to be formed with only one shareholder – a single member company.

✓ Draft ARTICLES OF ASSOCIATION of which the final version needs to be signed by the promoter(s) (and dated and witnessed). Articles can be drafted using the pro formas accompanying the Act with the addition of customised clauses. A charitable company must adopt an objects clause and incorporate it within its Articles (model Articles are available for charitable companies, CICs, Right to Manage companies etc.).

✓ Appoint initial directors of whom full personal details (name, address, date of birth, occupation) will be required both for the Register of Directors and formation publicity (although for public disclosure a service address rather than a director's private address can be used and the actual day of birth is not made part of the public record).

✓ Complete and submit form IN01 (CA06ss9 & 14) to CH with fee and a Statement of Compliance (CA06s1068). CH has powers to:

- stipulate in which form it must be lodged. This could mean that such documents must be lodged electronically (s1069);

- require standard contents; and

- require it to be authenticated by a particular person.

✓ PLCs must obtain a 'certificate to commence trading' from CH, before trading. If a PLC trades before it has this certificate the directors can be held liable for the company's debts etc.

✓ Open bank accounts, appoint auditors, solicitors, obtain a VAT number, notify HMRC (although HMRC is automatically notified of the formation of every company and will contact the officers directly).

Certificate of Incorporation

Following its acceptance of the above, and to evidence the formation and existence of the company, CH issues a Certificate of Incorporation which states:

1. The company's name in upper case (although this does not prevent it using upper and lower case as long as the name itself is identical) and with 'Limited' (or LTD) or 'Public Limited Company' (or PLC).

2. The registered number. This entirely distinct (and never re-used) number remains unchanged with the company throughout its life (no matter how often its name is changed).

3. The date of incorporation.

4. That the company is limited by shares or guarantee or is unlimited.

5. That it is an LTD or a PLC.

6. The country of registration (England and Wales, Scotland or Northern Ireland).

The certificate is conclusive evidence that the legislative requirements have been met and the company is registered and exists as a legal person. The certificate is no longer required to be displayed but should be kept safely since a lender asked to loan funds to the company may wish to see it as formal evidence of the company's existence.

Under CA06s1065 CH can be asked for a certified copy of a company's certificate of incorporation.

Name

The name of the company, as shown on the Certificate of Incorporation, must be displayed/used:

- on the outside of the registered office (unless this is a private residence);
- at every place of business. In default, every director and the Secretary are liable to an initial fine plus an additional fine for every day this is not effected;
- on all business letters including external emails, purchase orders, notices, website and official publications;
- on the common SEAL (and any securities seal) of the company; and
- on all invoices, bills of exchange, purchase orders, orders for money etc.

Failure to comply renders those at fault liable to initial plus daily fines.

Date of incorporation

This date (D) is used as the start point for filing time limits.

- D: Incorporation – the company is brought into existence as a legal person, liability of the members is limited, etc.
- D plus 9 months: Notify CH of Accounting Reference Date (i.e. its FINANCIAL YEAR END).
- D plus 12 months: Latest date for making up first CONFIRMATION STATEMENT.
- D plus a year plus 9 months (if LTD) or 6 months (if PLC) – file accounts.

Preservation

A replica of the Certificate of Incorporation is often inserted as the first page of the printed Memorandum and Articles. On any change of company's name, CH issues a Certificate on Change of Name which then stands in place of the original Certificate of Incorporation. The Certificate of Incorporation (or Certificate on Change of Name) should be kept safely and permanently.

CH Web Incorporation Service (WIS)

As an alternative to forming a company as above or using formation agents, for £12 CH's WIS can be used which means the new company can be incorporated virtually instantly. However the standard set of Articles accompanying CA06 must be used. This may not suit all companies although there is nothing to stop the new company being set up with those Articles which would enable it to commence business, one of the first items of which could be to convene a general meeting to pass a Special Resolution altering the Articles to a version which fits the company's particular requirements. The changed Articles must be filed with CH within 15 days.

Memorandum of Association

KEY POINTS

- Every pre-CA06 company was required to have a Memorandum of its aims – i.e. a document setting out full details of the objects for which the company was formed.

- CA89 diluted the requirement for objects clauses and a few newly-formed companies used the single line (cover-all) objects clause, *to be a general commercial company.*

- CA06 abolished the need, other than for charities, CICs and Right to Manage, companies to have or retain objects clauses at all.

Content

The Memorandum of a CA06 company cannot be changed and must state

1. The names of the promoters, although once INCORPORATION is completed this is of purely academic interest.

2. For a company limited by shares: a statement of the number of shares taken by each promoter, although again this is of interest only on formation since thereafter additional shares may be issued. A CA06 company does not need to have an authorised share capital unless the shareholders require it, in which case it must be included in its Articles. In the Memorandum of a company limited by guarantee, the maximum amount of each guarantee(s) must be stated

3. The name of the country (England and Wales, Scotland or Northern Ireland) in which the REGISTERED OFFICE is to be situated. Pending the implementation of EU proposals to relax this restriction,

UK companies can have their registered offices only in their country of registration. Although the actual address of the registered office need not be stated in the Memorandum, under CA06s9, on INCORPORATION a note of this address must be filed with CH (form IN01). Any alteration in the address of the Registered Office of the company must be filed with CH using form AD01. On the change of a Registered Office, a 14 day period is allowed during which both old and new offices are valid for the service of notices.

Pre CA06 companies

Pre CA06 companies' Memorandums were (and still are unless altered) required to contain:

- A statement of the total number of shares (and their various categories if applicable) that the company was authorised to issue. Whilst this is valuable information to creditors, since (at least in theory) it shows some of the funds available as security for their debts, the amount and type of share capital has always been subject to alteration. If the company was a PLC, the share issued capital had to be at least £50,000 of which 25% (i.e. at least £12,500) had to be paid up.

- The objects of the company. These, often extremely numerous, clauses are a public statement of the business the company was formed to undertake, and effectively act as a limitation on its directors' authority to conduct business.

Under CA89, companies were instead permitted to have a short form objects clause, e.g. 'the company will be a general commercial company'. Effectively this would mean that it would be very unlikely that the company could ever act beyond its powers. Such a clause was rare, mainly since banks were averse to lending money to a company with such unrestricted aims or objects. Those concerns over using an abbreviated objects clause reflect the original purpose of stating the objects – to protect those dealing with the company by confirming the nature of the business to be carried on by the directors. It may be feasible to use the abbreviated clause for a subsidiary, or joint venture company where lenders' concerns could be overcome by the parent guaranteeing the subsidiary's debts. CA06s39 states that (other than for charitable companies) the validity of an act of a company cannot be questioned on grounds of 'lack of capacity'. Companies that wish to (a charity must) retain objects clauses must include them in their Articles.

Deemed change

CA06 gives effect to one important change regarding the objects clauses of companies already in existence in that even if such companies do not change or re-write their Articles, the objects clauses in their Memorandums are now deemed to be part of their Articles (the company's Constitution). If such companies wish to change their Articles they must ensure that the objects clauses form part of the re-write – or (if feasible) that a decision is taken to do without an objects clause. All updated or altered Articles are required to be filed at CH within 15 days of the resolution approving them.

Minutes

Content and use

Generally minutes should record:

1. *The constitution* under which the meeting is taking place. This may be fairly obvious for a board meeting since the directors are meeting with the authority of their appointments (and in accordance with their duty under company law) to take decisions to operate the company on behalf of and for the benefit of the owners, whilst taking into account the interests of the other company stakeholders (the company itself, employees, creditors, consumers and society / the environment). They must also act in accordance with the internal rules set out in their Articles. Where there is a meeting of, for example, a sub-committee of the board, the terms of reference of that committee should be set out in the minutes of its first meeting as well as in the minutes of the appointing body.

2. *The administration*: when and where the meeting took place and who was there. Minutes should record the board members present,

as well as advisers in attendance and any comings and goings of members during the meeting (and the points of the meeting at which such entrances and exits occurred).

A note of any absentees (and whether for acceptable reasons) should also be made.

3. *The information:* data (e.g. reports) on which decisions were taken (including a note of whether these were tabled or distributed previously). The information that was provided demonstrates the basis on which decisions were taken and, by exception, information that was not available (which might be of considerable importance should the company get into difficulties – see WRONGFUL TRADING)

4. *The official back-up:* details of which registers were sealed, initialled, etc. and which reports were considered.

5. *The decisions:* whilst the content will differ according to individual company requirements, it is usually considered preferable for minutes to record decisions (and any dissent) rather than detailed discussion and arguments for and against the matter and reasons for arriving at it. It is also generally agreed that the briefer the minutes the better – although they should contain sufficient information to enable a third party to understand the reasons for decisions taken, which may mean at times that some commentary should be included to explain the basis for the decisions. This is a particularly important for companies operating under FCA rules.

6. *The authority:* Minutes (of both board and general meetings) should be signed as a true record of the preceding meeting at the next following board meeting.

   Under CA06s249, signing the minutes grants them status as evidence (in Scotland, *sufficient evidence*) of the proceedings, and they can be produced as such in Court. Some Articles stipulate that if the minutes are approved and signed then they are *conclusive evidence* of the proceedings, meaning that it will be virtually impossible for anyone to challenge them later.

7. *The record:* Once the minutes have been drafted they should be approved in principle by the chairman with drafts sent out to all members. Ideally this should happen within three to four working days of the meeting. If (a) board member(s) object(s) to the wording or substance proposed, and the objection has general support, the draft

minutes should be changed. Although this can be done by alteration, it may be preferable for a fresh version, incorporating any agreed change(s), to be prepared. If members wish to make more substantial amendments this may require further drafts until there is a consensus that the record is an accurate reflection of what was agreed. Seeing decisions in a written – and formal – format can sometimes generate a rethink -second thoughts can be valuable.

8. *Dissemination and protection:* The minutes should be sent out to board members (with extracts for others affected by board decisions) as soon as possible after the meeting. This means the minutes may be able to act not only as a record of the board decisions, but also as prompts to those required to effect decisions, since some directors' recollections of what they agreed and/or were required to do may be hazy. Those in receipt of copies may also need to be reminded of the need for adequate security. Minutes should be a true, fair and accurate record which is of particular importance should the company need to produce a certified copy of a minute to a third party, for example to evidence a board member's authority to sign a contract, ratify a bank mandate etc.

Inspection

Although the board members can access the minutes of their own meetings, the company members (i.e. the owners) have no such right (although they have a right of access to the minutes of their own (company) meetings – AGMs and (E)GMs). Others with rights of access include:

- The Auditors since they will need to check whether any commitments which would affect their audit, have been entered into or authorised to be entered into by the board;

- The FCA (for companies operating in the financial services arena) who may also request minutes and papers of board committee meetings;

- The HSE if investigating an accident etc.; and

- The Court.

Drafting guidance

The following examples should be regarded as guidance only. Under both versions, references to the later explanatory notes have been included – indicated by the bracketed numbers shown on the right.

Example: Draft minutes – 1

ANY COMPANY LIMITED   182 *(1)*

MINUTES of a BOARD MEETING held on 30th March [year]

At [address] at 10.00 a.m.

Present:

XYZ (in the chair)

ABC

DEF

GHI

In attendance: JKL (Company Secretary)

(Mr. TSS, auditor was in attendance for items covered by Minute 3 i and ii)   *(2)*

An apology for absence due to illness was received from UVW and this was accepted. Those present signed the attendance book.   *(3)*

The board reminded themselves of the seven duties of directors set out in the Companies Act 2006 and confirmed that in taking all decisions they would continue to take account of these duties and bear in mind the disparate interests of the company's stakeholders.   *(4)*

1. MINUTES
The minutes of the board meeting held on 29th February [year] previously distributed were taken as read, approved and signed   *(5)*

2. DIRECTORS' INTERESTS
The register recording interests of board members as advised to the company was laid on the table.   *(6)*

3. RISK CONTROL

The Secretary tabled an updated statement of risk control which would form part of the forthcoming Annual Report, as a result of an investigation and report recently completed by the Risk Control sub-committee of the Board. This was ratified. It was noted that an updated Delegated Authority chart had been issued to all employees and agents, reminding them (amongst other matters) that on no account should bribes be offered or taken and/or that product prices should be discussed with competitors, that there should be no exploitation of personnel in the supply chain or elsewhere and that tax evasion was not permitted.   *(7)*

4. SHAREHOLDER MATTERS

It was resolved that a share transfer covering 500 Ordinary shares in the company from Mrs MNO to Mr PQR be and it hereby is approved and that a share certificate in the name of Mr PQR be issued and the required entries be made in the Register of Members. The Secretary was asked to write to Mr PQR welcoming him as a shareholder. *Action: JKL*   *(8)*

A report from the Secretary recommending that responsibility for the share registration work of the company be placed with Share Registrars Ltd. was accepted and the terms of the contract approved. The Secretary was requested to make the necessary arrangements in liaison with the chairman. *Action: JKL*

(Mr DEF, having previously notified the company that he had a consultancy agreement with Share Registrars Ltd did not take any part in this discussion or decision.)   *(9)*

5. FINANCE

i) Management accounts. The accounts for the month of February and the cumulative 11 months were tabled and discussed in detail. The favourable comparison with budget was welcomed, as was the managing director's opinion that the trading and financial situation would continue to show improvement, both in real terms and against budget. It was noted that the situation regarding discounts and promotional payments was still being clarified and additional controls would be introduced from the commencement of the new financial year.

A number of estimated provisions were listed for possible incorporation in the year end accounts. *Action: ABC*

ii) Depreciation. It was agreed to change the company's accounting policies so that depreciation would be charged on vehicles, office equipment and computers at 33.3% p.a. straightline. It was noted that this change would have to be recorded in the published Accounting Policies.

iii) Capital expenditure.

    a) It was agreed that a further five production units at a cost of around £40,000 each could be purchased in stages over the remainder of 2XXX to allow the sale of [detail]. Mr UVW (whom failing, the Secretary) would authorise each item bearing in mind the effect on cash flow. *Action: UVW/JKL* (10)

    b) The chairman referred to Capital Expenditure Project form number 13/2XXX for the investment in [detail] which projected a first year return of 14% rising to 17% in year 2 on a fully absorbed basis. The project was approved for implementation no earlier than 31st December [year] *Action: ABC*

iv) Cash flow. The latest projection for the period ending 31st December [year] was tabled, discussed and approved

v) Investigations for the replacement of the company vehicles allocated to six area managers would be carried out. The guidance of the auditors as to the company's and individual's tax situation would be sought. *Action: GHI*

vi) Bank Mandate. The Secretary reported that the company's bankers had requested that a new mandate on the main drawing account be completed. It was resolved that the company operate the No 1 Main Drawing account in its name with the Finance Bank Plc on the terms and subject to the restrictions set out in a new mandate a copy of which initialled by the chairman for the purposes of identification is attached to these minutes, and that the Secretary be and he hereby is empowered to take such actions as might be necessary to give effect to this resolution. *Action: JKL* (11)

vii) Borrowings. The Secretary reported that in the absence of Mr UVW he had negotiated an additional £200,000 overdraft facility with the Finance Bank on the same terms as the existing facility. This additional borrowing was available for the eight weeks until end August [year]. Although he had expected to receive documentation requiring board approval to evidence this borrowing this had not arrived before the meeting.

It was resolved that the chairman, ABC and UVW (whom failing the Secretary) be and they hereby are empowered to sign such documents and take such actions to provide the company's bankers with the documentation they required in order to facilitate the advance of this additional borrowing requirement.

The Secretary was instructed to let each board member have copies of the relevant items and documentation when these were to hand.

The Secretary confirmed that even with this additional borrowing the limits in the Articles had not been breached. *Action: XYZ, ABC, UVW, JKL*   *(12)*

6. CURRENT TRADING
The managing director reported that [synopsis of report.........]. An analysis showing the deterioration over a five year period of sales of the main product was tabled and it was agreed that the deadline for delivery of supplies of Project X needed to be brought forward to compensate for the expected shortfall in sales in the latter part of the calendar year. *Action: ABC*

DEF requested that his dissent from this course of action be noted in the minutes with the note that in his opinion not enough was being done to incentivise the sales force and he had serious doubts concerning the effectiveness of the recently appointed sales manager.   *(13)*

7. PERSONNEL
A report from the divisional director (Personnel) had been sent to all members and the contents were accepted. It was agreed that negotiations should commence with employee representatives to try to agree the wage increase with effect from 1st July [year] along the lines outlined in the report.

It was noted that all employees and agents had been further reminded of their obligations for compliance with the Bribery, Modern Slavery and Tax evasion legislation by re-issue of the delegated authority chart / code of ethics (with explanatory data) referred to in item 3 above.

8. PROPERTY

The following items were noted: *(14)*

Little progress had been made on any of the pending rent reviews which would update the list accompanying the agenda for the meeting other than the following:

- [Facility]: Approval was granted to a letter of response to the landlords requesting that an extension to the user be agreed.

- [Facility]: Evidence thought to be misleading had been submitted by the landlord's agents.

- [Facility]: The landlord's agents had reduced their figure for the reviewed rent to £13,500. Negotiations continued.

- [Facility]: The sale was proceeding with exchange of contracts expected for mid-July and completion by 1st August. It was noted that receipt of the sale monies had not been built into the cash flow forecast and that if this sale completed as anticipated part or the whole of the additional overdraft facility would not be needed.

- [Facility]: The possibility of selling the business and licensing or underletting the lease was being pursued urgently.

Insurance: The Secretary would draft a letter to be sent to all landlords of leased premises requesting that the interest of the company be noted on the insurance policies to ensure any liability in the event of loss was minimised. *Action: JKL*

(Mr DEF apologised and with the permission of the chairman left the meeting) *(15)*

9. SAFETY MATTERS

i) The monthly report was accepted, no actions being required

ii) The Secretary reported

    a) that he had investigated the requirements of the current health and safety legislation regarding fire precautions in the workplace and tabled a brief synopsis of the action he felt it was necessary for the company to take in order to comply with the requirements. The board requested him to obtain detailed cost estimates for the various requirements with, in each case, an indication of the proposed timetable for implementation of the recommendations.

b) that he had commissioned reports to determine whether there were any asbestos containing materials in the two newly acquired company's properties Action: JKL   *(16)*

10. SEALING
The Secretary produced the Register of Sealing (and documents signed as deeds) to the board and approval was granted to the affixing of the company seal to items numbered 345 to 357 and 359 to 361, and approval granted to the signing as a deed of item 358. The chairman was authorised to sign the register in evidence of this approval.   *(17)*

11. BOARD MEETING TIMETABLE
The dates of future meetings of the board were confirmed as 28th April, 30th May, 30th June, 28th July, 31st August, 29th September, 25th October, 23rd November, and 21st December.

The Secretary would inform Messrs DEF and UVW.   *(18)*

Chairman _____ 28th April [year] *(19)*

Action points: *(20)*

Welcoming shareholder JKL _____ [Completion date]

New Share Registrars JKL _____ [Completion date]

Provisions in accounts ABC_____ [Completion date]

Capex products purchase UVW(JKL) _____ [Ongoing]

and so on

Notes:

1. Ideally minute pages should be consecutively numbered to try to prevent fraudulent alterations. The subject of each minute (where applicable) should be indexed cross-referencing provided. Some companies use the year to delineate minutes e.g. 2018/X etc. – changing to 2019/X for minutes of the first board meeting in the following financial or calendar year.

2. Stating the exact period of attendance of advisors, and of members, if not present for the whole meeting, is advisable.

3. It is arguable that only if an apology for absence is accepted that the absence is permitted. In some boards if no apology is made, that fact is stated in the minutes (i.e. 'No apology was received from....' which underlines the implied obligation that directors should attend). Under Reg. 81 Table A CA85, if a director does not attend board meetings for six months or more without permission of the board, he can be removed from the board.

   Some charities require their directors to sign an attendance book. This is not a legal obligation but underlines their implied duty to attend.

4. CA06 places explicit duties on directors and to be able to demonstrate that they were aware of such duties, wording such as this could be inserted in the minutes once a year as a reminder – and in the minutes of any board which a director is attending for the first time so that newcomers have the point brought to their attention.

5. Ideally the chairman should initial each page of the minutes except for the last which should be signed. See 19 below.

6. Under CA06 there is an implied requirement to record items in which directors have an interest – e.g. indemnities, loans, potential and/ or actual conflicts of interest etc. It may be prudent to maintain a Register of Directors' Interests into which details of such items are entered and to have this available at each board meeting so that all members are made aware of interests. This may also assist the Secretary should an item of business require there to be a *disinterested quorum*. This register can be updated regularly if the concept of requiring directors to complete a statement of their interests each year is adopted.

7. Listed PLCs, and companies with shareholders not on the board, should consider incorporating in their ANNUAL REPORT a statement of risk and control mechanisms devised as well as the fact that these are regularly assessed by the board. Being able to use the defence (e.g. for an allegation of bribery) that 'reasonable steps have been taken' would seem to indicate that it needs a constant re-assessment of the possibility. A record of board attention to this subject may be of assistance in meeting this aim.

8. Directors of many LTDs have the right to refuse to allow a transfer of shares to a person of whom they do not approve (entitling the company to be termed private). It is probably unlikely that an LTD

would need to retain external registrars to deal with its share registration work although such services are often used by listed PLCs.

Placing the initials of the person due to deal with the item enables the minutes (already a document of record and reference) to act as a means of encouraging prompt action. It becomes virtually impossible for the person to claim at the next meeting 'I didn't realise you wanted me to do that'!

9. Depending on the Articles' requirements, it is important that any director with an interest in the subject matter should declare that interest and that the point be noted. DEF's interest with Share Registrars should have been entered in the Register of Directors' Interests – see 6 above. The provisions of the Articles should be checked – some require an interested party not only to refrain from voting or the discussion, but also to leave the room whilst the matter is being discussed. Conversely the Articles of some private LTDs state that directors can have interests in third parties with which the company is trading – hence a conflict of interests may be virtually impossible.

10. Drafting a decision in this way leaves some leeway for delay should the circumstances at the time warrant such delay and also covers the situation should UVW not return.

11. Where a lengthy document is required to be approved, rather than repeating the whole item in the minutes, a copy could be attached to the minutes. It should then be numbered either consecutively after the last page number for that meeting's minutes, or take the number of the last page, with a designatory letter added for each page of the item. Banks prefer their standard form of resolution used which may prevent this short cut.

12. Reference needs to be made to the Articles to ensure the board are acting in accordance with them. These often set out requirements and restrictions on board activities, particularly any constraint on the maximum amount the board can borrow on behalf of the company. If such pre-set figures need to be exceeded the Articles should first be changed as otherwise the directors will be acting *ultra vires* and could be held personally liable (here) to repay the excess borrowed if the company does not repay it.

13. A director can exercise his common law right to have his dissent recorded.

14. To save the time of the meeting, it may be possible to distribute a report (as here) with the agenda and simply report on any updated information since the issue of the agenda.

15. Ideally all directors should be present for the whole meeting – and there is a presumption that this would be the case – otherwise the time a director arrived and/or left should be minuted.

16. The Health and Safety Executive (HSE) has recommended that safety should be a regular item for discussion by the board. This is sound advice not least since it may demonstrate that the company took and takes safety considerations seriously. It might be best if there were a regular safety report – at the very least the board could review the results of the regular *Responsible Persons'* inspections regarding fire safety required to be carried out at every place of work. As part of a safety investigation the HSE have the right to inspect board minutes. Where safety is of particular concern in the activities of a company it may be prudent to place it higher up the agenda (although the location of an item of business on an Agenda should not be taken as an indication of 'importance').

17. Provided the word Deed appears on a document it no longer needs to be sealed and can instead be signed by two signatories. Thus neither the seal nor a register of items sealed need to be retained. However both provide an additional measure of control – not least to ensure that authority for commitment to contracts is made at the highest level in the company. The use of a Register of Seals (and/or of subsequent board approval of all entries provides board authority for the items. It also enables details to be noted of items signed as deeds where the use of the seal has been dispensed with.

    The chairman should sign under the last number authorised at the meeting and should add the date. Ideally the number of each seal entry in the register should appear on the item sealed as a cross-reference of authority.

18. Meetings arranged in the absence of colleague(s) can clash with other commitments already entered into, hence early advice of meeting dates is essential. The dates of board meetings may best be arranged on a rolling 18 month basis, with the immediate six months dates fixed, the following six months subject to some leeway and the third six months indicative only.

Progressively each six month section becomes firmer with additional outline indications tacked on.

19. Inserting a place for the chairman to sign and adding the date (of the next planned meeting) emphasises the importance of signing (as well as improving the presentation of the minutes themselves). Any requirements of the Articles regarding approval of minutes should be checked.

20. Some companies that utilise the action point concept, list the points at the end of the minutes and insert required *completion dates.*

These minutes are based upon versions provided for the boards of actual companies although there are other equally effective versions. A company's chairman/board should decide the way it wishes to record its deliberations. However the importance of correct meeting control and minute taking is perhaps underlined by the comments made by the DBIS inspectors' report on the Phoenix/MG Rover collapse. One could be forgiven for describing it as an excellent example of how not to do it (see COMPANY SECRETARY).

Example: Draft minutes – 2

ANY OTHER COMPANY LTD   431 *(1)*

MINUTES of the [x]th ANNUAL GENERAL MEETING held on Thursday, 24 October 2XXX at [address] at 10.00 a.m.

Present:

ABC (in the Chair)

HIJ

KLM

NOP

12 shareholders

In attendance: AAA (Secretary) and BBB (Auditor)

1. NOTICE

The Secretary read the notice of the meeting   *(2)*

2. DIRECTORS REPORT for the year ended 30 June 2XXX

The chairman referred members to the Report and Accounts for the year ended 30th June 2XXX and the balance sheet as at that date. He requested BBB (of accountants – name) to read the audit report which he did. *(3)*

The chairman proposed, NOP seconded and it was resolved unanimously that the report and accounts of the company for the year ended 30th June 2XXX and the balance sheet as at that date be and they are hereby received. *(4)*

3. DECLARATION OF DIVIDEND

The chairman referred to the payment of an interim dividend in January 2XXX and to the fact that the board were recommending payment of a final dividend of 2p per ordinary share. He proposed, KLM seconded and it was resolved unanimously that the company should pay a final dividend on 27th October 2XXX in respect of the year ended 30th June 2XXX of 2p per ordinary share to the holders of ordinary shares registered on the books as at 1st October 2XXX. *(5)*

4. RETIREMENT BY ROTATION OF DIRECTORS

The chairman stated that in accordance with the Articles of Association and as set out in the notice of the meeting, Mrs EFG and Mr KLM were retiring by rotation and each being eligible, had submitted themselves for re-election. The chairman proposed, Mr HIJ seconded and it was resolved unanimously that the re-election of both retiring directors could be put to the meeting as one motion. *(6)*

The chairman proposed, Mr K Jones, a shareholder seconded, and it was resolved unanimously that Mrs EFG and Mr KLM be and they hereby are re-elected directors of the company.

5. AUDITORS

It was proposed by Mrs EFG, seconded by the chairman and resolved nemo contendare that Messrs [Name] be and they are hereby re-appointed auditors of the company until the conclusion of the next following AGM on terms to be agreed by the directors. *(7)*

The meeting terminated at 10.25 a.m.

Chairman   29th November 2XXX   *(8)*

Notes:

Under CA06, LTDs no longer need hold an AGM unless members (or the company's Articles or the directors) so require. If an AGM is held, minutes must be taken and (since October 2007) preserved for ten years (although it may be wise to preserve them for the life of the company – as is still required for earlier minutes).

1. The pages should be numbered consecutively. Often minutes of general and board meetings are kept in the same folder and numbered consecutively as a single record. This can pose a problem should a member wish to inspect them, since although members have a right to see the minutes of general meetings, they have no right to see the board meeting minutes. Thus the minutes would have to be separated and the page numbering might need explanation. Minutes of meetings of shareholders must be kept at the registered office. There is no restriction regarding the location of minutes of board meetings, although both they and minutes of GMs should be kept securely and under confidentiality protection.

2. There is no requirement to read the notice of the meeting but it can be helpful (if only to cover the arrival of latecomers)

3. Similarly there is no requirement for the auditors to read the audit report (which they will already have had to sign) but again it does little harm and, at least, identifies the auditor to the members.

4. The members have only a right to receive accounts already approved by the directors – they have no right of approval or rejection.

5. The members can approve, reduce or reject a final dividend: but cannot increase it. Using a dividend striking date prior to the meeting should enable all the calculations to be carried out, and even cheques drawn/credits prepared, on the assumption that the dividend will be approved. Once this happens, the payments can be despatched (or the amounts transferred) so that members receive them on the due date. Listed PLCs must give notice to the Stock Exchange of a board meeting at which there will be consideration of dividend declaration and (if so) of its approval.

6. The re-election of directors *en masse* can only take place if the meeting has previously approved (as here) that the re-election can take place in this way.

This can be a valuable time-saver if there are numerous proposed re-elections.

7. *Nemo contendare* is a Latin tag meaning no one objected to the proposal.

   Although everyone voted in favour of all the previous proposals, in this instance, whilst no-one voted against, there were abstentions.

8. Best practice suggests that the minutes of AGMs and (E)GMs should be approved and signed by the chairman at the next following board meeting (i.e. not being left until the next following general meeting, which could be well over a year later.)

Compilation and approval

The detail generated in using a dynamic AGENDA may provide an initial guide to the content of the minutes. In addition the Secretary will almost certainly take his own notes during the meeting and from both sources can draft a first version of the minutes. This is usually considered (and edited) by the chairman and possibly a second (or further) draft(s) generated until a final version for approval by the board is available. Best practice indicates that minutes should be approved at the next following board meeting. Articles may state that if the Chairman signs the minutes they become conclusive evidence that that was what took place which means that it may be virtually impossible to challenge them later. Once the minutes are signed, ideally notes and drafts may be best destroyed so that only the version eventually approved is available. Minutes should not however simply be *nodded through*.

Case study: Approved but not remembered

In *Muncipal Mutual Insurance v Harrap*(H), H claimed that the board had taken a decision, an assertion which they denied. When, under legal discovery rules, the minutes were produced in Court, and one month's board minutes showed the disputed decision, the directors claimed it was a mistake. However it was pointed out that the following month's board minutes evidenced that the board had confirmed the previous minute *as a true record*.

Names and name changes

Publication

The corporate name, registered number and office, and the country of incorporation must be shown:

- at the registered office (or SAIL used for records retention/ inspection);

- at all places where business is transacted (although no longer on their exterior);

- on all business letters and purchase orders;

- on all official publications and notices;

- on any website operated by the company (where the VAT number, if applicable, must also be stated);

- on all bills of exchange, promissory notes, cheques, money orders, etc.; and

- on all invoices, receipts and letters of credit.

These rules also apply to all communications with third parties. Thus all communications sent by e-mail (or fax) to a third party must also comply. It is not necessary for a business card or compliment slip to bear these details, although if such a slip was used to handwrite an offer or confirm a contractual commitment this might create a 'business letter' to which compliance would apply. Indeed this could be a protection since the legal entity would then be clearly committed and liable rather than the signatory having personal liability.

Case study: Whose name?

In *Hamid v Frances Bradshaw Partnership*, a director signed a contract bearing the trading name of a company (of which he was sole shareholder/director) but not the company name. Since there was no indication he was signing on behalf of the company he was found to be personally liable for the contract.

Business names

Formerly where a business traded under a name which was not its corporate name, under the Business Names Act 1985 (BNA85) it was required to state this fact and, if it was a company, it was also required to state its corporate name, registered number and office and country of registration on all business letters, orders, invoices, purchase orders and demands for payment of debts. Although BNA85 has been repealed, its requirements are re-enacted in CA06ss1192/9.

A company must also display at all premises where business is carried on, its corporate name and an address where official documents can be sent or served, and, should anyone request that information, it must be supplied in writing within five days (failing to do so renders the company liable to a fine).

Example: Statement of trading and corporate name and registration

BLOGGS PEGS is a business name of BLOGGS LTD

[Registered in England, No.111222333, registered office address]

Thus a retail company must display in every shop a notice stating the corporate name and address for service of documents, again complying with the basic rule, that even if the transactions are of little value, everyone has a right to know the legal identity and address of the (in this case) *legal person* with whom they are trading, and to know to what address any formal communication (e.g. regarding a dispute) must be sent. Such units are also required to display the name of the owner of the shop. It must be said that both requirements are more noted for breach than observance.

In *DTI v Cedenio* it was held that a sole trader did not breach BNA85 where, in a business letter, although he stated that he was the author of the letter he did not state that he was the proprietor of the business; neither was he obliged, having given an address for the business, to state that this was an address on which legal notices could be served.

Choosing and changing its name

1. A company can choose and change its name to another provided it does not offend certain rules.

2. The name must not:

    *   duplicate an existing name (on the company register);

    *   be misleadingly similar to an existing company's name;

    *   be misleading in giving an inappropriate indication of company type or of its activities;

    *   be offensive or criminal (both in accordance with criteria as laid down by the Secretary of State);

    *   infer a local or central government connection;

    *   contain more than 160 characters and/or certain banned symbols and must contain certain words as required by the Secretary of State (e.g. Limited, Ltd or LTD, Public Limited Company, Plc or PLC, etc., as applicable);

    *   other restricted words only if the permission of bodies controlling such use has been obtained and not withdrawn.

It is also wise to check whether any company is already using the name as a registered trade mark, since attempting to use a protected name may generate an infringement or an action for *passing off*. There is a trend to use combinations of letters and symbols to form *original* names. Since some of these symbols have caused problems at CH, there are restrictions regarding their use.

3. The company needs to pass a special RESOLUTION at a general meeting.

    Under CA06 only 14 days notice is required but if the Articles specify more (e.g. 21 days) that notice must be given (unless notice was waived in whole or in part). Alternatively the resolution could be passed by written resolution provided 75% of the total voting strength is in favour.

4. Within 15 days of the passing of the resolution, a printed copy of it, certified as such by the Secretary or a director, together with the current fee, must be filed at CH (electronically if preferred).

Example: Meeting notice and draft resolution

ANY COMPANY LTD

Notice is hereby given that a (n) (Extraordinary) General Meeting of the company will be held on Monday, 18th December 2XXXfor the purpose of considering, and if thought fit passing the following resolution as a SPECIAL RESOLUTION

'THAT the name of the company be changed from Any Company Ltd to Another Company Ltd'

By order of the board

Company Secretary   16th November 2XXX

Example: Wording for CH notification

SPECIAL RESOLUTION ON CHANGE OF NAME

Companies Act [1985 – 1989] OR [2006]

Company 0009876543 ANY COMPANY LTD

At a(n) (Extraordinary) General Meeting of members of the above-named Company, duly convened and held on 18th December 2XXX the following SPECIAL RESOLUTION was duly passed:

THAT the name of the company be changed to Another Company Ltd

Signed_____ Secretary 30th December 2XXX

Accompanying the resolution must be the required fee and form NM01 (Notice of change of name by resolution under CA06s78). This resolution can be filed electronically.

5. CH issues a Certificate of Incorporation on Change of Name. If the date of the name change is critical, or the company wishes to ensure that no one else can use the new name before the change can be effected, it may be safer to form a shell company with the new name and then for old and new companies (by both passing Special Resolutions simultaneously) to exchange names on a set date.

Control

For many years companies have been required to change their names if:

- their name is too like that of an pre-existing company;

- information provided to support the use of the name was misleading;

- any description of activities in the name is misleading; or

- the name of an oversea company is such that it could not have been approved for use in the United Kingdom.

There is detailed guidance on sensitive words in the CH Guidance Note. However further control over company names is now exercised by the Company Names adjudicator's office and additionally, if a company wishes to use, and thus objects regarding, a name already registered, it may be able to challenge the existing name. The person owning the existing name will only be able to resist the challenge if it can show:

a) the name was registered before the objector obtained any value or goodwill in it;

b) the company using that name has already operated under the name and/or has incurred costs preparing and/or using the name;

c) the company was registered in the ordinary course of company formation and is available to the objector on commercial terms of company formation;

d) the company was formed in good faith;

e) the objector's interests are not adversely affected to any significant extent.

However, if the objector can prove that the purpose in registering the name was purely to try to obtain value from a subsequent legitimate user (i.e. it was deliberately and purely set up using a name that was thought might in the future be desired to be used by a legitimate business) the tribunal can order the original company to change its name and if it does not comply, the tribunal will effect the change for it, allocating a name of its own choosing! This legislation is retrospective so even companies formed speculatively before October 2008 are affected.

This *too same a name* protection does not extend to companies registered in the Isle of Man, Jersey or Guernsey which have their own jurisdictions. Any company which is registered in one of those jurisdictions, and trades on the mainland only through a third party (i.e. they do not have a place of business on the mainland which would classify them as an oversea company – see TYPES) cannot be prevented from using the same name as a company registered in Great Britain.

Case study: Not too similar?

Most applicants to the Tribunal have won (i.e. the decisions went against those who had previously set up companies trying to *reserve* a name speculatively to be able to sell it profitably). However in the case concerning Zurich Insurance Company (ZIC) against Zurich Investments Ltd (ZIL), the applicant (ZIC) lost. ZIL had been set up in the Isle of Man and it was later decided to change the name of a UK registered company to ZIL. The Tribunal felt that this was purely an administrative action not intended to conflict with (the already existing) ZIC and one made *in good faith*. Thus ZIL can continue to use that name although many might feel that ZIL would surely have some connection to ZIC which it does not and that ZIC were let down by the protection!

'Too similar' name objection and monitoring

Although CH can prevent the registration of a company name which is the same as or *too like* an existing company name, there have been instances where this has taken place. Companies have 12 months within which to object to the registration of a new name which they feel is too like their own. Once the 12 month period has expired there is no right to require a change. Companies concerned to protect their names should monitor the list of proposed/new company names regularly so that any objections can be lodged before the time limit expires – using the CH website, anyone can check the current register for their own company and therefore see whether there is a new company with too similar a name.

Although registering a company name at CH should protect that name in terms of preventing another company using it as their corporate name, this does not necessarily prevent commercial use. Trade Marks are distinct from company names and action to protect such assets may be necessary.

Case study: Need to protect name

In *IBM v Web-Sphere Ltd*, IBM registered 'Websphere' for software products as a Community Trade Mark (CTM) in 1998. In 1999, a competitor company, Publiweb Ltd, changed its company name to Web-Sphere Ltd and registered three domain names using that new corporate name. A CTM owner is entitled to prevent other parties using an identical mark in relation to identical products (and may be able to prevent use in relation to similar goods). IBM sued Web-Sphere Ltd for passing off their product as if it were IBM's. Web-Sphere Ltd. argued that this could not be so since it was merely using its company name but this failed and the company was held to have infringed IBM's CTM. The High Court also required Web-Sphere Ltd to change its name and to cease using the domain names.

A UK Patent Office survey disclosed that over 80% of small and medium sized organisations had not registered the name of their businesses as trade marks; 44% did not think they have enough protection and 1% didn't know whether they had protected their name at all!

Developments

1. If the company has permission to omit 'Limited' (or 'cyfyngedig' for Welsh companies) from its name (which can be effected by submitting form NE01 to CH) and the Secretary of State has determined that permission to omit should be rescinded, or where a company has been restored to the register having previously been removed from it, the directors can resolve to change its name and then lodge form NM05 with CH.

   If the Articles permit a name change other than by special resolution form NM04 can be used.

   If a company wishes to change its name to one which requires permission from a third party, form NM02 can be used, with form NM03 used if and when the required permission is granted.

2. The Company, LLP and Business Names etc. Regulations 2014 removed a number of sensitive words from a list of those that

previously could not without specific permission be used as part of a company name. Those removed (i.e. now made available) include 6 very common words on the previously proscribed list – Holding, International, Group, European, National and Board. It is felt that allowing wider use of such words will pose *no harm to the public*.

In addition there are a number of changes regarding words etc. that seek to differentiate one company from another but that in many cases would be seem to be *the same'*– thus 'Stone Company Ltd' would now be regarded as being *the same as* ' Stone and Company Ltd' (although previously these companies would not have been so regarded).

Words such as Exports, Group, Holdings, Imports, International and Services are now disregarded when comparing names to see if they are the *same*.

Thus 'Widgets Galore Exports Ltd' will not now be regarded as the *same name* as 'Widgets Galore Ltd' and would be allowed by CH. The effect however is that the unscrupulous may not be prevented from forming similar-named companies incorporating such words. It may be advisable for legitimate companies to form companies themselves using such words to prevent this.

For example if you own Widgets Galore Ltd, you might want to form Widgets Galore (Export) Ltd, Widgets Galore (Imports) Ltd, Widgets Galore (Holdings) Ltd and so on. Of course if a third party formed a competing company there could still be an action if losses were incurred as a result of such *passing off*. Expert advice should be taken.

Nominee shareholdings

KEY POINTS

- Under previous legislation companies needed two share-holders – to satisfy this requirement parent companies could hold (say) 99 shares leaving 1 share to be held by a director.

- This is now unnecessary as Single Member Companies have been permitted since 1992.

- Safeguards are essential if a nominee shareholder is to be used.

Directors as nominees

There is no reason to continue with the device of someone holding a share on behalf of the main shareholder in a subsidiary simply to create a second shareholder as making the company an SMC is permissible. However, if a company originally had two shareholders (e.g. its parent held 99 shares and a director held the other) and the single share is transferred to the parent (the subsidiary becoming an SMC), entries must be made in the Register of Members, and CH must be informed that the company is now an SMC. The sole member's entry in the Register should read 'On [date] this company became a single member company'. If an SMC subsequently issues shares to a new shareholder, or the parent transfers some of its holding to additional member(s) the note 'On [date] this company ceased to be a single member company' must be added to the former sole member's account and CH must be informed.

A difficulty may arise where a director (or some other appointee) is the nominee holding the single share, there is a disagreement, and they leave the company. In order to register the transfer, either to another nominee or to the parent company, the nominee's signature is required on a stock transfer form (STF), which may be difficult to obtain. Indeed a refusal to sign might be used as a lever to obtain an enhanced settlement.

Administration

If it is decided to create a nominee holding or to appoint a new nominee, a declaration of trust together with an undated STF relating to the share(s) and signed by the nominee should be obtained.

Example: Draft Declaration of Trust for nominee shareholder

This Declaration of Trust is made by me (Name) of (Address) on this (Date) concerning the One share of (Nominal Value) held by me in (Company).

I confirm that I hold the above share on behalf of, and as Trustee for (Name and Address of Beneficial Owner) who is the legal owner of the share. I confirm that any dividends received by me in respect of my holding this share on behalf of the said (Owner) will be immediately remitted by me to (Owner), or immediately disposed of in accordance with any instructions issued by (Owner).

I also confirm that on receipt of instructions from (Owner) I will immediately transfer the share as directed, in anticipation of which instructions I have today signed a stock transfer form which has the identity of the transferee left blank.

Signed _____ Witness _____

Provided the nominee has previously signed an STF then should the majority owner ever wish to change their nominee (or simply to transfer the share into its own name), the name of a new holder can be inserted in that STF, the form can be dated, and lodged with the share certificate to effect the transfer. Obviously such a signed STF should be preserved safely. Stamp duty will not normally be due.

Proxies

Authority

The authority for company members to appoint another person to act as their proxy (on their behalf) is found in the Articles which may stipulate requirements re drafting and submitting the forms – and even specify a wording. It is usual for a company to despatch a proxy form with the notice of a meeting and to state that it must be lodged (at the registered office or office of the share registrar of the company) by a set time before the meeting. Under CA85 Table A reg. 62, the required time for lodging cannot exceed 48 hours before the meeting (or 24 hours before the operative date where the poll is to be taken after the meeting) – although of course there is nothing to stop a member submitting their proxy earlier. In the CA06 pro-forma LTD Articles, any time limit can be set by the company in its Articles (providing the limit is not earlier than those in CA06s327(2) ignoring non-working days), so companies adopting the pro forma would need to add specific requirements in this regard. Although it is administratively preferable for members to use the standard printed form, the use of an alternative is usually allowed provided the instructions are clear.

Form

Proxies can be either general or specific. A general proxy simply appoints another person to act and vote on behalf of the member in accordance with the proxy's) own views – which may of course have been dictated to them by, or agreed with, the member. Specific proxies, or two-way proxies, allow the member to indicate, for each resolution to be considered by the meeting, how his votes must be cast. Wording allowing a proxy to vote as he thinks fit on items legitimately before the meeting (e.g. a motion to adjourn, vote of thanks etc.) could also be included.

The wording used in proxy forms may sometimes be specified in the Articles.

Example: General proxy

GENERAL PROXY Bloggs Manufacturing Ltd

I, [name] of [address] being a member of Bloggs Manufacturing Ltd hereby appoint [name of proxy], or failing him/her, [name], as my proxy to vote in my name and on my behalf at the [type of meeting e.g. ANNUAL, [EXTRAORDINARY] GENERAL MEETING of the company to be held on [date] and at any adjournment thereof [as he/she thinks fit]

Signed _____ Date _____

Example: Specific proxy

SPECIFIC PROXY Bloggs Manufacturing Plc

I, [name] of [address] being a member of Bloggs Manufacturing Plc hereby appoint [name of proxy], or failing him/her, [name], as my proxy to vote in my name and on my behalf at the ANNUAL GENERAL MEETING of the company to be held on [date] and at any adjournment thereof as is stated below:

Resolution 1 Adoption of accounts for the year ended

30th June 2XXX and Balance sheet as at that date FOR / AGAINST*

Resolution 2 Payment of dividend FOR / AGAINST*

Resolution 3 Re-election of directors

J Bloggs FOR / AGAINST*

A N Other FOR / AGAINST*

Resolution 4 Re-election of Auditors FOR / AGAINST*

Resolution 5 Authority for directors to agree

the auditors' remuneration FOR / AGAINST*

Signed _____ Date _____

*Delete as appropriate. Unless the way a vote is to be cast is indicated, the proxy will vote as they think fit.

Proxy administration

1. It is usual to insert 'the Chairman of the meeting' as the first choice proxy with space to allow the member to delete this and insert an alternative.

2. A proxy need not be a member of the company (CA06s324). (This is so even if the Articles state a proxy must be a member.)

3. A listed PLC must provide a three-way proxy – not only allowing members to vote either *for* or *against* but also to *withhold their vote* (i.e. as a form of protest which the member feels may not be strong enough to warrant a vote against the matter).

4. It may be helpful to suggest that members give the person acting as their proxy, a copy of the form of proxy to aid identification when attending the meeting.

5. Proxies should be date and time stamped on receipt. A member could file a subsequent proxy (before the final time limit) in which case any proxy revokes one lodged earlier.

6. An analysis of the proxy forms should be made as soon as the required time of deposit has passed so that (where specific proxies are used) voting strength for and against each item of business is known in advance.

7. The ARTICLES should be checked for clarification of QUORUM requirements.

   If the Articles are silent regarding the quorum (other than for single member companies where the quorum is obviously one) CA06s318 states that this should be two members in person or by proxy or representative.

8. Under the Electronic Communications Act and CA06, company members can submit proxy forms electronically.

9. Under CA06s324 members of companies limited by shares are allowed to appoint more than one proxy – each representing part of their holding.

Revocation

Proxies are revoked by:

- receipt of a notice of termination either prior to the meeting or to the vote to which the proxy relates or, if a poll is required, before the time for the poll to be taken – CA06s330.

- the submission of a later proxy in place of one filed previously;

- the death of the member; or

- the attendance by the member in person at the meeting, although it would be safer to check the position (i.e. who is going to vote) if both member and proxy are present.

Operation

The use of the authority vested in a proxy (person) depends on the ARTICLES. Although historically some companies restricted the powers of proxies, CA06 overrides any such restrictions. Proxies have a right to speak and vote on a show of hands and join in the request for a poll. As noted above, a proxy does not have to be a member of the company even if the Articles so specify – CA06 overrides the Articles.

Calling for a poll

The full power of shareholding can usually only be felt when a poll is called since then all votes eligible (rather than a single raised hand per shareholder regardless of whether they have 10 shares or 10,000) can potentially be counted. A poll can usually be demanded or called by:

- the chairman;
- any two members (which includes proxies and representatives of corporate shareholders); or
- any member(s) holding 10% or more of the share capital.

The pro forma Articles for an LTD accompanying CA06 also allow the directors to demand a poll.

Thus an individual proxy, unless speaking for member(s) holding 10% or more of the share capital, can only join in the request for a poll.

Some listed PLCs have changed their Articles and abolished voting by show of hands – since that could be criticised as being undemocratic. Thus all votes are conducted by poll and business is resolved by (potentially) the full voting strength.

Representatives

Corporate or institutional members should not grant a proxy but should appoint someone as their representative. To do so, requires a resolution of the board (or governing body) of the entity or institution naming the person to act on its behalf. Such a representative acts in all respects as an individual member of the company with all the rights of such a member. There is no need to lodge the letter of authority prior to the meeting – effectively the representative attends in exactly the same way as do natural persons – although requiring advance notice of the name of the representative may be prudent.

Electronic proxies

The EU Shareholder Rights directive requires listed PLCs to give their members at least 21 days notice of a GM (which is not an AGM), but this can be reduced to 14 days provided:

- the shareholders approve (by special resolution), every year, the shortening of such notice; and

- shareholders are able to cast their votes by electronic means available to all of them.

The wording for such a resolution could run as follows:

'That any meeting other than the Annual General Meeting of the company be properly convened providing 14 days notice is given to members entitled to attend and vote.'

Quorum

KEY POINTS

- Articles usually stipulate that a minimum number of members must be present before a meeting is validly convened.

- If that minimum number is present the meeting is 'quorate' but the situation should a member leave and the number fall below the minimum should be addressed.

Board meetings

The ARTICLES may stipulate a quorum. The new model Articles for an LTD state that the quorum can be fixed from time to time by the directors themselves but it must never be less than two (and if it is not fixed, it will be two) – virtually the same provisions as those in Table A of CA85. Reference should also be made to any Article governing directors' interests, since some stipulate that if a director has a personal interest in an item for discussion then they may not be counted as part of the quorum for that item – that is there must be what is called a *disinterested quorum*. If so, at least the required minimum number of directors who are not interested in the matter must be present. If the number of directors is small and the quorum requirements are high, the fact that a director is disqualified from being counted as part of the quorum could mean there is delay in gaining proper authority for decisions as the meeting could be *inquorate* (and valid decisions could not be made). Failing to abide by the requirements of the Articles renders those responsible personally liable for any losses to the company occasioned thereby since they are acting *ultra vires* (beyond the powers given them by) the Articles.

General meetings

Other than in a single member company where the sole member is the quorum (in which case all decisions taken by the member should be recorded either by a written resolution or by minutes of that person's *meeting* simply by the member notifying the company of his decision), normally the quorum is two persons personally present. Proxies (and representatives) can be counted towards the quorum. However where one person acts as proxy for two members that person alone cannot form a quorum. A meeting proceeding in the absence of a required quorum is *inquorate* and anyone acting on decisions purporting to be taken at such a meeting could be held liable.

Case study: Ignorance is no excuse

In *Smith v Henniker-Major* a director wanted the company to follow a course of action to which he knew his three co-directors were opposed. Failing to notify his colleagues that he was convening a board meeting, and acting on his own at that *meeting*, he purported to pass a board resolution approving the matter. However he overlooked that not only was failing to give notice of the board meeting to his colleagues a breach of company law, he was also acting *ultra vires* the company's Articles which stipulated that for a board meeting to be validly constituted the quorum was two directors. The Court of Appeal stated that the resolution he purported to pass was a *worthless piece of paper* and since he acted in breach of the Articles (i.e. *ultra vires*), he was personally liable for any loss occasioned as a result of the implementation of the 'decision'.

Conducting business

Usually, if within 30 minutes of the time set by the notice of the meeting, a quorum is not present, the meeting cannot proceed and must be adjourned. However Table A CA85 stipulates that if a quorum was present at the commencement of the meeting but then later the meeting ceased to be *quorate* because a person forming part of the quorum left (or was disqualified, for example because of a conflict of interests), then, providing there are at least two members present, a meeting can continue.

Single member quorum

In a company where more than one member is entitled to attend, the Court has power to authorise the holding of a meeting even though it is known in advance that only one person will be present (either in person or by proxy). Thus in a case where the minority shareholder refused to attend meetings (for which the quorum was two) and at which the business to be conducted was his dismissal by the majority shareholder, the Court allowed the majority shareholder to act alone to conduct the business.

If there is only one holder of a class of shares (e.g. preference shares) the decision of that person (which would be best confirmed in writing signed by that person) on behalf of the whole class (see CLASSES OF SHARES) will be binding even though no *meeting* as such has taken place.

Record inspection and retention

Policy for document and records preservation

To ensure that all the documents required to be made available are protected and able to be displayed, a policy such as the following could be adopted.

Example: Company policy for document protection

Document and records preservation [Company] PLC/LTD

1. Responsibility for preserving the various books, registers and records of the company, to comply with legislation and in accordance with business practice is delegated to [the Secretary].

2. Such responsibility includes:
   - ensuring safe storage with reasonable accessibility whilst the items are current;

- provision of adequate back up systems capable of providing current record data, should the original be lost for any reason;

- preserving records in accordance with a procedure and timetable to be devised, and in archives.

3. The terms of retention as set out in *The ICSA Guide to Document Retention* (subject to any extension, but not contraction, of the suggested time limits for reasons particular to the company) are to be adhered to at all times

4. Suitably secure premises/facilities will be utilised for this purpose. Such premises etc. must be protected from rodents, fire and flood, intruders etc.

5. Checks will be made that all records held electronically can still be accessed before any change of system/software is finalized.

6. [The Secretary] will monitor changes in requirements and effect appropriate alterations.

7. A report on compliance with this policy will be made annually to the board of directors.

Promulgation

Those responsible for admitting visitors to the company need to know how to deal properly and efficiently with such inspections and enquiries as legally required.

In reality, personal inspections are rare and most people wishing to check such data will find it much easier to access the company data filed at CH even though it may be somewhat out of date (e.g. details of the shareholders as disclosed by the most recent Confirmation Statement could be up to a year out of date).

Suggested procedure

1. Identify all those having a right of access and the records to which such rights apply.

2. The credentials of the person requesting access to the records should be checked in order to ensure that they have the right to access (or make a request to access) the record requested. Shareholders' names should be checked against the members' register, creditors against the purchase ledger, debenture / loan holders against their register, and so on.

3. They should be conducted to the interview room. Those with a right of inspection will be interviewed by the Secretary, whom failing the assistant Secretary, whom failing the chief accountant. Should the visitor require copies of the documentation – charges as laid down may be levied. An invoice should be raised and payment obtained before the visitor leaves [or before inspection]. A company representative should remain in the interview room throughout the visit to ensure the protection of the record. A note of the inspection should be made in the visitors book and the fact notified to the Chairman immediately and also reported at the next following board meeting.

    Those without an immediate right of inspection will be advised that their request will be passed to the board for decision and they will be advised of the decision within 48 hours.

Charges

The charges for inspection and copying (although there is no obligation to provide copying facilities) are as follows. The company can also charge for any costs incurred in delivering a copy.

a) Register of members: inspection – £3.50 each hour or part thereof; copies – £3.50 for first 50 entries, £31.50 for next 950 entries or part thereof, £20 for next 4,000 entries or part thereof and £25 for every subsequent 5,000 entries or part thereof.

b) Directors service contracts and/or indemnity provisions, resolutions and meetings, report under s805: inspection costs as above; copies – 20p per 1,000 words or part thereof.

c) Register of Debenture holders: inspection as above, copies – 10p per 500 words in the trust deed.

'Internal' bodies access

These records are shown below with details of those with rights of access. Unless otherwise stated the records should be held at its registered office or SAIL or with CH. If such records are held in an electronic format, the records should be held at the registered office and CH informed. If a SAIL is used all the records must be held there.

A
Register of Members

Access: on application to the directors

The board must within 5 days allow the inspection or apply to the Court (telling the person wishing to inspect that it has done so) for permission to resist the inspection because they feel it is 'not a fit purpose'.

'Fit purposes' could include:

- to check/correct personal details;
- to contact other shareholders for pressure purposes;
- for regulators checking money laundering;
- in consideration of a takeover;
- for research;
- for stockbrokers before a transaction; and/or
- to enforce a judgement (e.g. a dividend stop notice).

Whilst the reasons for resisting an inspection could include purposes that:
- are unlawful;
- would breach the Data Protection Act;
- enable a third party to check credit or identities of shareholders;
- facilitate the marketing of investments or commercial products;
- might result in the threatening, harassment or intimidation of shareholders; or
- seek to market securities, and so on.

If wishing to resist an inspection, taking legal advice may be appropriate.

B
Register of Directors and Secretary

Register of Directors Shareholdings – PLCs only

Register of significant shareholdings/substantial interests – listed PLCs only

Overseas branch register (with Register of Members)

Reports on disclosures under CA06s793 notices – listed PLCs only

Contract/Statutory declaration for purchase by company of own shares

Register of persons of significant control (copy must be lodged at CH)

Access: by members – every working day. By others – on application to the directors

C
Minutes of General Meetings

Directors' service contracts (with Register of Members) (must also be available for inspection at AGM.)

Access: by members only (who must also be sent a copy if requested).

D
Register of Debenture/Loan holders
(in place where Register of Members is held)

Access: by members, and debenture stock/loan holders.

E
Statutory declaration of payment out of capital for redemption or purchase by company of own shares

Access: by members and creditors.

Additional requirements

The above notes cover only corporate records where there is a requirement to preserve them and to make them available for inspection. The preservation of a whole range of other records is required – to comply with legislation, for commercial reasons and since they form part of the history of the company.

Detailed consideration is essential for the safe protection and accessibility of such records. In view of any space limitations the possibility of electronic scanning might be examined although great care should be taken and reference should be made to the British Standard 's 'Code of practice on the legal admissibility of information stored on electronic document management systems'. Under the Civil Evidence Act 1995 computer generated records are admissible as evidence although it may be necessary to prove these were properly created and are accurate.

Retention periods

The records referred to above must be held for at least the life of the company. However since a company is a legal person, it can not only be dissolved, liquidated, wound up, struck off etc., but also, by order of the Court, it can be resuscitated (see RESURRECTION OF COMPANIES) to face a liability claim. Hence it may be safest (other than for companies which have never traded) to retain such records for at least (say) 6 years beyond the end of a company's life. Since the purpose of resuscitation is to enable a company to respond to a liability claim it would be prudent to keep liability insurance records for at least the same length of time. Records other than those stated above may be held for shorter periods and guidance should be sought in each case. However, this process may now be unnecessary since the Third Parties (Rights against Insurers) Act 2010 avoids the need for company resuscitation and enables actions to be lodged directly against insurers (provided they are known of course).

'External bodies' access

A considerable number of other regulatory bodies have rights of access to the company premises and records, and it is essential to be prepared for such visits and to brief those responsible in the company to deal with them.

Procedure

1. Representatives of organisations on the following list have a right of access to company premises, may have a right to inspect records and interview employees and may also have a right to remove records, data and registers, etc. Denial of access to some of these bodies can be a criminal offence.

2. The receptionist/gate keeper on duty should establish the agency represented and inspect their credentials to ensure their *bona fides*. They should be conducted to the waiting room and the company representative stated should be contacted. The contact will then be responsible for dealing with the enquiry.

a) Government and statutory regulatory agencies

Department of Business, Energy & Industrial Strategy (DBEIS formerly DBIS), Financial Conduct Authority (FCA), Serious Fraud Office (SFO), Competition and Markets Authority (CMA), European Union inspectors (EU).

Scope:

- *DBEIS*: Under company legislation, power to investigate company affairs, ownership, dealings in shares, including insider dealing. The exact nature of the investigation must be ascertained.

- *FCA*: Under the Financial Services Act 1986 the FCA has powers to investigate the affairs of all companies operating under its aegis. The FCA also has authority under the Financial Services and Markets Act 2000 to regulate all financial business in the UK and investigate instances of market abuse and manipulation including insider dealing. It has a wide range of disciplinary and enforcement powers.

- *SFO* has powers to investigate matters of fraud in excess of £2 million and to be of public concern as well as matters arising from the Bribery Act.

- *CMA* to investigate whether supplies of goods or services breach the principles of the Fair Trading Act 1973, the Competition Act 1998, the Enterprise Act 2002 and the Consumer Rights Act 2015 and can gain access to inspect records of any company which is suspected of infringing the prohibitions set out in those and ancillary Acts.

- *EU* inspectors have rights (without notice) to enter the premises of organisations of member states under the Communities Act 1972. In doing so, the inspectors are supposed to act in accordance with the laws of the member state (and in concert with its domestic regulatory agency) concerned.

Persons dealing: Secretary (whom failing assistant Secretary, whom failing chief accountant).

Actions:

- Advise chairman and board, corporate lawyers, and public relations staff (to deal with media requests for information).

- Meet representatives and endeavour to ascertain requirements.

- Check requirements with corporate lawyers.

- Endeavour to assist investigators whilst ensuring the minimal potential damage to the company name and reputation.

- Write report of visit, requirements, action carried out, records inspected/removed.

WARNING

Taking legal advice may be essential since those questioned may not have a right to silence. Refusing to answer questions, even those felt to be self-incriminatory, can generate sanctions including imprisonment, although there is a right against self-incrimination in competition legislation. Oral questions (usually posed during a *dawn raid)* tend to relate to questions about the documents.

Material questions are usually asked in written form and via a *section 26* notice.

It is also essential to try to obtain copies of everything seized during such a search, although some agencies will not allow this, undertaking to provide copies of the documents seized within a week.

b) Statutory reporting agencies

HM Revenue and Customs (HMRC), Health and Safety Executive / Local Authority (HSE/LA), Trading Standards Officers (TSO), Pensions Regulator (PR), Rating authorities (RA), UK Border Force (UKBF).

- *HMRC*: Powers of access tend to be exercised by the Audit Department of the Inland Revenue, or the Compliance units of the Dept of Work and Pensions (DWP), which are charged with the duty of checking the validity of the way an employer has paid and deducted tax from employees and workers. The DWP also has rights under the National Minimum/Living Wage legislation to check that employers are paying at least the wage rates specified to those entitled (and to bring criminal prosecutions if not) – which may be extended to investigations regarding payments under the new Apprenticeships scheme.

HMRC has wide powers of access and seizure in respect of its VAT collection duties. The penalties for, even totally accidental, errors in VAT collection and payment can be severe. Presumably additional powers will be granted as a result of the implementation of the proposals regarding prohibition of tax evasion.

- *HSE and/or LAs* have rights under the Working Time Regulations 1998 to inspect records of hours worked by those opting out of the maximum 48 hours worked per week rule.

- *TSOs* have rights under the Consumer Protection Act 1987 to ensure compliance with such legislation.

- *PR* has rights under various Pensions Acts to check compliance, in particular that pension contribution deductions made from employees wages have been paid to the appropriate trustees and that, where necessary, access to the provider of a stakeholder pensions is provided and the deductions made are being paid over. These rights have been extended to cover the records of the NEST pension arrangements following auto-enrolment.

- *RA* have a right of access for the purpose of checking the valuation for the purposes of the Uniform Business rate (or any appeal in respect thereof)

Persons dealing: Chief accountant/personnel director (whom failing finance director, whom failing Secretary)

Actions:

- Meet representatives and establish nature of enquiry.

- Provide information required.

- Advise chairman and board and corporate lawyers (via Secretary).

- Ensure if errors are found that systems are changed to avoid a repetition, whilst those responsible should be disciplined if procedures have not been followed correctly. HMRC have a right to pursue an individual employee if through their actions tax has been underpaid in respect of payroll liabilities.

- Write report of visit, action required and effected.

c) Emergency and utilities services

Fire, police, Health and Safety Executive, Factory Inspectorate, Environmental Health Officers, gas, water and electricity utilities:

- *Fire*: right of access to premises mainly for the purposes of checking compliance with the Regulatory Reform (Fire Safety) Order 2005 (i.e. that there is a Responsible Person appointed for every location and that they regularly conduct inspections of the premises – dated reports on which should be made available)

- *Police:* unless in the belief, or in connection with such belief, that a crime has been or is about to be committed, or is being committed, or in *hot pursuit* of a suspected person, or accompanying Government and Statutory Regulatory Agencies the police have no immediate right of access to premises other than with the permission of the owner/occupier.

- *Health & Safety Executive (HSE), Environmental Health Officers (EHOs) and Factory Inspectors* have a range of powers which vary from industry to industry.

Operators of large (and potentially hazardous) facilities are obliged (under the Control of Industrial Major Accident Regulations 1988) to file and keep up to date details of plans and emergency evacuations etc. which will require an interface with the appropriate department which may well wish to check the site. EHOs also have rights of access under the Food Safety Act 1992 to check that food preparation, storage and serving areas are suitable. HSE inspectors have a right of inspection of Certificates of Employers Liability (hard or electronic copy) and, if investigating a safety breach or accident, the right to inspect the minutes of the board.

- *Utilities* have rights of access to read meters and, if leaks / breaks are suspected, to rectify on an emergency basis which could even entail forced entry out of hours.

Persons dealing: Personnel director (whom failing Secretary, whom failing personnel manager)

Actions:

- Meet representative and establish problem.
- Rectify if required and possible.
- Update procedures, if required.
- Write report of visit and action effected.

d) Others

- *UK Border Force*: to check the right to work in the UK (and the copy documentation related thereto) of all employees (and ex-employees for up to two years after they have left), and employees transferred under the Transfer of Undertakings (Protection of Employment) Regulations, and, if using immigrants from outside the EU, that the employer has the appropriate licence to permit such employment.

Persons dealing: Personnel/HR manager (whom failing Secretary)

Action:

- Be prepared to produce copies of relevant evidence (in a form which cannot be altered) and, if applicable, the licence.
- *Department of Transport*: to inspect transport (fleet) operators licence and administration.

Persons dealing: Transport manager (whom failing Secretary)

Action:

- Be prepared to produce operators licence and back-up records etc.

- *Local Authorities:* have an increasing range of obligations – see above re Trading Standards. In addition they are responsible for ensuring compliance with environment protection, food safety and storage etc. legislation.

Persons dealing: Personnel/HR manager (whom failing Secretary)

- *Landlords and agents:* to inspect condition and use of premises, assess value for insurance, prepare dilapidations ('*wants of repair*') reports, under the provisions of leases and licences.

Persons dealing: Secretary (whom failing assistant Secretary, whom failing chief accountant)

Action:

- Meet: representatives – since most leases state that (say) 48 hours notice of such inspections must be given there should be no need to allow immediate access unless it is an emergency, although good landlord/tenant relations may require a positive and helpful approach. If a dilapidations notice (or schedule of '*wants of repair*' i.e. a requirement to put or keep the premises into good order and repair) is served, refer to the lease for the right to serve/procedure to be followed (and for the situation regarding the costs of service of the notice).

Note: Any other bodies with rights of access for particular industries (e.g. Charities Commission for charitable companies, etc.) should be identified.

Registered number and office

KEY POINTS

- A company's registered number is unique to it.

- The number can never be changed (although the company's name can).

- The registered office must be located within the country of registration.

Consistent identification

Although a company can change its name (by special resolution), its business (by changing its objects clause), its type of registration (an LTD can RE-REGISTER as a PLC and vice versa) etc., and its ownership (by change of guarantor or shareholder), etc., the one constant unchanging evidence of its existence is its unique and unalterable registered number. Although under CA06s1066, CH has powers to adopt a new form of registered numbers there are currently no announced plans for this, and if it were implemented, there would be a 3 year period, during which both old and new numbers would be acceptable, so that stocks of letter-heads and other stationery could be exhausted and equivalents bearing a new number originated.

For the purposes of the official lodgement of papers (matters concerning the corporate entity, legal actions, notices, etc.) and to comply with the principle that all those dealing with the company have a right to know with whom they are dealing, and where they are located, every company must have – and promulgate – its registered office. The registered office can only be situated within the country in which the company is incor-porated, although there are EU proposals that would allow a company to move its registered office within the EU – in which case it would be bound by the corporate laws of the country in which its principal office was situated. On registration, the registered office must be advised to CH (form IN01), and all subsequent changes of address must be notified on form AD01 (CA06s87). The country of registration (but not necessarily the address within that country) must be stated in the Memorandum. Around 50% of companies registered in England and Wales have their registered office in London or south-east England.

Promulgation

The company name must be displayed at every place at which the company undertakes business (but no longer on the exterior).However exterior display is required for the registered office (unless it is a domestic residence). Details of the company registration (name, number and registered office and country of registration) must also be shown on all invoices, order forms, letterheads, websites and monetary documentation. This includes external e-mail communications (and faxes). There is no requirement to put such details on business cards or compliment slips – although should they be used to make or accept an offer, contract etc., the legally required details would best be added to ensure it is the company not the individual that is party to the contract. Under CA06 the Secretary of State has powers to stipulate where the company name must be displayed.

Changing the location of the registered office

Any alteration in location of the registered office must be filed with CH using form AD01, since all communications from CH are sent to the registered office, if it is changed and there is no postal redirection, official communications may go astray. This could result in the company failing to respond to CH requests including failing to file its accounts within the required time limit, in turn leading to prosecution and fines for the directors – and even to the company being struck off the register (thereby incurring costs for reinstatement).

On notifying CH of a change of registered office, a 14 day period during which both old and new offices are valid for the service of notices is allowed. If a company is required to move in an emergency (for example because of terrorism, fire, flood or other disaster, etc.) the penalties for failing to notify the change of registered office to CH are waived, provided notification of the new office is made within 14 days of the enforced move being known.

'Company hi-jacking'

There have been numerous instances of unauthorised persons filing with CH a form purporting to evidence a change of registered office to a location under their own control. From that location they proceed to trade and take on credit as if they were the original company. Anyone suspicious, on checking the company's file at CH would find a change of address, as it would be reasonable to presume, validly filed. The fraudsters then abscond owing substantial sums to unpaid creditors who would understandably think they were owed the money by the original company. Regular checking of the company's details on file at CH might be prudent. Alternatively the company could either add its own name (with the private or email address of the Secretary) to CH's Monitor service so that all changes to the company's own records are notified to that address and/or use the CH PROOF service under which a company commits to file all key items electronically which (needing both an authorization code and a password) should provide greater protection. Having signed up to this system any subsequent hard copy notification will be rejected by CH – unless separately accompanied by form RP03. (See REGISTRAR for erroneous data correction methods.)

Problems can also arise if a company acquires premises formerly used as the registered office of another company that has failed to inform CH they are no longer there. Post should be *returned to sender* and CH should be informed by recorded delivery that the other company is no longer at that address. CH can then contact the officers of that company and request advice of its new registered office. CH can now go further and change the registered office of that company to the private address of one of the directors.

In order to deal with the above problems CH has made available form RP07 (Application to remove a disputed registered office address) to enable a company to correct the record of their own company or advise the movement of a vacating company from their new address.

Note: For companies formed electronically, since one of the options is to make the service address [for directors] the registered office, answering *yes* means that any future change of the registered office will automatically mean the service address also alters. If this is not the preferred address, form CH01 changing it will have to be filed. Alternatively on formation insert a specified address (even if this is the current registered office).

Administration

Advertising the address of the registered office is required so that everyone knows where official or legal notices can be served. However the means by which such documents are processed after delivery may also need to be given attention as there have been instances where documents requiring attention have not been correctly actioned.

Case study: Expensive inactivity

In a case concerning money said to be owed by a leading UK insurance company (at the time a FTSE100 company), documents giving notice of the intent to apply to the Court for a winding-up order against it for failure to pay, which were legitimately served by a creditor in north-east England, were filed rather than acted upon by the company at its head office in London. Because there was no response, the winding up petition was listed for a Court hearing, to the considerable embarrassment of the company, whose bankers indicated that unless there was immediate clarification they might need to dishonour the company's cheques. The judge refused to accept the company's explanation and promise to pay in order to permit delisting of the application unless they produced the creditor in Court to confirm personally that he had been paid. The company had to pay the creditor, transport him to London and accommodate him in a hotel prior to the hearing!

A responsible person should thus oversee the receipt of post and ensure such notices are brought to the prompt attention of someone in authority.

Disclosure

The registered number helps identify the legal person and the registered office confirms its location. Both items must appear on all business letters and communications (including external emails), invoices, websites, statements and order forms etc. In view of the requirement also to state the country of incorporation, it is normal to use a form of words such as the following, and to instruct printers to incorporate them on all such business stationery.

Example: Wording for incorporation on company letterheads etc.

Bloggs Manufacturing Co. Ltd. Registered in England No 123456789

Registered office: Bloggs House, 1, Bloggs Rd, Bloggsville, Bloggshire, BL1 SH1.

Notes:

1. The names of directors are no longer required to be shown on letterheads, unless one is named, in which case all must be named. However where the printing of a name merely indicates a person-alisation of corporate notepaper (e.g. 'from the office of [name of director or 'The Chairman]') DBEIS is record as stating that this is not normally regarded as being a breach of this requirement.

2. Fines can be levied against both company and officers for failure to comply with these requirements.

Registrar of Companies

INTRODUCTION

- The UK Registrar of Companies was set up in 1844 and is now an Executive Agency of DBEIS. It aims at being fully digital by 2019.

- It maintains records on over 3.5 million current companies which is both a repository of data on those companies and a means by which the public can access their statutory records.

- Dissolved companies records are held by CH for 20 years.

Locations

The main company registry for English and Welsh companies is in Cardiff:

Companies House
Crown Way, Maindy
Cardiff CF4 3UZ
www.companieshouse.gov.uk

Telephone (all departments) 0303 1234 500 with a satellite office now located in London at:

4 Abbey Orchard Street
Westminster
London SW1P 2HT

The records of companies registered in Scotland are located at:

Companies House
4th Floor, Edinburgh Quay 2
139 Fountainbridge
Edinburgh EH3 9FF

The records of companies registered in Northern Ireland are located at:

Companies House
2nd Floor, 32-38 The Linenhall
Belfast NI BT2 8BG

At each location, search, inspection and copying facilities (subject to charge) are available for all callers usually between the hours of 9.00 and 5.00, Monday to Friday (excluding Bank Holidays). However, CH offices (except Belfast) clear their letterboxes at midnight each day, and items placed in these boxes, even if posted there after an office has closed, but before midnight, are regarded as having been filed on that day.

The service

Information on CH requirements and data available is freely available and includes:

1. *Guidance notes* (regularly updated) on a variety of corporate compliance subjects

2. *Monitor* – a service which enables subscribers to nominate certain companies in which they are interested (which, for security reasons, can include itself) so that each time an item is filed in respect of such companies, they are automatically sent a copy.

3. *Direct* – a subscription service which enables subscribers who wish to obtain information on any specified company on a regular basis to do so at any time by direct access. Charges £4 per month are deducted from an account or float paid in advance. It covers around 130 million documents going back 20 years.

4. *WebCheck* is a web-based service which enables those paying by credit card to access information on companies electronically and virtually instantaneously.

   Both Direct and WebCheck services indicate the status of companies using 'A' if a company is in administration and 'V' it if is subject to a voluntary arrangement.

5. *'Scan on demand'*. Since 1995 all company data has been reconstituted in virtual format and is available on demand. Earlier records

are progressively being reconstituted in virtual format. Where this has not taken place records are available on microfiche. Until all files are available electronically, CH operates a service whereby (on an individual basis) copies of data not available in virtual format can be requested electronically, accessed and scanned internally and then made available electronically.

6. *PROOF* stands for PROtected Online Filing facility. Companies which sign up to this service commit themselves to file all documents electronically. Thus any paper documents (if, for example, filed by fraudsters to try and *hijack* the company – see below) are rejected. CH provides on-line guidance on using PROOF.

7. CH produces a DVD/ROM every month containing details of all active companies on the register as well as those in liquidation, receivership, and of all companies dissolved, struck off, etc., in the previous 12 months. The information includes the name, number and address of the company, its type, year end, and dates of the latest annual return and accounts. It also includes details of companies dissolved in the previous months. The charge is £30 for a single DVD or £300 for a year's subscription.

Filing requirements

All CH required data must be filed on or before set time limits, and in an appropriate format. Hard copy documents must be submitted:

- bearing the company's registered number;
- on plain white matte A4 paper between 80 and 100 gsm weight (or else of a background density not greater than 0.3)
- using black ink, with clear legible writing of uniform density or in printed format (but not using a dot matrix printer);
- letters must not be smaller than 1.8 mm with a line width of not less than 0.25 mm;
- have a margin all round not less than 10mm wide.

Documents submitted other than in the above formats (including for example four-colour annual reports) will be rejected. Hard copy forms, returns etc., can be sent by post or delivered by hand to each office. Electronic filing is preferred by CH. Users must obtain an authorisation code and a user password.

Receipt

If filing hard copy, it is advisable to be able to evidence receipt (to resist a claim of late or non-filing), so either the name of the subject company should be added to the Monitoring service, or a covering letter or duplicate form should be sent with each item filed. The original letter should request that CH receipts a copy letter (or the copy form) and returns it. CH is prepared to do this (by affixing a bar code sticker to the copy) provided a pre-paid return envelope is provided.

Example: Letter to CH requesting receipt for item filed

LETTERHEAD
Registrar of Companies
Crown Way, Maindy
Cardiff CF4 3UZ Date

Dear Sir

A Bloggs & Co. Ltd Reg. Number 12345678987

I enclose form [number – in the following example – AP01] relating to [e.g. *'the appointment of an additional director to this company's board of directors'*].

Kindly acknowledge receipt by signing and returning the attached copy letter. A stamped addressed return envelope is attached.

Yours faithfully

J. Bloggs

Secretary

Enc. Copy letter

Form [number]

Reply paid return envelope

[On copy for return in addition to the above wording]

I acknowledge receipt of the document referred to above.

Signed _____

Registrar of Companies

Much of the data required to be filed is subject to time limits, with fines for breaching such limits and/or non-compliance. There are four separate filing time limits – most FORMS, including the CONFIRMATION STATE-MENT must be filed within 14 days of their effective date;

- certain ordinary RESOLUTIONS and all special and extraordinary resolutions must be filed within 15 days of being passed;
- details of CHARGES must be filed within 21 days of creation
- details of new shares issued must be filed within 28 days of board decision re allotment.

Rather than remembering which time limit applies to which filing, it may be more convenient to assume that all items are subject to the shortest, 14 day, limit. Fines for late filing most of the forms are rarely applied. However a company's annual accounts and its Confirmation Statement must not be filed late, since this could generate prosecution, a fine and even the company being struck off the register. Further, under CDDA86s3, anyone responsible for *persistent late filing* at CH can be prosecuted and, if the action is successful, disqualified from acting as an officer of all UK companies during the period of disqualification (ranging from 2 to 15 years).

Accounts

Although smaller and dormant companies (as well as companies whose annual turnover does not exceed £10.2 million etc.) can claim exemption from having their accounts audited, they must still file their accounts at CH. LTDs must file within 9 months of their Accounting Reference Date (ARD – see FINANCIAL YEAR END) and PLCs within 6 months of their ARD. A late filing penalty (of varying amounts depending how late the accounts are filed) is applied. Although there is a strict approach to the time limits re accounts, if it is the first time a company has late-filed and the delay is not more than three days; or the accounts were filed in time but had to be returned for amendment and the corrected accounts are returned within 14 days, the penalty may be waived. In addition to the late filing penalty charged to the company, individuals responsible may be made subject to personal fines following a criminal prosecution and CH may take action to strike the company off the record. If the company is subsequently restored to the register, penalties may be required in respect of the late (or non-) filing of data during the period the company was 'off the register'.

If there are exceptional difficulties in filing accounts by the due date, providing CH is contacted *before* the deadline for filing, it may be possible to obtain an extension. If this is carried out by telephone it would be advisable to confirm all the details including the date and time of the call and person spoken to in a letter or email to CH. All calls to CH are recorded and kept for a year.

If a company has a complaint against a CH procedure – or member of staff etc., it can appeal to the CH adjudicator.

Dormant companies accounts

A company which has not traded (i.e. has had *no significant accounting transactions*) within the year being reported on, can claim exemption from audit and need only file an abbreviated balance sheet and notes (i.e. there is no requirement to file a profit and loss account or a directors' report, although the latter must be sent to the members). If a dormant company does not wish to prepare a set of accounts, form DCA can be completed, although CH recommends that this form should only be used where the company has never traded.

Routine filing matters

Each year companies must file a Confirmation Statement. The first such statement must be made up to the anniversary of the company's incorporation and must be filed within 14 days of that return date. Thereafter a company must make subsequent returns to a date no later than the anniversary of the previous return date. The date can be brought forward before such anniversary but not deferred, and must be filed within 14 days of the date chosen. Changes to the company record in the year following the submission of the Statement can be made without charge.

The Statement can be filed electronically, via the company's own file available through the CH website. The data can simply be updated and the appropriate fee paid. However companies wishing to file hard copy must download a blank return form, complete all the details themselves and pay a filing fee of £40.

Failure to file the Confirmation Statement can involve those responsible being fined, being given a criminal record and could mean the company is struck off the register.

Non-form filing

As well as the forms which must be filed, companies are also required to file:

- Details of their Constitution (the Articles) and any changes thereto. Such changes will normally require Special resolutions which will also need to be filed.

- Certain ordinary RESOLUTIONS. The following resolutions must be filed within 15 days: i.e. those that authorise:

    - an increase in the authorised share capital;
    - the directors to allot shares (although these are now only applicable to companies registered pre CA06, unless there are restrictions on issuing additional shares for CA06 companies which do not need an authorised share capital); or
    - a voluntary winding up of the company.

- Special resolutions and extraordinary resolutions.

Format of resolution for filing

The following is a draft of the format that should be acceptable.

Example: Wording of resolution for filing at Companies House

Company Name Registered number [12345678987]

Ordinary/Special/[Extraordinary] Resolution(s)*of [Company Name]

At a general meeting of the members of the above-named company duly convened and held on [date] at [time] at [the registered office of the company] [address], the following resolution(s) was/were* duly passed:

THAT _____ [detail]

Signed _____ Director/Secretary _____ *

Date _____

*delete as applicable

Data correction

If mistakes occur in filing documentation at CH, the correct information should be filed under cover of form RP04. If the company has committed to electronic filing (i.e. uses PROOF) since the second (corrected) filing can only be filed in hard copy, it will also be necessary to send with these documents the *consent to paper file* form (PR03). The effect is to second file not to correct the first file – so both will be shown on the company record. Incorrect information on the following forms can be corrected using this process:

- AP01, 02,03 and 04
- CH01,02,03 and 04
- TM01 and 02
- SH01 and AR01.

Unfortunately in addition to accidental inaccuracies, CH is aware of several deliberate *misfilings* by fraudsters. There are at least two versions:

a) *Celebrity kidnapping.* Several well-known, personalities have discovered that, without their knowledge, they have been *appointed* to a company's board.

   The purpose presumably is for the company to advertise the fact of such *appointment* to boost its reputation or support some other fraud etc.

   Obviously the filing of the *appointment* was carried out fraudulently and the company can correct the record using form RP02A. (As a variation on this, a person could *appoint* himself to the board and then claiming to be a director, try to commit the company to expenditure, take on credit etc. (as in b). Anyone checking would find an apparently legitimate appointment record at CH.).

   Appointments as a director can now only be made with confirmation from the company that the appointee has signed a 'consent to act' form.

   In addition, form RP06 is now available to those fraudulently appointed to allow the removal of details of a person who has not consented to act as a director.

b) *Company hijacking.* There have also been numerous instances of a company's registered office being *changed* by fraudsters to an address under their control from which they proceed to take on credit as if they were the company itself.

   Having obtained goods, services, etc. they then disappear. To correct the record form RP02B should be used. Using the CH PROOF facility since filing then requires a user code and password may help prevent such frauds.

Finally if a filing failed to meet the requirements, the original filer can send a hard copy replacement with form RP01. The document will not automatically replace the original since CH will consider each filing on its merits.

Although payment can be made by cheque or credit card, those responsible for filing in respect of a number of companies can apply to open a credit account at CH.

A salutary tale

Following the High Court making a winding up order against Taylor & Son Ltd (T) the Official Receiver advised CH of the order but failed to quote the company number. CH incorrectly applied the winding up order to Taylor and Sons Ltd (TS) – a successful and solvent 100-year old company which was informed it was *in liquidation*. CH rectified its error, but not before it had advised credit agencies etc., that the (wrong) company was in liquidation. This led to a total loss of confidence of TS customers and suppliers and to the company actually going into administration.

TS successfully lodged a claim for negligence against CH. The Court stipulated the only liability CH had was to the company itself (i.e. not to those who suffered as a result of its failure – employees who lost their jobs etc.) although even that is likely to amount to over £8 million. The case underlines the need for companies to quote registered numbers when interfacing with CH although here it was completely outside the company's control.

Re-registration

Private to public

To re-register an LTD as an unlisted PLC (CA06ss90/6) the company must:

1. Have an issued share capital of at least £50,000 of which 25% or more must be paid up in cash. If there is insufficient authorised capital to permit this then the members must first pass an ordinary resolution (which must be lodged with CH within 15 days) increasing the authorised share capital; and then issue shares for at least the minimum amount (details of which must again be notified to CH within 28 days of allotment).

2. Pass a special RESOLUTION (which could be a written resolution) stating that it wishes to re-register as a PLC.

3. Alter its MEMORANDUM and ARTICLES, changing its NAME so that it ends 'public limited company' (or 'plc', 'Plc', or 'PLC' or 'CCC' standing for Cwmni Cyfyngedig Cyhoeddus if it is a Welsh plc), insert a statement that it is to be a PLC, and remove any restrictions (e.g. the directors right to refuse a share transfer) which are incompatible

with PLC status. A company which does not have its Memorandum in the format required under CA06 will be required to transfer any required objects clause into the revised Articles.

4. Appoint a Secretary (if it does not already have one) and notify CH within 14 days of the appointment.

5. File a copy of the change of name resolution with CH within 15 days of it being passed, together with:

   - a printed copy of the Articles and (if appropriate) amended memorandum;

   - an auditors statement regarding an accompanying balance sheet which must not be more than six months old, reflecting the tighter timetable for filing of; PLCs accounts, and must bear an unqualified auditors report and show that net assets exceed the paid up share capital and reserves;

   - (if part of the paid up capital is represented by a consideration other than cash) an expert's opinion on the asset's value;

   - the appropriate fee.

6. CH then issues a certificate of re-registration as a PLC.

Note: Because of the variety of filing time limits it may be preferable to regard all items to be filed with CH as needing to be filed within 14 days.

Public to private

To re-register a PLC as an LTD (CA06ss97-101) the company must:

1. Pass a special resolution resolving that the company is to be an LTD, thus changing its name from ending PLC to LTD.

2. Alter the name in the Articles of Association, and (for pre CA06 companies) in the Memorandum.

3. Send to CH (within 15 days) a copy of the change of name special resolution and the altered Articles and (if appropriate) the Memorandum.

There follows a 28 day delay to allow time for any minority shareholder who wishes to apply for cancellation of the resolution. However if all members of the company endorse the special resolution, the 28-day period can be waived. CH then issues a certificate of re-registration in the new LTD status and name.

Unlimited companies

An LTD can re-register as an unlimited company (CA06ss102-104), an unlimited company can re-register as an LTD (CA06ss105-108), and a PLC can re-register as an unlimited LTD company (CA06ss109-111). Legal and financial advice should be taken.

Resolutions

Ordinary

Any resolution which is not special or extraordinary is classified as ordinary. At GM ordinary resolutions are used to obtain approval by means of a simple majority of the votes that are actually *cast* in person or by proxy. Hence if only some of the votes are *cast* then an ordinary resolution is passed if 50% plus 1 of the shares that are actually voted are in favour. Any shares not voted are effectively disenfranchised – the effect of the shareholder deciding to abstain. The following ordinary resolutions must be filed with CH within 15 days of being passed:

- for a company with an authorised share capital (i.e. those pre CA06 companies and CA06 companies that have such a restriction), any resolution increasing it;

- a resolution authorising the directors to allot shares (unnecessary for companies formed under CA06 unless required by the company's Articles);

- a resolution voluntarily winding up the company; and

- a resolution revoking an elective resolution. Continued use of elective resolutions may be somewhat pointless as a result of CA06 allowing LTDs to dispense with holding an AGM.

Special notice (of an ordinary resolution)

Two ordinary resolutions require *special notice* being given to the members – that is at least 21 days notice with full details of the proposal and any objections or representations of the other party(ies) directly involved. They are required for any resolution relating to an auditor other than their re-election or to set their remuneration and the removal of a director (see DIRECTORS – REMOVAL)

Note: Special notice has nothing to do with Special resolutions.

Special

Special resolutions are required to:

- alter the company's objects clause

- alter the company's Articles

- change the company's name

- RE-REGISTER an LTD as a PLC, an unlimited company as an LTD, or a PLC as an LTD

- disapply any pre-emption rights of shareholders (the right of pre-emption gives existing shareholders the right of first refusal to subscribe for any newly issued shares in proportion that their own shares bear to the total issued)

- authorise the purchase by the company of its own shares or the provision of assistance to allow the purchase of its own shares. Under CA06s724, a company can purchase (out of its distributable profits) a maximum of 10% of its issued share capital. The shares purchased are held *in treasury* in the company's own name. They are not cancelled since this would lead to a reduction of capital which is subject to separate rules but such shares have no voting or dividend rights whilst they are in treasury. This may be a simple method of acquiring shares for later use (for example in an employee share scheme) rather than needing to issue more shares. CH must be informed using forms SH03 and 04. If shares in treasury are to be cancelled form SH05 must be used.

- reduce the company's share capital. For a PLC, a resolution to reduce share capital can usually only be effected provided the Articles allow for it (if they do not they must first be changed – which will mean obtaining the permission of the members) and under a scheme of arrangement which needs Court approval and notification to CH using SH06. The reduction is only effective when CH issues a certificate to this effect. However, under CA06s641 an LTD can reduce its share capital by special resolution and Court application, or by the directors swearing a solvency certificate (s642) stating, under all their names and the date that each of the directors has formed the opinion that there are no grounds on which the company would be unable to pay its debts for the year ahead, or, if the winding up of the company is expected to commence within a year, that the company will be able to pay its debts.

- any resolution relating to business stated in the company's Articles to require a special resolution.

Under CA06, the notice required for special resolutions is reduced from 21 to 14 days notice (unless a company's Articles specify the longer period). At a meeting the approval of 75% of the votes cast in person or by proxy is required. Copies of all special resolutions must be filed with CH within 15 days of the date of the resolution.

Extraordinary

Extraordinary resolutions are needed to resolve:

- any matter stated by the company's Articles to require an extraordinary resolution
- that a company cannot continue in business by reason of its liabilities and should be wound up

- to grant certain powers to the liquidator in a members voluntary winding up

- that assets of the company in a winding up can be distributed to the members *in specie.*

Extraordinary resolutions require 14 days' notice and the approval of at least 75% of the votes *cast* by members present in person or by proxy. Since all resolutions (subject to an individual company's Articles stipulations) require 14 days notice there is no longer a difference between the requirements for Special and Extraordinary resolutions, both of which must be filed at CH within 15 days. CA06 does not refer to extraordinary resolutions, the legislators perhaps assuming that special resolutions will be used. However a company should refer to its Articles since if they stipulate certain business must be passed 'by an ExtraOrdinary resolution' this should be followed.

Written

To reduce the time and resources that LTDs were perceived to 'waste' in convening meetings to consider business, CA89 authorised members to pass resolutions without meeting. A copy of the proposed resolution must be sent to each member (either electronically or in hard copy) with a note of how to indicate agreement (s296) and, ideally, a cut off date, after which, if not ratified, the resolution would fail. If no cut off date is specified, the proposal fails 28 days after the date (*the circulation date*) on which it was dispatched. Where the members are distant from the company it may be advisable to send hard copies by recorded delivery so that some record of posting exists, and to suggest that the same precautions are taken when returning the signed copies. It might also be advisable to request that shareholders who are not known personally to the company, should have their signatures witnessed.

Originally, a written resolution required unanimous agreement and if just one member did not agree, or simply did not reply, the resolution failed. However under CA06s288 written ordinary resolutions can now be passed if there is a simple majority (50% plus one or more) of the *entire* voting body, whilst written special resolutions are passed if there is 75% support from the *entire* voting body. Thus if using a written resolution there needs to be a much higher level of agreement compared to the situation where the same resolutions are considered at a meeting where a simple majority for an ordinary resolution or 75% for a special resolution is needed but only of the votes actually *cast*.

The company's auditors must be sent a copy of the resolution (failure to do so attracts a £500 fine) although the auditors no longer have their former power to state that if the resolution *concerns them* the written process had to be abandoned and a meeting convened.

Once the resolution is passed, a copy certified by a director or the Secretary must be recorded in the minute book. If the resolution is such that, had it not been passed using the written process it would need to have been passed as a special resolution, or as an ordinary resolution required to be notified to CH, then CH must be notified within 15 days.

A written resolution cannot be used to remove a director (s168) or an auditor (s510) from office. Such proposals can only be effected at a properly convened meeting (where the subject has a right of reply with the notice and at the meeting) by an ordinary resolution subject to special notice.

If wishing to transact the following business using written resolutions there are additional requirements regarding the need to provide full explanation re:

- disapplication of pre-emption rights;
- financial assistance for the purchase of own shares;
- purchase of own shares;
- payment out of capital; or
- approval of directors' service contracts.

Members holding 5% or more of the voting strength of the company (or any lower limit allowed by the Articles) can request that a written resolution be put to the members at a properly convened meeting.

Wording

Legal advice may be advisable when framing the wording for a resolution relating to other than routine items, as clear wording is essential particularly about the operative date. Thus it may be better, rather than resolving:

> *'That the report of the directors and the annual accounts for the year ended 30th June 2XXX, together with the Balance sheet as at that date are accepted'*

to word it:

> *'That the report of the directors and the annual accounts for the year ended 30th June 2XXX, together with the Balance sheet as at that date be and they are hereby accepted'.*

The word *hereby* indicates that the resolution was passed on and became effective on the same date as the minuted decision. However with resolutions where the operative date is dependent on the actions of some third party (for example, the change of the company name is not effective until the date of the certificate of incorporation on change of name issued by CH) the wording might be:

> *'That the name of the company be changed from ANY COMPANY LTD to ANY OTHER COMPANY LIMITED and that the new name be operative from the date stipulated by the Registrar of Companies.'*

Filing with CH

The following resolutions must also be filed:

- any resolution passed unanimously which would otherwise have been a special resolution;

- any resolution passed unanimously by a class of shareholder which would have required a specified majority; and

- any resolution directed by the Secretary of State requiring the directors to change the company name to include the word *limited* (i.e. where formerly there was a dispensation not to use the word)

The following format should be acceptable.

SPECIAL RESOLUTION ON CHANGE OF NAME

Companies Act [1985] or (2006]

Company 00123456789 ANY COMPANY LTD

At an [Extraordinary] General Meeting of members of the above-named company, duly convened and held at [address, usually the Registered Office] on [date] the following SPECIAL RESOLUTION was passed:

THAT the name of the company be changed to
ANY OTHER COMPANY LTD

Signed_____ Secretary [Date_____]

A change of name resolution is currently the only one that can be electronically filed at CH.

Minority protection

Any resolution (or any other action e.g. paying an interim dividend) the effect of which is that a member with a minority shareholding is disadvantaged is illegal. If, for example, X holding 90% of the shares purports to pay a dividend but only to those members holding more than 10% of the shares, the minority shareholder(s) could bring an action for unfair prejudice. If the majority shareholder were also a director, there could also be a basis for a DERIVATIVE claim as this could amount to a breach of trust and/or breach of one of the basic statutory duties of directors, i.e. to treat all members equally.

The Elective regime

To relieve LTDs (only) from administrative obligations, which again may have been more perceived than real, CA89 introduced the *elective regime*. This allowed shareholders if acting unanimously (i.e. every entitled vote had to be cast in favour) to *elect* to allow their company take certain actions. Whilst such resolutions could be passed at a meeting, they could also be passed by a written resolution (which also originally required 100% unanimity) in which case the members did not even have to meet. Elective resolutions mainly related to AGM business and, since CA06 allows LTDs to dispense (subject to their Articles) with holding AGMs, to a large extent elective resolutions were rendered superfluous by that Act.

Under the Companies (Resolutions of Private Companies) Order 1995, provided all the members agree, the requirement to give 21 days notice of an elective resolution could be waived.

The elective regime was restricted to:

- Give, renew or extend directors' five-year authority to ALLOT shares. The effect was that the directors could allot shares within a limitation either in time or number of shares, (within the limits in the Memorandum unless those requirements were first changed) without convening a meeting and seeking such permission from the shareholders at the time. CA06 companies are not required to have an authorised share capital (unless specified in their Articles) and their directors can issue shares they feel are appropriate (unless there are restrictions on such powers in the Articles).

- Dispense with laying the accounts before the AGM – although the accounts are still required to be sent to each member.

- Dispense with holding an AGM. CA06 abolishes the need for LTDs to hold AGMs unless the Articles state one must be held (or the directors or shareholders require it).

- Reduce the percentage required for sanctioning short notice of an EGM from 95% to 90%. CA06 allows short notice providing 90% of the voting rights agree (although a company's Articles can stipulate a higher threshold of up to 95%)

- Dispense with annual re-appointment of Auditors (in which case the auditors are deemed to be re-elected automatically). If an LTD does not hold AGMs the auditors simply continue in office.

All elective resolutions were required to be filed at CH within 15 days of being passed.

If passed at a meeting, the minutes evidencing the adoption of the elective resolution(s) needed to be prepared and preserved in the ordinary way. If passed using a written resolution, the requirements relating to recording of such resolutions applied.

If an LTD re-registered as a PLC, elective resolutions ceased to be effective on the date of the re-registration. An elective resolution was also able to be revoked by the members passing an ordinary resolution (which itself had to be filed with CH). The effect was that a shareholder who acquired shares after an elective resolution had been passed was subject to it unless and until he could muster sufficient support to pass an ordinary resolution revoking it.

CA06 is silent concerning elective resolutions and effectively abolishes the concept (unless of course the principle has been written into a company's Articles) although if all the members are in agreement, obviously they can resolve all legal business. If unanimity is not possible, either the written resolution process could be used or (probably safer) a meeting should be convened.

Resurrection of companies

Action

The actions that could generate application to the Court for resurrection are those concerned with claims for damages in respect of personal injuries or claims under the Fatal Injuries Act 1976 or Damages (Scotland) Act 1976. Such claims would mainly be generated by application on behalf of former employees who have become subject to a condition which became apparent only after the company was removed from the register but which can now be proved to have originated prior to that date. It can take many years for diseases caused by industrial activity (e.g. mesothelioma, caused by inhaling asbestos fibres) to manifest themselves. If it is alleged that the condition originated as a result of a person working for a company (now defunct), the company can be resurrected to face the claim. However under the Third Parties (Rights against insurers) Act 2010, those who allege loss against a company that is wound up, insolvent or cannot meet a claim for damages can now sue its insurers directly i.e. the company would not have to be resurrected in order to face the action.

Alternatively, if the claim is against a now defunct subsidiary but it can be proved that it had a parent company which exercised sufficient direct control over that subsidiary, it may be possible to pierce the VEIL OF INCORPORATION that normally exists between parent and subsidiary companies and for the action to be taken directly against the parent.

Administration

Shareholders or guarantors allowing their companies, or parent companies allowing their subsidiaries, (other than companies that have never traded) to be struck off should ensure they keep details of the records (particularly the insurers) of such defunct companies in case such an action is brought in accordance with the above relaxation. It may be prudent to keep company statutory books, etc., for 'life of the company' plus (say) six years (or even longer in view of the Court's powers to extend the period).

Certificates of Employers Liability insurance

The principle of allowing a company to be resurrected in order to face liability claims flows from the realisation that some claims for liability may not arise for some time after they originated. From 1999 the legally required annual Certificates of Employers Liability insurance were required to be kept for 40 years and had to be displayed at every place of work. The requirement to keep these certificates has been abandoned, as has the obligation to display the annual certificates, provided the details are kept electronically on a system to which every employee has access. (e.g. it could be included within an employee handbook, regularly updated). It might be prudent, despite the relaxation, to continue to keep a copy of each future certificate – possibly with the statutory books – so that there is evidence of the insurers at relevant times.

Seal

KEY POINTS

- A company's agreement to a contract can be evidenced by applying the company seal to the document.

- Alternatively the document can be 'signed as a deed' by two directors or a director and the Secretary.

- Recording such approved contracts in a Register is prudent.

- Items subject to such a procedure should be approved at the next following board meeting.

History

Using a seal to evidence a person's agreement to a contract originated over a thousand years ago when, to indicate their acceptance of its terms, those who could neither read nor write could press their signet ('signing') ring into hot wax on the document. Sealing wax was replaced by an adhesive red sticker but even that has now been dispensed with and a company can 'sign' its agreement by having its seal simply impressed onto a page of a document evidencing a contract. Applying the seal with its use evidenced by an entry in a Register of Seals ratified at a board meeting, is an effective control over – as well as being a useful record of – commitments entered into by the company.

Adopting the seal

CA89 made the use of a seal optional (unless the company's Articles required its continuation) allowing 'deeds' to be created by them being signed on behalf of the company by two directors or a director and the Secretary. However if a company wishes to use a seal subject to the Articles giving authority for its use, a seal bearing the name of the company must be commissioned and produced at a board meeting, with a board resolution passed adopting it. An impression of the seal must be made on the page alongside the resolution. If the company changes its name and wishes to continue using a seal the process should be repeated with the new seal (its predecessor having been destroyed).

Requirement for use

Originally seals were used to create deeds which were needed for:

- freehold property transactions and leases lasting three years or more;

- sales and purchases of British ships (or shares in such ships);

- *gratuitous promises* i.e. transactions where there was no consideration for the value being given; and

- confirmation of the legitimacy of share certificates. The Articles of many pre-CA06 companies limited by shares state that a share certificate will only be a valid document of title if it bears the common seal of the company. Thus if a company limited by shares decides to dispense with using a seal it would need to change its Articles if they include such a wording to be able to continue issuing valid share certificates.

Sealing procedure

To ensure adequate time is allowed to gain board authority to the item:

1. Documents required to be sealed should ideally be submitted at least two weeks before any critical date (flexibility may be needed).

2. The seal can be witnessed by two directors, or a director and the Secretary.

With Articles authority, the seal can also be witnessed by one director and a person authorised by the board – usually known as an 'authorised counter-signatory'. Many large companies that undertake a great deal of sealing, delegate witnessing the seal to other officers. As noted if documents are to be signed *as deeds* rather than sealed then they can only be witnessed by two directors or by one director and the Secretary or in Scotland (only) by one director and an authorised counter-signatory.

3. At least one signatory must know personally of the content and purpose of the item to be sealed.

4. Other than for the approval of the following items, a brief synopsis of the content of the document must be prepared and initialled by the director ultimately responsible for the commitment of resources, etc., evidenced by the document::

    a) Share certificates. Many companies use a securities seal which is affixed by the person or organisation responsible for the company's share registration work under terms of authority granted by the board.

    b) Renewals of leases, or new leases which have board approval.

    c) Agreements where the capital value in total (either separately or should the document be one of a series, cumulatively) is less than [say] £5000.

    Any synopsis should be kept in the register of seals until the sealing has been approved by the board, and will be preserved subsequently for [set period].

5. The register of seals (and/or of documents signed as deeds) will be completed with every item sealed being given a sequential number. The same number will be placed on the document itself and also on any synopsis.

6. The register of seals will be produced at each board meeting so that all members (if they wish) can inspect details of all items sealed between board meetings. With board approval the chairman can initial under the latest entry. The affixing of the seal to a document grants the authority of the company to the item and thus the seal needs to be adequately protected.

Dispensing with the seal

Under CA89, companies were permitted to dispense with their seals. If use of a seal is to be abandoned it might be advantageous to consider the following:

1. Are there adequate procedures for ensuring items needing the equivalent of the affixing of the seal receive the degree of authority they require? Formerly because items needed to be sealed they had to be processed via the board. Lacking the need for a seal, the authority of the company could be *improperly granted* at too low a level – and possibly without a full appreciation of the possible consequences.

2. Are there procedures in place to provide evidence of the authority of those who will sign deeds instead of these being sealed?

3. Has explanation of the relaxation been given to those used to receiving a sealed document (e.g. overseas organisations) to avoid them querying the change?

4. Is there a rule such as the following to provide back-up authority for those actually signing documents that would otherwise be sealed?

   'Every six months, the board will approve a resolution authorising (named) directors and the Secretary to sign on behalf of the company, documents which otherwise would have been sealed. Copies of such a resolution, authenticated by the chairman, will accompany each document signed to avoid any questioning of the authority.'

   This should also help avoid questions from those who are not aware of the option to dispense with the seal and have been accustomed to receiving documents that have been sealed. Requiring a six-monthly repeat/update of the authority itself, should help negate any challenge as to its currency.

5. To ensure appropriate drafting solicitors must be briefed to refer to documents as a deed if they are to be so regarded and not to be sealed. A wording such as 'Executed as a deed, for and on behalf of Any Company Ltd by (two directors or one director and the Secretary or authorised counter-signatory' should be incorporated.

Further relaxations

The principles of the Regulatory Reform (Execution of Deeds and Documents) Order 2005 are that:

- sealing a document no longer makes it a deed automatically;
- a third party can rely on a document signed by two directors (or a director and Secretary);
- solicitors signing on behalf of the company are now assumed to have the authority to bind the company in all transactions (not only transfers of land as they could previously); and
- a corporate director can bind the company for third parties if a representative of the corporate director signs a deed (the company should retain a copy of the appointment of the representative).

CA06 allows the sole director of an LTD where there is no Secretary to appoint an *authorised signatory* so that a second signature is available for documents requiring dual signatures, whilst under s47 the company can by deed empower a single person (either for a specific purpose or generally) as its attorney to execute deeds or other documents on its behalf.

Register of Seals

There is no legal requirement to keep such a register although many companies do since it not only provides a record of the commitment to the contract, but can also record brief details of the content, date of approval and signatories, and the destination of the item after sealing/signing. If entries are numbered in the register subsequent approval of the board to the affixation/signing can be achieved by a simple board minute:

> *'Approval was granted to the affixation of the seal (signing as a deed) of items numbered [X] to [Y] and to item number Z signed as a deed in the Register of Seals. The Chairman initialled the register under item [Z].'*

Cross referencing can be obtained by inserting the register number against the seal impression.

WARNINGS

1. Many overseas organisations not only prefer contracts to be under seal but also require confirmation by a Notary Public, etc. Retention and use of a seal may avoid a considerable waste of time trying to explain the above diluting legislation. Usage of the seal is simple, time efficient, inexpensive (a seal can usually be obtained for under £25) and subject to little challenge. Dispensing with it negates these advantages and may create time-consuming (but avoidable) explanations.

2. Retaining the seal means the document has to be passed through a procedure such as above. (As one experienced Secretary said on one of my seminars 'I'm never getting rid of the seal – it's the only way I find out what's going on.')

    Needing a contract to be sealed may also mean avoiding commitment being granted at too low a level in the company.

3. Experience indicates that sometimes when reference to all other records has failed to identify the operative date of a disposal or acquisition, the Register of Seals can provide the required date.

Shareholder agreements

KEY POINTS

- The internal rules under which directors operate their company are contained in its (owner-approved) Articles (lodged at CH).

- If owners wish to agree items not subject to public scrutiny at CH they can enter into a shareholders agreement

- Anything in such an agreement that would have needed to be passed by a Special Resolution, must be filed at CH.

- Provisions in the Articles and the shareholders' agreement must not be in conflict.

Persons of significant control

Other than listed or quoted PLCs most other companies are required to create and lodge with CH, a register of persons of SIGNIFICANT CONTROL. The purpose, for those dealing with the company, is to identify anyone who could control to a significant extent the activities of the board and thus of the company. In some shareholders' agreements (particularly those that state that they 'override the Articles') there could be instances of such 'significant control' which should be disclosed. Since the price companies pay for 'limited liability protection' of the shareholders investment is disclosure of information about the company, a shareholders' agreement which overrides the Articles breaches this principle. Effectively there could be matters kept private about the operation of the company which those involved with it (e.g. creditors) might prefer to know.

Paragraph 12 of Schedule 1A CA06 requires that any and all individuals (including corporate bodies) where the (combined) control meets the conditions of a person with significant control must provide information to the company so that the information about them and the interest(s) can be included in the register. Where shareholders are not on the board, since a shareholders' agreement may be confidential between them (i.e. unknown to the directors) there is a possibility that the information required will not be made known to the directors and thus not included in the register. Those who are party to such information in that kind of agreement are required to make themselves (and the arrangements) known to the company and then, if they meet the conditions for 'significant control', entries must be made in the register. Failure to disclose – or to answer a request for disclosure – is a criminal offence and can lead to shares being disenfranchised.

Companies should advise members of this requirement in case there is such an agreement of which the directors are ignorant.

Agreement to discuss the possibility of selling the shares

On a more basic level an agreement could cover situations where existing shareholders simply wish to divest themselves of their holding. Thus the agreement could stipulate that should one or more member(s) wish to withdraw from the company, the other member(s) will have the right to purchase, or find purchasers for, that member's shares (i.e. a right of pre-emption or first refusal on the shares), rather than them being sold to an outsider. There may be some protection in the Articles as many give the directors powers to refuse to register a transfer of shares to a new shareholder – unacceptable to them. It might be preferable to address the possibility in advance as the following draft illustrates. This version does not, subject to the wording of the Articles, actually bar any sale or transfer of the shares but simply requires the member to discuss it.

Example: Deed of agreement

This Deed of Agreement is made this day of 2XXX between XYZ, ABC, DEF and GHI, who comprise all the shareholders in ANY OTHER COMPANY LTD (a limited liability company registered in England under number 1112223334).

It is hereby expressly agreed by and between all four parties hereto that none of them will sell (individually or collectively) all or any of the shares he holds in the company without first discussing it fully with, and to the satisfaction of, the other members.

In witness whereof this Deed of Agreement is signed this day of 2XXX

Signatures of all members and witnesses _____

Since an agreement is unenforceable unless there is a consideration, such a document (and the following alternatives) should always be described and signed as Deeds (or incorporate a nominal consideration).

Right of pre-emption

Effectively this is a right of first refusal given to the other members to buy any shares that a member may wish to sell.

Example: Deed of pre-emption

This Deed of Pre-emption agreement is made this.... day of.... 2XXX between the two members of ANY COMPANY LTD (the company) a limited liability company registered in England No 112233445566, whose registered office is at [address] namely XYZ (owning approximately 70% of the issued shares of the company) and ABC (owning approximately 30% of the issued shares of the company).

Both the parties hereto, Messrs XYZ and ABC, hereby voluntarily, separately and expressly agree that in the event of either wishing to dispose of his shareholding (or any part thereof) in the company, he will first offer it for purchase by the other party hereto.

The offer must be in writing specifying a price per share, and any other conditions of sale, and must be posted by recorded delivery to the last known private residential address of the shareholder (the recipient) stipulating an expiry date. The recipient will have 56 days to make a decision whether to accept or reject the offer. If at the end of 56 days from the date of posting of the offer (as evidenced by the recorded delivery slip) no agreement or rejection of the offer has been received then the offer will lapse and the offering shareholder will be at liberty to offer the shares elsewhere at a price not below that used in the offer to the other shareholder. In the event, and on each and every occasion, if the shares have subsequently to be offered at a lower price than that originally calculated, the shares will first be offered at that price to the other shareholder (as set out above)

In witness whereof, etc.

Signatures of both parties and witnesses to each.

_____

Date _____

It is important that the exact basis of the appointment of a valuer of shares is set out in the agreement or Articles and that those requirements are strictly adhered to.

Agreement allowing for calculation of value and veto on alternative member proposed

This version involves the auditors as witness to the negotiations which may help clarify the situation in the event of dispute.

Example: Deed of agreement for calculation of value and veto on alternative member

This Deed of Agreement is made this day of 2XXX between XYZ and ABC (the parties) both of whom own and control shares in ANOTHER COMPANY Ltd, a company registered in England No 111122223333.

It is hereby expressly agreed between the parties that should either party wish to dispose of the shares held in their name or the name of their spouses as their nominees, or of any of such shares, that they should first offer such shares to the other party, and will only be able to dispose of such shares elsewhere after the other has indicated in writing that he does not wish to acquire the shares.

The valuation to be placed on the shares shall be calculated by the auditors to the company, Messrs Accountant & Auditor, or such other valuer as the parties may jointly agree, or in the absence of agreement, by a person appointed to carry out such valuation by the President for the time being of the Institute of Arbitrators.

In the event of such shares being offered at the price stated by the auditors, the member will have 56 days (from the date that the disposing member confirms the intention to dispose in writing to the other member, a copy of such dated offer being sent to the auditors) to consider the offer. If at the end of this period no acceptance has been received, the member may offer the shares elsewhere. On receipt of an offer from a third party full details of such third party will be given to the remaining member, who shall have a right to veto in writing the person to whom the shares would otherwise be transferred. Any veto shall be sent by post within seven days of the remaining member being made aware of the identity of the third party, a copy of the veto will be sent to the auditors.

In witness wherefore the parties have signed this Deed of Agreement this [number] day of [month] 2XXX

Member

In the presence of:

Witness (Name) _____

(Address) _____

(Occupation) _____

Case study: Costly ignorance

In *T A King (Services) Ltd Cottrell (C) v King(K)*, K's motor business needed capital and C agreed to refinance it, taking 75% of the shares in consideration. When C died, the company gave the shares under transmission to C's widow. K objected since the Articles stated that on the death of a shareholder, their shares had first to be offered to the surviving shareholder, i.e. himself. After a costly High Court action the shares were required to be transferred from Mrs Cottrell back to her husband's estate, the executors of which then had to have the shares valued and offered to K. If K wanted the shares he would have to pay for them, the money going to C's estate; if not, the executors would then be able to deal with the shares in accordance with C's will.

Ironically whilst he was alive C (since he had 75% of the shares) could have passed a special resolution changing the requirement. However, there might have been a clause in a shareholders' agreement under which C undertook not seek to change the Articles in this way.

Other clauses

Clauses could also be included in such an agreement covering:

- the granting of enhanced voting rights to some directors if the board is deadlocked. This device is sometimes used in Joint Venture (JV) companies, but, since one of the principals effectively may then have board control, such enhanced voting rights could need to be recorded in the register of Persons of Significant Control:

- other methods (than the foregoing) whereby a member can realise the value of the shareholding;

- situations where unanimity of shareholders is required before action can be taken; or

- a mechanism whereby if the shareholders are deadlocked, a decision can be arrived at.

This last item reflects fairly numerous instances where there is an equality of votes (e.g a *quasi-partnership* with two shareholders each holding 50% of the shares). This seemed fine when the company was set up and the parties were in agreement, but should there later be a dispute, deadlock can result – which is even more problematic if they are also the only directors and/or they are married or in a civil partnership. The logical result here would be for one shareholder to sell his holding to the other, although that in turn may give rise to a dispute as to the value of the shares. Without agreement at the time and/or in the absence of a shareholders' agreement regarding share price valuation, it may be necessary to apply to the Court for determination of the situation. The Court has wide-ranging powers – it can order that the company's conduct be regulated; require the company to refrain from certain activities; or authorise civil proceedings to be brought in the name of the applicant. The Court could also order that one party's shares should be bought by the other, and, if the parties cannot agree a valuation, the Court will determine this. Alternatively, the party in dispute could apply for the company to be wound up since obviously the *quasi-partnership* has come to an end. Court action can incur fees, so some kind of negotiated settlement might benefit everyone.

Employer shareholders

Employees have the right to surrender some of their employment protections in exchange for being given shares worth at least £2,000 in their employing company. This option can be made available to both new and existing employees – although no-one must be put under duress to agree to the arrangement. The employment rights surrendered include being able to:

- claim unfair dismissal (except for those which are automatically unfair);
- claim redundancy pay; and
- make a request for flexible working or time off for training.

This option has not been taken up by many, not least since the employee-shareholder is likely to be a minority with no say re dividend policy or strategy, whilst conversely (for example) being unable to obtain redundancy pay etc., should the company fail. The arrangement must be covered by a written agreement, and any employee or prospective employee wishing to participate must be provided with independent legal advice.

Significant control registers

KEY POINTS

- Seeking to improve transparency regarding the ultimate ownership and control of companies and assist in the prevention of money laundering, tax evasion, and terrorism financing, SBEEA15 requires LTDs to compile a Register of Persons of Significant Control.

- Details of those entered in the register (and changes thereto) must be filed at CH.

Register content

Entries are required to be made for all persons (real or corporate). There are five conditions of control – those who:

- hold more than 25% of the shares;

- can exercise more than 25% of the voting rights;

- can appoint or remove a majority of the directors;

- can exercise significant control or influence over the company;

- can exercise significant control or influence over the activities of a trust or firm which meets the above conditions.

Where there is a disclosable shareholding the amount of such holding must be quantified within three bands – between 25% and 50%; between 50% and 75% and over 75%.

(Note that the wording is 'above 25%' etc. so if a holding is a level '25%' disclosure is not required. Thus there are no persons of significant control in a company where there are four shareholders each holding 25% of the shares (unless other means of exercising control, as set out above, are open to one or more of them)

The personal details required are name (individual or corporate), address, country of residence, nationality, date of birth (where this is to be made publicly available the actual day of birth is withheld), date of entry into the register and nature of the control. If there is concern that someone whose details must be included in the register could be subject to violence etc. application can be made to CH to have details protected and concealed from public viewing.

Any and all individuals (including corporate bodies) where the (combined) control and influence meets the conditions must provide information to a company so that the Register is accurate – i.e. there is an obligation to disclose where (possibly) the company would not otherwise know of it (e.g. where any of the above conditions are met by virtue of detail set out in a SHAREHOLDERS AGREEMENT to which non-shareholding directors may not be party). The company itself has a duty to 'take reasonable steps' to identify those whose details should be included in the register and should a shareholder fail to respond to a request for such information the company can disenfranchise their shares.

Forms

There are nine FORMS dealing with recording this additional disclosure and filing it at CH. The company must file a form of declaration for each person affected – e.g.PSC01 for an individual with control. For such a person the form (which must be signed by a company officer) requires the following information:

- name, date of birth and nationality:

- date the control being declared was acquired:

- service address (This does not have to be a residential address – but, if not, the residential address must be supplied on a part of the form that will not appear on the public record. PO Box numbers cannot be used unless the number is part of a full service address); and

- the nature of their control (e.g. share ownership, voting rights, appointment/removal of directors, significant influence or control).

If the control is exercised through a firm or a trust over which the individual has control then the nature of control must be declared

Who controls?

Examples of persons (other than those holding shares) who could exercise control over a company could include the following:

- the founder who no longer holds a directorship and yet regularly attends board meetings (whether formal or not) and has a constant input on the proceedings; and/or

- a person who influences one or more directors but not necessarily within a formal board meeting; and/or

- a director who, owning an asset being used by the company, exercises control over its use by the company; and/or

- a former CEO, but now retired, director, who attends board meetings as a 'consultant' but whose opinions are often followed by the board (particularly where he may have helped appoint many of the current board).

In many ways a non-director shareholder or person exercising control could be compared to a 'shadow director' (i.e. *a person in accordance with whose directions or instructions the directors of the company are accustomed to act* as defined by CA06s251) and their details would need to be entered in the register.

Like the controls regarding shadow directors, details of those giving professional advice (e.g. lawyers, auditors, consultants etc.) are not subject to disclosure. Similarly suppliers, customers, lenders, employees acting in the course of their employment, directors (including a non-executive with a casting vote), and groups of employees in an employee-owned company normally will not be regarded as persons requiring to be entered.

Shareholder control

The shareholders of many companies enter into SHAREHOLDERS AGREEMENTS the full content of which may not be known to non-shareholding directors. Some such Agreements state that their contents 'override the Articles'. If such Agreements do override the Articles (and sometimes even if they do not), the effect could be that the signatories are persons of significant control or influence. Where the contents of a shareholders' agreement are unknown to the directors, it is possible that the information required to be disclosed by this legislation will not be made known and thus not included in the register. Those who are party to such information in such an agreement must make themselves (and the arrangements) known to the company and then, if they meet the conditions for 'significant control', provide details to enable appropriate entries to be made in the register.

Other bodies capable of exercising control

As well as shareholders exercising control, third parties could have similar rights. Accordingly if a relevant legal entity (RLE) can exercise control (e.g. share ownership, voting rights, appointing/removing directors, or other control or influence), details of that entity must also be disclosed as must details of any trust or firm which can exercise control. An RLE is a legal entity which would have been classified as a PSC had it been an individual and must (unless excepted) itself keep a PSC register showing any person or body which can exercise control over it

Disclosure and updating is also required of 'other registrable persons' (ORP) or of a firm or trust over which it has control. An ORP is any of the following:

- a corporation sole;
- a government department;
- an international organisation whose members include two or more countries or their governments); and/or
- a local authority/government body.

Disclosure of control by RLEs and ORPs is achieved using the appropriate PSC forms and providing similar details to the individual as set out above. If such information has not previously been filed with CH details must be provided in the annual CONFIRMATION STATEMENT.

Types of control requiring registration

The statutory guidance providing examples of 'significant control or influence' suggests registration of persons with the following powers ('absolute rights over') would be required:

a) adopting or amending the company's business plan;

b) changing the nature of the company's business;

c) making additional borrowing (except for the protection of a minority);

d) appointing or removing the CEO;

e) establishing or amending any profit-sharing, bonus or other incentive scheme of any nature for directors or employees; or

f) granting options under a share option or other share based incentive scheme.

In addition, details of a person with veto rights over the appointment of a majority of the directors (or those that have a majority of the board voting rights) would be required to be registered.

However where a person has veto rights over fundamental matters purely in order to protect minority interests and/or where decision rights are derived from the person being a prospective purchaser of the company, those instances are unlikely on their own to constitute control or to require registration.

Examples of control to be exercised by the fifth category (i.e. over the activities of a trust or firm which meets the four original conditions) include the rights to:

a) appoint or remove any of the trustees or partners of the trust or firm (other than by Court application) and/or

b) direct the distribution of funds or assets and/or

c) direct the investment decisions of the trust or firm and/or

d) amend the trust or partnership deed and/ or

e) revoke the trust or terminate the partnership.

Failing to respond within a month to a request for information concerning those with significant control over the business could result in a criminal conviction, a fine and up to two years imprisonment.

Scope of disclosure

Not all persons who have control need to be entered in the register since the rules distinguish between those with control who are 'registrable' and those who are 'non-registrable'. If a person has control only because they have significant control in what is called a 'relevant legal entity' (RLE) they may be non-registrable. An RLE is a legal entity which would have been classified as a PSC had it been an individual and (unless excepted) must itself keep a PSC register. Thus:

- If XYZ owns all the shares of A Ltd., XYZ must be entered in the PSC register of A Ltd.

- If XYZ holds all the shares of A Ltd and A Ltd holds all the shares in B Ltd, although A Ltd must be entered in the PSC register of B Ltd, XYZ does not have to be entered in B Ltd's register as they are a non-registrable RLE of B Ltd.

- However, if XYZ held all the shares in A Ltd., and A Ltd held 50% of the shares in B Ltd; and at least 25% of B's shares were owned directly by XYZ. XYZ would need to be recorded in the PSC register of B Ltd. (because XYZ does not **only** hold an interest in B Ltd through its shareholding in A).

Non-disclosure

Almost inevitably there will be instances where, despite the law placing on a person with significant control and influence an obligation to make themselves known to the company, this will not happen. If a company suspects that there is a PSC in relation to it, it has the right (and duty) to require information regarding such an interest to enable it to complete its PSC register and notify CH. If, despite repeated requests, a person fails to respond or provide such information, a company has a number of options. It could, for example, freeze:

- ownership, so that the interest cannot be transferred (thus rendering invalid any contract to sell);

- the rights attaching to the interest;

- the exercise of any rights attaching to the interest (e.g. effectively disenfranchise the holding);

- any payment in respect of the interest (e.g. prevent the payment of dividends.

Failing to reply to a request for information and/or keeping the required records could result in a criminal prosecution, imprisonment of up to two years and/or a fine.

If 'restrictions action' as above has been taken the company must state in the Register – 'The company has issued a Restrictions Notice as required by paragraph 1 of Schedule IB of the Act'.

Access

The PSC register (even one without any entries) is required to be kept at the registered office (or SAIL) and must be made available to anyone with a 'proper purpose' for inspection and/or copying (for which a small charge can be made).

Statutory books

KEY POINTS

- Several registers are required to be held either by a company at its Registered Office or SAIL or at CH.

- Such registers are known as the statutory books which must be kept updated and copies of entries notified to CH within time limits.

- Statutory books are subject to inspection.

The registers

Register of members. The name and address of each member must be entered. A company limited by guarantee must enter the amount of the guarantee given by the member whilst a company limited by shares must enter the number/types of shares held (and transfers into and out of their holdings), calls on, and the nominal value of the shares. If it is a single member company the register entry relating to their sole holding should bear the phrase 'this is a single member company'. Companies with large numbers of members usually keep their register in a computerised form – if so, CH must be informed.

Details must also be filed with CH each year in the CONFIRMATION STATEMENT. However, because of fears of identity theft, unwanted mailings etc., public information is restricted. Thus in listed PLCs, addresses of those holding under 5% of the shares are not disclosed, whilst for LTDs, the private addresses of shareholders are not shown.

If new shares are issued CH must be informed within 28 days of their allotment being granted by the board. Transfers of existing shares between existing holders or to new holders do not have to be notified as such transactions will be declared each year in the Confirmation Statement.

Register of directors and secretaries. Full details (name, and any former name, address, date of appointment and date of resignation/removal) must be given for both directors and Secretaries. In addition, dates of birth and nationality for each director must be provided. Under CA06 all directors can opt to conceal their private address and nominate a service address for public scrutiny. Both company and CH must, however, be told the director's private address. Although CH must be told the full date of birth, only month and year are made available publicly to try to prevent identify theft.

Before any new director is appointed the company has to confirm that it holds a formal 'consent to act' signed by all appointees (see DIRECTORS APPOINTMENT).

Register of directors' share interests. Although holdings of shares in a PLC of which a person is a director must continue to be recorded, this register is no longer required for LTD directors. (However if an LTD director has an interest in a third party which does business with their company – and could thus conflict with their duty to the company – then that interest should be recorded and could usefully be placed in this register omitting the word '*share*' from the title). If an interest arises after appointment then as soon as the director is aware of it, they must declare it. Similar entries could be made for any indemnities or loans etc. given to the director. PLCs might need a separate register for these potentially conflicting interests.

Register of substantial interests. Where a member of a listed PLC holds a beneficial interest of 3% or more, a non-beneficial interest of 10% or more, or a combined (beneficial and non-beneficial) interest of 10% or more, this must be recorded in this register. Changes in the holding through each percentage point (up or down) must also be notified. Non-beneficial interests of 5% are also now required to be disclosed (but not the variation of percentage points between 5% and 10%).

Register of Persons of Significant Control. Full details of anyone who has an interest in the company which legislation defines as giving them control (as is set out in SIGNIFICANT CONTROL) must be recorded in this Register and notified (with any changes) to CH. The nature of the interest must also be disclosed.

Register of debenture and/or loan stockholders must contain details of name, address, holding (and changes thereto) of every stockholder.

Register of charges. Formerly, regardless of whether or not a company had created any charges (i.e. had borrowed money against the security of, or mortgaged, company assets), a register of charges was required. Full details of all charges over assets of the company and by whom they had been taken were required. However this requirement is being abolished although details of specified CHARGES must still be filed at CH. It may be helpful to continue to keep this register if only as a reminder of the need to discharge the record of the charge at CH when the sums borrowed are repaid.

Register of seals. This register is not legally required but it is a useful method of recording details of how and when the seal was affixed to deeds, how the company became committed to the subject of the document, who witnessed the seal's affixation, a brief synopsis of the content, and the document's ultimate destination after being sealed. Even where a company has dispensed with the use of a seal, such a register may be a valuable method of recording such salient details of documents signed on behalf of the company as deeds – not least as one method of exercising control of the delegation of AUTHORITY (i.e. if the contract is required to be subject to sealing (or being signed as a deed) it requires board attention and thus denies those with less authority committing the company).

Compilation

Traditionally such registers have been held in hard copy format – and many still are in smaller LTDs. Combined registers giving all the required rulings are available from law stationers or can be supplied by formation agents as part of the company formation pack. Formerly some registers were required to be held at the registered office which would mean, if using a hard copy combined register, that it had to be held at that office. A problem could arise when the office of the Secretary was not at the registered office. Under CA06, if the company notifies CH of a single alternative inspection location (a SAIL) for such records (using form AD02) the registers can be held there.

The registers can be held in electronic format which, if there are linked computers in the office where the books are kept and the registered office or SAIL, this would both comply with the legal requirement as well as meeting the administrative requirements of a choice of inspection locations. There are proposals to abolish the right of physical inspection – leaving the details available at CH as a source of such information to interested parties.

Access and charges

Charges for physical inspection and copies are:

a) Registers of members, overseas branch register, directors share interests (PLCs only), members significant share interests (PLCs only),

- Inspection: £3.50 each hour or part thereof

- Copies: £1 for each of the first 5 entries, £30 for the next 95 entries, £30 for the next 900 entries, £30 for the next 99,000 entries and £30 for the remaining entries or part thereof.

b) Directors service contracts and/or indemnity provisions, resolutions and meetings, report under s. 805: 20p per 1,000 words or part thereof.

No charge for inspection of a register of Persons of Significant Control can be made although a charge can be made if providing a copy.

Retention and inspection

All the registers must be kept safely by the company and preserved for at least the life of the company (see RESURRECTION OF COMPANIES). Historically for two hours every working day, any member of the public could walk into the Registered Office of a company and demand to see its Register of Members. The creditors could demand to see that Register and the Register of Charges, and the members could demand to see all the Registers, however these rights have been (and continue to be) somewhat curtailed (see RECORD RETENTION)

Certificate of Incorporation

On formation, CH issues a Certificate of Incorporation bearing the company name, date and place of incorporation, and the company number. If the company changes its name a fresh certificate bearing the new name is issued. The Certificate should be kept safely as it evidences the existence of the company, and, if, for example, the company wishes to borrow money, a bank will usually insist on seeing it. If the Certificate is lost, or cannot be found, CH can issue a duplicate.

Types of companies

Unincorporated businesses

Sole trader

This is the simplest form of business; often operated from the trader's home, which keeps overheads low. A sole trader has personal unlimited liability and all his assets (other than those for 'the necessities of life') can be seized to settle the debts of his business should it become insolvent and fail.

Committees

Those elected to a committee (for example of a social or sports club etc.) have personal liability for the debts of the business. If a committee employs staff, gardeners, cleaners etc., any breach of employment legislation could create personal liability on the committee members themselves – including unlimited compensation if discrimination was proven. The personal position of the committee members would be better protected by making the organisation into a company limited by guarantee with the committee as its board of directors.

Partnership

If two or more people go into business together they form a partnership whether or not they enter into a partnership deed. Individually however their situation is similar to the sole trader and the club committee members – joint and several personal liability for all the debts of a failed business. Since 2001 partnerships have been able to limit the liability of their principals by becoming a Limited Liability Partnership (LLP).

Co-operatives

The first known co-operative was set up in the early 1840s in Toad Lane, Rochdale when 28 workers formed the Rock Equitable Pioneers Society to run their own food shop. During the following 170 years, the co-operative movement spread throughout the UK and then worldwide.

Business names

CA06ss1200/8 stipulates that, in running a business, if individuals use a trading name other than their own personal name(s), then on all note-paper, orders, invoices etc., the name(s) of the principal(s) behind the business name must be stated. Thus everyone dealing with the business will be made aware of the identity of the person (real or legal) with whom they are trading since, if there is a dispute, legal action cannot be taken against a name.

Incorporated bodies

a) Private company limited by shares

The word 'company' is derived from the Italian 'com' (with) and 'pagnia' (bread) since businesses of groups of people with shared personal liability was often decided over a meal. Private companies constitute the largest proportion of those registered at CH. An LTD limited by shares can issue from one to many million shares although around 80% of such companies have a share capital of under £100 and around 90% have five or fewer shareholders. Often an LTD's Articles allow the directors to restrict who owns the shares (that is the directors have the right to block a share transfer to a person they do not wish to be a shareholder) – hence these LTDs being referred to as *private companies*. Unless they act fraudulently, usually once a shareholder has paid for their shares in full they cannot be asked to pay more into the company – even if it fails with massive debts.

b) Private company limited by guarantee

Where the company will not *trade* in the normal sense of the word and/or is thus unlikely to fail in an insolvent manner (e.g. sports clubs, Chambers of Commerce, flat management companies, etc.) an LTD can be formed by members who do not subscribe for shares (and thus create a fund of share capital in theory available for the creditors) but simply undertake that should the company fail they will contribute the amount of their guarantee (usually £1 up to a maximum of £10 each) to pay off the creditors. Normally the company will be required to state 'Limited by Guarantee' at the end of its name although, with CH permission, the last two words can be dispensed with. The word 'Limited' can also be omitted from the name under CA06s60 if it is a charity and/or has an exemption from the Secretary of State. Since there are no shares, there can be no dividends. A guarantee company cannot be a PLC.

c) Company with unlimited liability

Such a company does not limit the liability of its members. This means that in any insolvent failure, any unpaid creditors can sue the shareholders themselves for their losses; so the shareholders of such a company have the same exposure to debt as have sole traders, club committee members or partners of an unlimited liability partnership. Unlimited companies are not obliged to file accounts at CH unless they are members of a group also comprising limited liability companies. In addition, such a company can reduce its share capital without following the procedure required of other types of companies.

d) Royal Charter companies

The Royal Charter is the oldest type of company – used since the 13th century when obtaining a charter signed by the monarch of the day was the only method by which entrepreneurs could limit their liability. The first two Charter companies were the Universities of Oxford and Cambridge, although the concept was quickly taken up to create cities – raising towns to a status where they could *conduct commerce* in their own corporate name – the first being Liverpool granted a charter by King John in 1205. This is presumably the origin of the phrase 'the Mayor and Corporation of [City name]' used when entering into contracts with such bodies. There are just under 1,000 such companies, and are mainly used by professional bodies which do not trade in the accepted meaning of the word, although many own LTD or PLC trading subsidiaries.

e) Statute companies

These are companies formed by individual Acts of Parliament. Such companies mainly pre-date the innovation of limited liability company law in the 1850s since this was formerly the only method other than the Royal Charter, by which members' personal liability could be limited. Whilst a statute company must comply generally with company law, they are also bound by the particular terms of their constitution.

WARNING

Whilst it is still possible to form both statute and Royal Charter companies this should really only be considered where it is certain that their business and the rules under which they will operate are unlikely to alter. Changing the terms of reference/ operation for either of these types of companies is expensive and time-consuming since it could require an amending Act of Parliament and/or application to the Privy Council.

f) Single member company (SMC)

The Companies (Single Member Private Limited Companies) 1992 Regulations allowed companies to be formed with just one member. If additional members are generated by an ALLOTMENT or transfer of shares, not only do additional accounts need to be opened in the register of members, but also the fact has to be drawn to the attention of anyone inspecting the corporate records. Thus in the share account of the original member, a note must be inserted such as 'This company is no longer an SMC' with a note of the effective date – and CH must be informed.

Conversely, should a company with two or more members become an SMC, then in the remaining member's account in the register of members, a note 'This company is [now – date] an SMC' needs to be entered – and again CH must be informed.

At general meetings of an SMC, the sole member is a quorum. Contracts between the sole member and the company (particularly if the sole member is also the sole director) should also be recorded in writing or set out in the minutes of the board meeting(s). There are initial and daily fines for every officer in default of these requirements.

Where a company not set up as an SMC carries on trading with only one shareholder, after six months the remaining shareholder loses their limited liability protection and has potential personal liability for the debts of the company should it fail.

The danger for a company where there is one shareholder and that person is also the sole director is that should the sole director / shareholder be unable to act (e.g. dies, is declared bankrupt, or is sectioned under the Mental Health Act) there is no-one with capacity to appoint a new director. The company will be unable to continue to trade until the ownership of the share(s) is determined – a process subject to considerable delay, during which it could fail. For CA06 companies this may be to some extent overcome since in the new pro forma Articles that accompany the Act (in the Companies (Model Articles) Regulations 2008), item17 states that 'personal representatives... have the right... to appoint a person to be a director'. This implies that it would not be necessary to wait for probate or letters of administration or similar to be granted to the personal representatives. The company should check the authority of the personal representatives claiming to act. If there is a Will this should be relatively easy, however if the shareholder has died intestate there may be difficulties proving the authority of the person wishing to act until letters of administration are granted. Where there is a Secretary at least there is an officer of the company who could carry out these checks – without this appointment the situation could be even more problematic. It might be prudent to insist the person claiming to act signs a form of indemnity protecting the company should they act on instructions that turn out later to be unauthorised. Legal advice should be taken.

The situation for a single person/director Guarantee company is even more problematical. Where a sole shareholder dies or is otherwise incapacitated, at least the share(s) still exist and can be transmitted to the Estate beneficiaries, trustee etc., but a guarantee cannot be transferred. It might be preferable to form an SMC with just one share so that the amount to be invested is small. Alternatively it might be suggested that the guarantor find a substitute who could step into the position should anything happen to them. The substitute would have to sign the same guarantee as the original guarantor, made in advance, but only coming into effect in the event, of the original guarantor's death.

The CA06 pro forma Articles for guarantee companies similarly state that 'personal representatives... have the right... to appoint a person to be a director'. Once again this implies that it would not be necessary to wait for the grant of probate or letters of administration. Legal advice should be taken.

g) Right to manage (RTM)

This is a company (usually a guarantee company) which enables long leaseholders in blocks of flats to take over the management of the building in place of their landlord. There are model Articles for RTM companies which must include an objects clause. Due to the nature of the *business* they are carrying on (i.e. it is essentially for their own benefit), the Constitution of some such owner-occupied property companies limited by shares sometimes include an obligation on the members to contribute pro rata to costs incurred in operating it – thus negating the normal limitation of liability of the shareholders to the amount they invested. RTM companies limited by shares usually allow joint members since often the members are married or civil partnership couples who jointly own a lease of their apartment in the property.

h) Public limited company

Subject to a company having:

- an issued share capital of £50,000 of which at least 25% (i.e. £12,500) is paid up; and

- excluded from its Articles any directors right to reject a share transfer; and

- a certificate or licence to commence trading from CH evidencing satisfaction that the required share capital has been subscribed; and

- appointed a Secretary (if one was not already appointed); and

- changed its name to end in PLC or Public Limited Company then an LTD can RE-REGISTER, or a new company can be formed as a PLC.

The external perception may be of a corporate body of considerable value and prestige although the issued share capital is tiny. Such a company should not be confused with a listed or quoted PLC, although it must be said this confusion is very widespread – and is often the reason some owners of LTDs take the step of re-registering their company as an unlisted or unquoted PLC (i.e. deliberately seeking to give to the outside world an impression of the company being far more substantial than it is).

i) Listed or quoted PLC

A PLC formed as above can apply either for a full listing on the Stock Exchange (i.e. become a traded company) or for a quotation on the Alternative Investment Market (AIM) provided they have at least the minimum amounts of share capital stipulated by the Stock Exchange from time to time. In addition, the company will have to commit itself and its officers to the listing rules applicable and to the UK Corporate Governance Code. Obtaining a listing is termed *flotation* and is a route chosen so that either existing shareholders can realise their investment and/or so that the company has access to additional share capital other than that sourced by existing owners.

j) Community interest companies (CIC)

Any LTD or PLC company which is formed for social enterprise, and/or those entities which intend to use their profits for the benefit of the local community or public can (unless they are charities) become a community interest company (CIC). A CIC is:

- subject to objective and transparent eligibility tests;
- required to produce an Annual Report and file it at CH showing how they are attaining their Objective(s); and is
- allowed to transfer assets to other similar bodies.

A CIC can issue shares, pay its directors and pay dividends subject to limits set from time to time by the Bank of England, although most of its profits are expected to be ploughed back to enable it to attain the company's social objectives.

If a company becomes a CIC its name must be displayed everywhere as (for example) *'J Bloggs CIC PLC'* or *'J Bloggs CIC LTD'*

k) Charitable incorporated organisations (CIO)

This concept (similar to a CIC) was enacted in the Charity Act 2006 for use by charities which have to register with the Charity Commissioners (CC) but not with CH (which might simplify matters for those running charitable companies since some aspects of charity and company law are in conflict). A CIO must adopt a constitution, and have a trustee body, and members. Whether the members have an obligation to contribute on winding up as members of guarantee companies do, may be optional. A CIO must:

- keep registers of its trustees and members;
- make the above details available publicly;
- file accounts and annual returns with CC; and
- advise CC of any charges it has created over the charity's property.

l) Employee owned companies

Although since the 1970s it has been possible for companies (mainly listed PLCs) to give their employees shares in the company for which they are working under tax-advantageous arrangements, the total number of shares capable of being made available is usually limited to 10% of the issued share capital. Other than this there have been very few companies where the employees alone constitute the shareholders – rather like a co-operative – and usually where initially the original owner gave his shareholding to the employees (e.g. the John Lewis Partnership).

m) Societas Europaea (SE)

An SE is a European PLC formed under the European Company Statute (ECS). The ECS contains a regulation allowing the formation of such a company under core company law provisions which apply throughout the European Union. An SE must have a minimum share capital of Euro120,000 and is available to commercial bodies with interests in more than one European country. An SE allows UK companies to engage in cross border mergers with companies from other EU member states. Thus rather than taking over a company in another member state a UK company can agree with the other company to form a jointly owned SE subsidiary or holding company. An SE can have either a single board (an *administrative organ*) or a two board system with a *management organ* reporting to a *supervisory organ* every three months. It must hold an AGM every year and within 6 months of its financial year-end.

n) European Private Company

SEs are only available for PLCs. Paralleling that development, however, is a proposal for private companies as set out in the European Council Regulation on the Statute for a European Private Company.

o) Oversea company

Under CA06s1044, any 'company incorporated outside the United Kingdom' is an 'oversea company' and within one month of it establishing a place of business here it must send CH the following information (form BR1):

- its Charter or Articles;

- the names of the director(s) and Secretary; and

- a list of persons in the UK authorised to accept service of notice on behalf of the company etc.

Under CA85 a *place of business* was usually deemed to be one where only administrative functions are conducted. Any other activity (e.g. *trading* or functions central to the operation of the business) usually meant that the location was defined as a *branch*. Under CA06 there is no difference between the two definitions – any place of business is required to register as a branch.

p) Joint Venture (JV) companies

To develop a new product or concept, two or more bodies may agree to set up and operate a jointly owned subsidiary company. In addition to framing the ARTICLES they will normally enter into a SHAREHOLDERS AGREEMENT setting out their relationship and the relationship they may have with those nominated to serve on the board. Any such arrangement would need to be checked for any declaration in accordance with the SIGNIFICANT CONTROL rules.

JV board appointees who are also directors of the owner companies can have divided loyalties. It is not impossible to imagine a situation where the interests of the JV itself and its owners are not the same. However, in taking decisions related to the JV, the JV directors must put its interests first (even though their own appointment is derived from one of the owners).

q) Dormant companies

Around 20% of all companies registered at CH are dormant and inactive. They are nevertheless required to file a confirmation statement and accounts each year – although instead of an actual set of accounts (which would be fairly skeletal) they can submit form DCA. At any time the company can be re-activated. It is widely thought that keeping a company on CH's Register (active or dormant) automatically protects its NAME. Whilst it should stop another company with an identical name being registered as a company (although even this may not be fool-proof), this does not prevent someone using the company's name without *Ltd* at the end. In this instance the claimant would need to institute an action for passing off or trademark infringement. Companies using names etc. as trade marks may find it advisable to also register a private company with those names. However the UK Patent Office states that over 80% of small and medium sized companies have not registered their names as a trade mark.

Even within the UK the protection given to companies whereby another company cannot have the same corporate name is not fool-proof. For example, a company registered in the separate jurisdictions of the Isle of Man, Jersey, or Guernsey etc. could have the same name as a company registered at CH at Cardiff, Edinburgh or Belfast. The mainland CH is unable to prevent this provided the *externally registered* company does not establish a place of business on the mainland (in which case it would be required to comply with the 'overseas' company provisions – see above) but merely operates via third parties (solicitors, agents etc.).

Veil of Incorporation

Corporate separateness

A company is a legal person created under company legislation with an existence entirely separate from its owners and its directors. It is also an entity totally separate from its own subsidiaries (even if it owns all the shares in those companies). The extension of this is that being separate entities, should a subsidiary (even if wholly-owned) become insolvent, the parent (unless it has guaranteed its subsidiary's debts) can simply wash its hands of, and walk away from, its subsidiary's plight and all its liabilities. The parent's loss would be restricted to the (probably nominal) value of its shares in the subsidiary.

Case study: Legal separation

In 1897, Salomon(S), a rather disreputable leather merchant, transferred his sole trader 'business' into a company that he set up – Salomon and Co Ltd – which promptly collapsed into insolvency. The company's creditors attempted but failed in their attempt to hold S personally liable for their losses as the company (even though he owned all its shares and was running it) was held to be a separate legal entity. This was (and still is so) even though a company could and can only act via its officers – in this case S himself.

(Nowadays had Salomon not regarded the interests of the creditors as *paramount* when his company was failing, (i.e. he allowed it to continue to trade ignoring the fact that the creditors could lose the money he owed them) he could have been required to contribute to their losses under the Insolvency Act 1986. His actions would almost certainly have been classified as WRONGFUL TRADING (or even fraudulent trading) as his whole intent seems to have been to avoid paying his creditors.)

However although the *veil* is automatically in existence, if it can be shown that a parent company or the parent board of directors exercised undue influence over the activities of a subsidiary, the parent could still be held liable as a result of such activities (indeed the parent company might be classified as a shadow director of the subsidiary, with potential liability should it become insolvent). There have been instances where Courts have allowed the veil of separateness to be *pierced* meaning that a claimant against a subsidiary could pursue a successful action directly against the parent.

Case study: Parent responsible (or not) for acts of subsidiary

In *Chandler v Cape plc* the parent company was held to have a duty of care to the employees of its defunct subsidiary company. Mr Chandler had worked with asbestos during his employment with a subsidiary of Cape plc, which, (by the time his mesothelioma was diagnosed) had ceased to exist.

The Court of Appeal held that since the parent company exercised control over its subsidiaries including dictating the overall health and safety policy of the group, even though the subsidiary could exercise a degree of independence, the parent company did have a direct duty of care to Mr Chandler. Since the parent company should have been aware at the time that contracting a harmful disease from asbestos dust was a distinct possibility, they had a liability to the subsidiary's employees. The *veil* in this instance was *torn* and liability could flow directly to the parent.

However, if there is no *direct* control between parent and subsidiary the *veil* may be impervious and the parent will have no responsibility for its subsidiary. In *Thompson v The Renwick Group plc,* Renwick (the parent) appointed a director with responsibility for health and safety to the board of a newly acquired subsidiary. Thompson (working for that subsidiary) handled asbestos and contracted mesothelioma. His attempt to hold Renwick responsible failed since the parent could not be shown to have **controlled** the activities of the (now-defunct) subsidiary for which Thompson worked – merely to have appointed a director to its board.

The director/company relationship

The *separateness* of parent company and subsidiary referred to above is mirrored in the relationship between the company itself and those that operate it. As a legal person formed under law the company has an existence separate from its owners (shareholders or guarantors) and its directors. However, despite the company being a separate legal person, it can act only via its directors. Since many of their actions are taken in the name of the company it can be held responsible for such actions, although this is not always the case.

Case study: Whose actions at fault?

In *Brumder (B) v Motornet Service & Repairs Ltd (M)*, B was sole share-holder and sole director of M. B suffered an injury at work and sought to hold the company responsible since he argued it had negated its obliga-tions to him under Health and Safety legislation.

The Court held that a claimant could not assert that the company had not done all it could to comply with safety regulations when it was only through the claimant himself that the company could take action to comply with those regulations and thus protect its employees.

Obviously where a person owns all the shares of the company and is also its sole director, the legal rule that company and person are totally separate entities (particularly if there is wrongdoing) may be difficult to defend.

Case study: Separateness was a sham

In *R v Sale*, S was the sole shareholder and director of a company which by bribing Network Rail employees had received the benefit of lucrative contracts with the rail company. S was found guilty of corruption but defended the seizure of the value of the contracts from the company by contending that it was the company rather than himself who had benefited. It was held that there was such a close link between the legal person of the company and the real person S that both had acted in the corruption and both should be held liable.

Similarly in Bilta (UK) Ltd (in liquidation) v Nazir & ors, all four directors of Bilta were involved in a scheme with a third party to create transactions (in the company's name) so it could fraudulently over claim VAT. The directors tried to pass the liability for their fraudulent activities to the company, claiming they were only acting in its name. They failed and the liquidator was therefore entitled to seek financial contributions from those involved in the fraudulent activities. In addition, by involving the company in such activities the directors had damaged the company and thus were in breach of their fiduciary duty to it.

The corporate protection

Being a separate legal entity, the company has liability for matters entered into on its behalf. Most such commitments are entered into by its directors. The directors should ensure that when they enter into commitments on behalf of the company that the company is identified as being the *persona* that has liability. Failure to identify this – and to identify the body exactly – could mean the director being personally liable.

Case study: Clarity of principal's commitment is essential

In *Hamid v Frances Bradshaw Partnership*, a director signed a contract bearing the trading name of a company (of which he was sole shareholder/director) but not the company name. Since there was no indication he was signing on behalf of the company he was found personally liable.

Voting and taking a poll

Authority to vote

There are three ways in which shareholders' powers can be exercised:

1. By attending and voting in person – giving the shareholder freedom of action to speak and vote.

2. By appointing a PROXY or proxies to attend, and (usually with restrictions) speak and vote in place of the owner.

3. By a corporate body appointing a representative. A representative is for all intents and purposes a member (since effectively the corporate shareholding body is actually present) and the representative can exercise all the rights of an individual member.

Preparation

If antipathy is expected (and it is rare that there has been no indication in advance) preparation is essential. Thus the board could ensure:

- the impact of opposition is negated or blunted by advance discussion;
- there is sufficient support so that opposition can be outvoted;
- only those entitled to speak do so – but are allowed to do so with courtesy;
- meeting administration is sound; and
- the media are given an adequate (and accurate) briefing.

Media

It is important that those who are to deal with the media are coached in such work, particularly in dealing with hostile or critical questioning. Unless well-prepared and well-briefed for this type of examination, reputations can be irreparably damaged and poor impressions created. Not for nothing is there a saying that reputations can take years to create but can be lost in a few seconds.

To try to ensure that any media report is accurate and balanced it may be advisable to prepare a press release. Advice should be taken but the following may provide a quick guide to the preparation of such a release.

CHECKLIST: The four ONLYs

✓ Only issue a release when something of interest to the target audience is to be featured.

✓ Only issue a release if it passes the *blind man's test*. This entails reading the release once only to someone who knows nothing of the subject matter and will have no chance to re-read it and asking them to state the story. Unless they can repeat the salient facts the release needs to be re-written – and probably shortened.

✓ Only issue a release to the particular part of the media who are likely to be interested in the item.

✓ Only issue the release if there is someone always on call ready and prepared to answer questions and provide additional data should the target media channel require this.

Out-thinking the opposition

Not only should friendly shareholders be canvassed to obtain their proxy (and support) if they are not attending, and tame proposers and seconders be told to avoid silences at the meeting when the chairman invites support, etc., but also it is essential that if hostility is expected, it is adequately prepared for.

CHECKLIST: Preparing for hostility

✓ Identify source and extent of support and of opposition.

✓ Check if *hostiles* have a right of attendance (if not, seek to exclude them).

✓ Consider possibility of an advance private meeting to avoid public confrontation.

✓ Monitor arrivals and arrange for security forces to be nearby to deal with any physical disruption. Ensure visitors sit apart from shareholders to aid accurate *show of hands* counting.

✓ Canvass proxies sufficient to ensure overcoming any potential opposition.

✓ Prepare a list of the questions least wished to be asked – and, more importantly, a crib of suitable answers.

✓ Brief the directors about the problem and controls.

✓ Brief media contacts and provide media trained spokesman to answer follow up queries.

✓ If hostile shareholders wish to make a point they should be allowed such a courtesy, answering the points made as far as possible and offering subsequent discussions if this is feasible.

✓ If questions are posed the answer can be stated to be posted on the company's website later.

Voting

1. The Articles should be checked as they may give guidance re QUORUM requirements, rights of attendance, special rules, who is to chair the meeting (it should not be assumed that the Board chairman will also chair the general meetings as some Articles state 'the members shall elect one of their number to act as Chairman') etc.

2. If a large number attend it may be helpful to arrange shareholder seating in blocks of (say) 20 and to arrange for the auditors act as scrutineers for a block of seats each. The use of scrutineers (announced by the chairman at the commencement of the meeting) seeks to show that an independent force is available. The scrutineers could also act as receptionists, asking shareholders to sign in, checking voting strength and ensuring only shareholders sit in shareholder areas to aid vote counting.

3. If a show of hands is required, each scrutineer should note the result from his section and hand it to the chief scrutineer (two such persons may be advisable for checking purposes).

Poll

Reference should be made to the Articles for guidance regarding calling and administering a poll which can usually be demanded or called by:

- the chairman;
- any two members (which includes proxies and representatives of corporate shareholders); or
- any member(s) holding one tenth or more of the share capital.

The chairman needs to:

- check that the member(s) making the demand has/have the required authority;

- appoint scrutineers to administer the poll; and

- set the date, time, and place for poll to be taken.

Since it is the owners' votes that are being counted and the Auditors are appointed by the owners, it may be sensible to request the Auditors to act as scrutineers.

Since proxies are usually required to be deposited 48 hours prior to the Meeting (excluding non-working days), the scrutineers' first task should be to check the proxies for authenticity and to tally the proxy voting strength for and against each resolution. Proxies should provide a space for the insertion of the number of shares/votes applicable.

At the meeting the list of proxies lodged must be compared with those shareholders present to ensure there is no double counting. Although a shareholder has a right, even having lodged a proxy, to attend the meeting, clarification of the status of the proxy must be sought.

On receiving a demand for a poll to be taken, the chairman usually has authority to require it to be conducted immediately, or at the end of the meeting or at some other date (in which case the meeting may have to be adjourned). The requirements of the Articles should be checked.

If a poll is demanded, the proxy cards provide evidence of the preferences of those not present. Additional voting cards need to be made available for shareholders present. Each scrutineer should distribute voting cards to shareholders present and not represented by a proxy – and after voting, collect and total them. The results from each area should be passed to the chief scrutineer(s) who will summarise the returns and pass the result to the chairman. Shareholders usually have a right to inspect details of a poll vote.

The future

Companies (having checked that there is no prohibition in their Articles) are now permitted to use e-mail to communicate with their shareholders and to do so must submit a resolution to them for permission to communicate electronically. If the resolution is passed, shareholders must be advised that they have the option of continuing with hard copy or opting for an electronic version, and that if they do not reply within 28 days they will be deemed to have opted for the electronic option. If they do not reply (or do not give an electronic address) they must still be sent a hard copy notification of a meeting referring them to the company website for full information re the meeting. They would not be sent (for example) the report and accounts – the shareholder would need to request these. Those who do not opt for electronic communication can be re-invited to do so once a year.

Case study: Using technology

In *Byng v London Life* the Court stated that that a general meeting could be validly held in several locations provided there were 'fully functional mutual audio-visual links' – i.e. so that everyone could see and hear and interact with all others. Whilst holding the meeting in two or three locations might be feasible, attempting to use more locations and trying to ensure everyone can see and hear everyone else must be virtually impossible.

It is possible to foresee a situation where general meetings could be held with shareholders remaining in their homes or offices etc. (connected via the Internet to the location where the meeting is physically being held) and being able to exercise their voting power in *person* having heard any points made in favour or against a particular proposal rather than signing a proxy well in advance of the meeting and without the benefit of hearing such arguments on the day.

Case study: The future is here

The AGM of fashion shoe manufacturer Jimmy Choo was held using online facilities. Each shareholder was given a user name and password plus a unique meeting ID which allowed them online access to the AGM.

Once a shareholder logged on, their shareholding and eligibility to vote was checked. They were then able to see the proceedings including visual aids and could register a vote at each resolution.

The company, advised by registration services provider Equiniti which set up the system, declared itself well-pleased with the result not least as the number of shareholders participating was greater than the number that would have been expected to attend physically.

Any company wishing to develop such a facility would need first to take authority to do so by changing their Articles – not least since at present there is no capacity to ask questions. This can to some extent be overcome by using a Frequently Asked Questions on the company's website. However lodging a question in such a way can only generate a written answer – and sometimes the answer simply begs more questions. In any case it is not the same as hearing an answer at the time. Body language can be an important part of the message.

Winding up

Types of orders

Members' voluntary winding-up

Where the purpose(s) of the company has/have been achieved and the assets are such that they are able to meet all claims likely to be made, and the directors can swear a declaration of solvency, this method of ceasing the company's existence can be utilised. Within five weeks of the directors swearing such a declaration, the members must pass a resolution winding up the company and advise CH.

Procedure: The directors swear a declaration of solvency and convene an (E)GM to appoint a liquidator. A notice is posted in the *London Gazette* and details are given to CH within 14 days. The liquidator sells the assets and settles the debts. A director has liability for the debts of the company (regardless of the timing of any resignation) for 12 months from the date he signed a solvency declaration.

Creditors' voluntary winding up

If the directors are unable to swear a declaration of solvency, they decide to wind it up and convene a creditors' meeting.

Procedure: An (E)GM is convened to pass a winding up resolution, to nominate a liquidator, and authorise the convening of a meeting of creditors giving at least seven days notice including in the *London Gazette*. At the creditors meeting, those present appoint a liquidator whose appointment terminates the powers of the directors (although they remain in office). The liquidator sells the assets and settles such debts as are possible.

Court ordered winding up

This occurs when:

- the company passes a special resolution to this effect;
- a judgement creditor has a debt of £750 or more and has petitioned for the winding up;
- the company has failed to comply with certain requirements; or
- the Court feels it is just to do so.

Procedure: The Official Receiver becomes the liquidator.

Striking off

Provided a company has not in the previous three months:

- changed its name;
- traded or conducted business;
- engaged in any activity (other than that connected with this application); and
- made a disposal for value of property rights then the directors can apply to CH for it to be struck off.

Procedure: A form DS01 (under CA06s1003) must be filed, with copies sent to any director(s) not signing the form and all other interested parties.

Notice of intent to strike the company off is inserted in the *London Gazette*. Three months later, provided there are no objections, CH can strike the company off.

Third party action

Administration and Administrative Receivership have similar names but very different objects. An Administrator has control of the company but tries to keep it (or at least part of it) operating whilst disposing of it (or part) as a going concern. Often at least part of the company may survive. An Administrative Receiver also has control of the company but seizes all the assets and attempts disposal (often at very reduced prices since speed is deemed essential). In the process the company will almost certainly be wound up. In both although the directors remain in office that will be without power.

a) Administration

The Enterprise Act now requires most companies approaching insolvency to apply for administration (rather than administrative receivership) and as a result of the credit crunch there have been a number of well-publicised companies – particularly retail chains – that have done so. Under this arrangement an Administrator is appointed (usually by creditors holding a charge over the assets) to try to save the company (and/or sell the whole or part as a going concern); or to sell assets (often at a discount to their true worth) to raise cash to keep part at least of the company going. Should the Administrator be successful, the (often slimmed-down) company may be able to emerge from Administration. Voluntary arrangements (i.e. agreements with the creditors) are also encouraged under the Enterprise Act. Wherever the name of the company is used, the words 'in Administration' must be added to bring the situation to the attention of all third parties – particularly current and potential suppliers and creditors. This is also important to customers – after all a customer wishing to return goods (e.g. if faulty), needs to be made aware of the state of the company, since it may not even exist in the near future and restitution may be problematic.

b) 'Pre-pack' administration (PPA)

Under PPA arrangements any potentially profitable part of a failing company is *hived off* (in advance of failure) and sold (often to the directors of the failing company), whilst the *rump* is allowed to fail. Since unsecured creditors may be involved in both parts they may have an incentive to go along with the concept in the expectation of at least continuing to benefit from trading with the continuing business whilst knowing they will lose their interest in the failed part of the company. During the last recession there were around 2000 *pre-packs*. To some extent PPA blunts the purpose of insolvency legislation which placed personal liability on directors, should they not regard the creditors' interests as *paramount*. That was devised to deter directors from running companies into the ground knowing they could walk away without liability. This scenario may not continue unabated following the *Wind Hellas* (WH) case. WH was registered in Greece but two weeks before it collapsed it re-registered as a UK company purely (claimed some unsecured creditors) to gain the benefit of the UK's *pre-pack* concept, with the original owners and management continuing to run the profitable part of the business. One unsecured creditor, hedge fund SPQR Capital, described the UK's situation as akin to running *an insolvency brothel.*

Whilst the pre-pack concept has been criticised, it can save jobs, albeit at the expense of the unsecured creditors. In 89 pre-packs effected in one month, 4846 out of 5478 jobs were saved. When HMRC (a major creditor of one company) tried to block an Administrator setting up a pre-pack, the judge held that the plan seemed the best way of saving 50 jobs – in the process saving the State paying unemployment benefits, as well as notice and redundancy pay – thus effectively passing what would have become the State's liabilities to the creditors! This was not the intention of the Insolvency Act although presumably it satisfies the thrust of CA06 requiring consideration of all the stakeholders – including Society – to be taken into account.

In response to these concerns a number of recommendations have been made:

- details of a proposed sale should be reviewed by a third party to increase transparency;

- connected persons should conduct a viability review to increase a new company chances of success;

- valuations should be prepared by a person with professional indemnity insurance;

- effective marketing should be undertaken to increase sales proceeds; and

- the insolvency profession regulation should be strengthened and there should be new regulatory objectives and stronger powers for the Insolvency Service.

c) Administrative Receivership

Since the thrust of current insolvency law is to try to save companies (via Administration) this alternative is now rarely used. The aim of an Administrative Receiver (AR) (appointed by a lender under authority given usually by a CHARGE) is to generate as much cash for the assets of the company as quickly as possible, which will almost certainly entail the immediate cessation of trading, whilst the assets are sold – often at a considerable discount since purchasers, knowing the urgency are able to strike a hard bargain. This was certainly the case in the recession of the early 1990s and many banks (who, since assets were charged to them, had the right to appoint ARs) were criticised for *pulling the rug* from organisations which might have survived had they been supported. Such actions were copied during the most recent recession which has prompted severe criticism not least as the aim in some of those instances seems to have been, in part, the enhancement of the bank's own property portfolios by enabling it to seize some of the assets of a failing company – the failure of which the bank had helped precipitate). The AR pays his own fees, and then repays any organisation with a charge over the assets (who was probably the organisation that appointed the AR), and then pays the unsecured creditors and shareholders (usually only a few pence in the pound – and often not even that).

Voluntary arrangements

Under a voluntary arrangement the creditors agree to support the company – normally by agreeing not to press for payment of their debt for a set period to relieve pressure on cash flow etc. This may allow the company time to *trade out* of its current solvency problems. Very often the creditors may be in the position of being virtually forced to agree to a *voluntary* arrangement simply since if the company fails they are likely to receive next to nothing. Alternatively, the creditors may be prepared to exchange their debt for shares in the company – a *debt-equity swop*. Should the company survive they can share in its recovery whereas if it fails they have probably lost no more than their, already incurred, doubtful debt.

Case study: Saved by the creditors

The Queens Moat House hotel group was saved from insolvency in the late 1980s by the actions of its bankers mainly since the credit they had advanced to the company was so great they could not afford to let their debtor go under as they would then be facing massive bad debts, severely affecting their own accounts.

Similarly in 2003 the Marconi Group (formerly the highly-respected GEC, in its day regarded as the 'bellwether' of the UK economy) was saved from insolvency by its creditors who agreed to a debt-equity exchange and finished up owning over 99.5% of the share capital of a listed PLC.

WARNING

If directors' personal liability is to be avoided it is essential that legal and audit advice is sought – the directors must be able to demonstrate they regarded the interests of the creditors as *paramount*.

Wrongful and fraudulent trading

KEY POINTS

- Following CA1856 being implemented it was criticised as being a little more than a 'rogues charter' and 'a means of devising the encouragement of speculation, overtrading and swindling' – allowing unscrupulous directors to walk away from a failed company without any personal liability for the debts, the costs of its failure having been passed to the creditors.

- To rectify this imbalance, the Insolvency Act 1986 introduced the concepts of the directors trading *wrongfully* (due to negligence or ignorance) or *fraudulently* (deliberate deception) for which they can be fined, imprisoned and/or required to make good any deficiencies to the creditors personally.

Wrongful trading

A director is held to have traded wrongfully, if he knew or, (critically), *ought to have concluded* that there was no reasonable prospect of his company's creditors being paid on their due dates or within a reasonable time thereof, or of the company avoiding insolvency and yet he allowed the company to continue to trade, thereby taking on more credit. If guilty of wrongful trading, a director can be made personally liable to contribute (without limitation) to any deficiency in assets to satisfy the company's creditors, and also be disqualified from acting as a director for a maximum of 15 years. Whether a company is insolvent (and should, therefore, cease trading rather than continuing to trade *wrongfully*) may be able to be judged fairly accurately with hindsight but may be difficult to assess at the time particularly as the directors may genuinely be working to try to save the company. The following outline tests may help but are no substitute for taking competent advice:

1. Is the company capable of paying its debts as they fall due (or shortly after)?

2. Do the assets of the company exceed the value of its liabilities?

3. Would the realisation of assets be sufficient to pay all its liabilities?

If the answers to any of these questions are 'no', then, unless it is known that the situation will improve before the debts become overdue, the company is almost certainly approaching insolvency, and unless the situation can be, or is reasonably expected to be, rectified swiftly, it should cease trading (i.e. stop taking on more credit). To do otherwise may involve the directors being made personally culpable. In assessing culpability, the Court will bear in mind the expertise of the person(s) concerned. Liability can be reduced or avoided, if it can be shown that everything that could be, was done to minimise the potential loss.

Case study: Qualifications enhance liability

In *Dorchester Finance Co Ltd & anor v Stebbing* there were three directors (all qualified accountants) two of whom left the running of the company to the other. The former often signed blank cheques for use by their colleague and made no enquiry of how the funds were used by him. When the company failed owing substantial sums all three directors were prosecuted. The Court found that the two *sleeping directors* (who claimed in court 'they didn't know' what was going on) had failed to apply the necessary skill and care in the performance of their duties (and indeed that they had failed to perform **any** duties as directors).

The Court stated that a director must in the exercise of his duties:

* show the degree of skill and care reasonably be expected from a person of his knowledge and experience (hence the expectations of three qualified accountants would be high in view of their professional training and qualifications);

* take such care that a man might be expected to take on his own account; and

* use the powers granted to him in good faith and in the interests of the company of which he is a director.

Directors must be proactive in the exercise of their responsibilities.

Action required

Immediately it is known that a company is insolvent, or it appears that it is approaching such a state, the directors need to take action – inactivity is not an option if personal liability is to be avoided. Whenever a company is wound up, an insolvency practitioner must investigate the position and the records and the actions of its officers. Each officer is required to complete a lengthy questionnaire – the answers to some of the questions (e.g. 'When were you first aware the company was trading wrongfully?') being potentially self-incriminating. If transactions were effected at under-value or at preferential rates, or a creditor was given preferential treatment this can result in a report being made to the Director of Public Prosecutions who will decide whether to prosecute for fraud. If the company is being wound up under a Court order, the report must be made to the Official Receiver. If the insolvency practitioner or the Official Receiver feels that the conduct of a director has been such that he is unfit to run a company then a report must be made in case legal action should be taken against those culpable.

Case study: Fraudulent concealment?

In *Contex Drouzhba Ltd v Wiseman and anor,* W caused the company of which he was a director to enter into an arrangement with a creditor whereby the company promised to pay the creditor within 30 days of invoice. However the director knew there was no way the company could meet the debt. The judge held that the director had been deceitful and that it was *inconceivable* that the status of director should protect him from personal liability. Accordingly he was held personally liable for the creditor's debt.

If insolvency threatens the board could:

1. **Cease trading and call a creditors meeting to consider a voluntary arrangement** (see WINDING UP). Whilst this may remove what credit confidence remains in the company, in many respects the last thing most creditors would wish is for the company to fail, as often they have a great deal (more possibly than directors or shareholders) at stake. If there is a chance that the company could trade out of the

position, the creditors may be prepared to accept a moratorium on their debt (or even a debt:equity exchange, that is taking shares in the company in exchange for extinguishing part or all of their debt). During the recent recession several retail chains (not all successfully) entered into such composition schemes with their creditors to buy time to try and trade out of their insolvency.

Case study: Disclaim the commitments

In the BHS company voluntary arrangement of 2016, the company stated it was unable to trade profitably in 87 of its high street outlets where, mainly because of 'upwards only rent reviews' the rents were totally out of step with neighbouring units. The company suggested to its landlords a compromise agreement whereby they should reduce the rents or it would appoint an insolvency practitioner to disclaim the leases – which would allow the company to walk away from them without penalty. The landlords had a choice – accept lower rents but occupied units – or empty units with no rent. They would then be left with large retail space but little chance of attracting new tenants – and certainly not at the level of rent currently being paid. Somewhat unsurprisingly the landlords agreed to discount the rents so the company could continue to trade. (The respite proved short-lived as within three months the whole company was put into Administration).

2. **Appoint an administrative receiver**. However this right belongs to a creditor usually a bank – which has a charge over the company assets. The directors can invite the creditor to appoint an administrative receiver. The almost inevitable result of this (since time is of the essence) is that the assets may be sold for much less than their true value – thus reducing the funds available to pay the creditors. As a result of the Enterprise Act 2002 this course of action is now increasingly discouraged (since it will almost certainly result in the winding up of the company) in favour of trying to save the company (or at least part of it) by means of a voluntary arrangement or administration.

3. **Petition the court for the appointment of an administrator**. This is only possible if the company has access to funds and/or it is thought possible that the company – or at least a profitable part of it – might

be able to be sold as a going concern and/or trade out of the situation. Using this alternative is encouraged under the Enterprise Act 2002. Most of the retail chains that crashed during the recent recession went into administration and in some cases part at least survived, albeit as slimmed down entities.

4. **Raise loans.** Although these could provide essential cash and allow the company to trade on, it can be argued being loans rather than risk capital they actually increase the liabilities – rendering the company, at least technically, insolvent.

5. **Source additional shareholder (i.e. risk) capital.** New capital could be sought from family and/or friends of the officers. If considering inviting employees to invest, the company should offer to fund financial advice for them, since the risk of failure may be high. When the former Rolls Royce company (not the current company) failed in the1980s, most of its employees suffered a *triple whammy* since as well as losing their jobs, many had invested in the company shares, and the company pension fund had also invested heavily in the company.

   Other sources of funds include loans from national and/or local government and even the EU; by advertising in the media for investors or even, if it is the only way the company can survive, approaching a competitor or supplier with a view to a merger.

6. **Try to amalgamate with another business**

7. **Seek a *white knight* to take over the company as a going concern**. *White knight* is a term mainly used when listed PLCs are subject to an unwelcome takeover bid and depicts a third party whom the board of the target company feel would be an acceptable purchaser – at least more welcome than the hostile predator.

8. **At all times, record (on an on-going basis) full details of every action taken,** by whom it was taken, the date on which it was taken, and the result.

Whilst the recording of such actions may not save the company, it may, since it is evidence of the positive action of the directors to regard the interests of the creditors as *paramount,* save the officers from being accused of wrongful trading and, if found guilty, being required to contribute to the assets available to the creditors. Advice should be taken. If genuine re-financing steps are being taken (even if they are subsequently unsuccessful), the directors' liability may be minimised or avoided. If it is thought that a company might be nearing the point at where it could be held to be trading wrongfully, it is *essential* that the directors take action and daily record details of their actions.

Case study: Creditors interests are paramount

In *Gwyer & Associates and anor v London Wharf (Limehouse) Ltd & ors,* a director of a company approaching insolvency made no effort to ascertain what were the interests of his company before voting on a board resolution. The Court held he was not only negligent but also in breach of his fiduciary duty to exercise his discretion independently and *bona fides* in the interests of the company. It went on to state that where a company was on the brink of insolvency the directors owed a duty 'to consider as paramount' the interests of the creditors.

Under recent initiatives, a company in financial difficulties, can use a process under which creditors' claims can be frozen for 56 days during which period efforts could be made to save the business. At the end of 56 days a creditors' meeting must be held at which the creditors (subject to gaining a 75% in value agreement) can extend the moratorium for a further month.

Directors and Officers Liability insurance policies should be checked to ensure that if found guilty of wrongful trading (which almost certainly would involve a degree of dishonesty) there is any cover under such a policy. The best policies may cover the defence costs – even of those then found guilty.

Case study: Directors not guilty

The collapse of hamper company Farepak, (the effect of which was that around 100,000 people who wanted to use their £37 million worth of deposits previously given to the company to fund their Christmas hampers, lost such *savings*) heralded considerable, and, at the time, understandable, criticism of the directors from a variety of sources, particularly the media. Perhaps partly as a result of such attention it was decided to prosecute the directors for breaching the Insolvency Act.

In Court, however, the directors were completely vindicated but their bank, HBOS, was held to be responsible and lambasted for the failure of the company. It was evidenced that the directors made *strenuous efforts* on no fewer than 15 occasions to arrange a rescue of the company. However not only did HBOS refuse to grant a loan of £3 million pending the sale of a subsidiary (an action that would have avoided the failure), HBOS (patronisingly referring to the depositors' money as *Doris money*) also forced the directors to continue taking deposits of around £4 million from the savers – money that they knew would almost certainly be lost. The decision to put Farepak into administration was taken by the (later disgraced) head of HBOS corporate bank (who presumably evaded being classified as a *shadow director* – and potentially personally liable – because the bank's actions and his requirements were (so-called) *professional advice!*)

Penalties

In fact, compared to the number of company failures, there have been relatively few actions against directors. However courts found:

- two directors personally liable to contribute £75,000 each to the assets available to the creditors of their insolvent company because they knew before the liquidation that it was likely to happen and yet continued trading to the obvious detriment of the creditors;

- a husband and wife liable to contribute £431,000 to the creditors of their failed company;

- a director liable to contribute £2 million to help pay off his failed company's creditors.

Fraudulent trading

The essential difference between wrongful and fraudulent trading is intent. Whereas under wrongful trading the director could be held culpable by negligence, carelessness or even ignorance, under fraudulent trading there must be proven intent to defraud the company's creditors – i.e. the company fails owing the creditors and it can be proven that those responsible were aware of the situation and rather than protecting the creditors, actually and consciously exploited them. Those responsible can be:

- held personally liable to an unlimited extent;

- disqualified from acting as a director for a maximum period of fifteen years; and/or

- fined and/or imprisoned for fraud (for a term increased by CA06 to ten years).

Notes:

1. CH's guide to liquidation and insolvency gives guidance to the documents that must be delivered to CH. However the guide is not comprehensive and anyone involved in such a situation would be well advised to contact legal representatives and not just rely on it.

2. Either by default or design the recent activities of some of those in charge of limited liability companies has led to the situation where some companies have grown *too big to fail,* i.e. their potential failure has forced the Government (i.e. the taxpayer) to bail them out.

Printed in Great Britain
by Amazon

83051130R00221